Vikram Chandra is the author of the critically acclaimed novel, *Sacred Games* (2007), which was a finalist for the National Book Critics Circle Award for Fiction. His first novel, *Red Earth and Pouring Rain* (1995), won the Commonwealth Writers' Prize for Best First Book and the David Higham Prize for Fiction. His collection of short stories, *Love and Longing in Bombay* (1997), won the Commonwealth Writers' Prize for Best Book (Eurasia Region) and was a *New York Times* Notable Book.

GEEK SUBLIME

Writing Fiction,
Coding Software

Vikram Chandra

FABER & FABER

First published in India in 2013 by Hamish Hamilton,
a division of Penguin Books India.

First published in the UK in 2014
by Faber & Faber Limited
Bloomsbury House
74–77 Great Russell Street
London WC1B 3DA

Printed and bound by CPI Group (UK) Ltd, Croydon, CRO 4YY

A CIP record for this book is available from the British Library

ISBN 978–0–571–31030–2

10 9 8 7 6 5 4 3 2 1

For Melanie,
Sri Sri Sri

CONTENTS

LIST OF FIGURES

ACKNOWLEDGEMENTS

This project has been supported by the University of California, Berkeley.

Thanks to Martin Howard for the images of the LEGO logic gates (http://www.randomwraith.com/logic.html); and to Alex Papadimoulis of TheDailyWTF.com for the dependency diagram.

For inspiration, aid, and insight, I'm grateful to Jennie Durant; Janet Miller; Maura Finklestein; Wendy James, for the loan of that PCjr; Margo True; David Harvey, with fond memories of 'the rapture of the freeways' and AH&AJ Computing; Balaji Venkateswaran; Jeff Kowalski; Sumeet Shetty; S. Sadagopan; Eric Simonoff; Julian Loose; Ethan Nosowsky; Alok Aggarwal; Telle Whitney; Maria Klawe; Roli Varma; Dominik Wujastyk; Arati Gerdes; Ida Mayer; Avnish Bhatnagar; Balajee Vamanan; Dipankar Bajpai; Raka Ray; and Kapil Kapoor, for his help and his invaluable books about the Indian literary tradition.

Luther Obrock translated all the poems from the Dhvanyaloka, and was unstintingly generous with his knowledge and ideas. He provided essential guidance through the subtleties of the dhvanikaras.

The translation of 'I will tell you a funny story' from the Bhaver Gita was a collaborative effort: thanks to Dilip Misra, Rakesh Mishra, and Monidipa Mondal for their help.

Thanks to Chiki Sarkar for helping me discover the shape of this book; and to Tanvi Kapoor and her team at Penguin India for their heroic efforts at bringing the project to fruition.

As always, I couldn't have started or finished the book

without support from my parents, Navin and Kamna; my sisters, Tanuja and Anupama; Vidhu Vinod Chopra; Anuradha Tandon; S. Hussain Zaidi.

I'm especially grateful to the two irrepressible *shaktis*, Leela and Darshana, for their timely interruptions and revivifying hugs.

NOTE ON TRANSLITERATION

Sanskrit words in this book have been rendered phonetically, without the use of diacritical marks: 'Shakti,' not 'Śakti.' Diacritics have been retained in direct quotations and the titles of cited works.

```
class Program
{
    public static void Main()
    {
        System.Console.WriteLine( "Hello, world!" );
    }
}
```

Even if you're the kind of person who tells new acquaintances at dinner parties that you hate email and e-books, you probably recognize the words above as being some kind of computer code. You may even be able to work out, more or less, what this little 'Program' does: it writes to the console of some system the line 'Hello, world!'

A geek hunched over a laptop tapping frantically at the keyboard, neon-bright lines of green code sliding up the screen—the programmer at work is now a familiar staple of popular entertainment. The clipped shorthand and digits of programming languages are familiar even to civilians, if only as runic incantations charged with world-changing power. Computing has transformed all our lives, but the processes and cultures that produce software remain largely opaque, alien, unknown. This is certainly true within my own professional community of fiction writers—whenever I tell one of my fellow authors that I supported myself through the writing of my first novel by working as a programmer and a computer consultant, I evoke a response that mixes bemusement, bafflement, and a touch of awe, as if I'd just said that I could levitate. Most of the artists I know—painters, film-makers, actors, poets—seem to regard programming as an esoteric scientific discipline; they are keenly aware of its cultural mystique, envious of its potential profitability, and eager to extract metaphors, imagery, and dramatic possibility from its history, but coding may as well be nuclear physics as far as relevance to their own daily practice is concerned.

Many programmers, on the other hand, regard themselves as artists. Since programmers create complex objects, and care not just about function but also about beauty, they are just like painters or sculptors. The best-known assertion of this notion is the essay 'Hackers and Painters' by programmer and venture capitalist Paul Graham. 'Of all the different types of people I've known, hackers and painters are among the most alike,' writes Graham. 'What hackers and painters have in common is that they're both makers. Along with composers, architects, and writers, what hackers and painters are trying to do is make good things.'[1]

According to Graham, the iterative processes of programming—write, debug (discover and remove bugs, which are coding errors, mistakes), rewrite, experiment, debug, rewrite—exactly duplicate the methods of artists: 'The way to create something beautiful is often to make subtle tweaks to something that already exists, or to combine existing ideas in a slightly new way . . . You should figure out programs as you're writing them, just as writers and painters and architects do.'[2] Attention to detail further marks good hackers with artist-like passion:

All those unseen details [in a Leonardo da Vinci painting] combine to produce something that's just stunning, like a thousand barely audible voices all singing in tune.

Great software, likewise, requires a fanatical devotion to beauty. If you look inside good software, you find that parts no one is ever supposed to see are beautiful too.[3]

This desire to equate art and programming has a lengthy pedigree. In 1972, the famed computer scientist Butler Lampson published an editorial titled 'Programmers as Authors' which began:

> Creative endeavour varies greatly in the amount of overhead (i.e. money, manpower and organization) associated with a project which calls for a given amount of creative work. At one extreme is the activity of an aircraft designer, at the other that of a poet. The art of programming currently falls much closer to the former than the latter. I believe, however, that this situation is likely to change considerably in the next decade.[4]

Lampson's argument was that hardware would become so cheap that 'almost everyone who uses a pencil will use a computer,' and that these users would be able to use 'reliable software components' to put together complex programs. 'As a result, millions of people will write non-trivial programs, and hundreds of thousands will try to sell them.'[5]

A poet, however, might wonder why Lampson would place poetry making on the same spectrum of complexity as aircraft design, how the two disciplines—besides being 'creative'—are in any way similar. After all, if Lampson's intent is to point towards the future reduction of technological overhead and the democratization of programming, there are plenty of other technical and scientific fields in which the employment of pencil and paper by individuals might produce substantial results. Architecture, perhaps, or carpentry, or mathematics. One thinks of Einstein in the patent office at Bern. But even the title of Lampson's essay hints at a desire for kinship with writers, an identification that aligns what programmers and authors do and makes them—somehow, eventually—the same.

~

Both writers and programmers struggle with language. The code at the beginning of this chapter is in Microsoft's C#, one of thousands of high-level programming languages invented over the last century. Each of these is a 'formal language,' a language 'with explicit and precise rules for its syntax and semantics,' as the Oxford *Dictionary of Computing* puts it. Formal languages 'contrast with natural languages such as English whose rules, evolving as they do with use, fall short of being either a complete or a precise definition of the syntax, much less the semantics, of the language.'[6] So these formal dialects may be less flexible and less forgiving of ambiguity than natural languages, but coders—like poets—manipulate linguistic structures and tropes, search for expressivity and clarity. While a piece of code may pass instructions to a computer, its real audience, its readers, are the programmers who will add features and remove bugs in the days and years after the code is first created. Donald Knuth is the author of the revered magnum opus on computer algorithms and data structures, *The Art of Computer Programming*. Volume 3 of the *Art* was published in

1973; the first part of Volume 4 appeared in 2011, the next part is 'under preparation.' If ever there was a person who fluently spoke the native idiom of machines, it is Knuth, computing's great living sage. More than anyone else, he understands the paradox that programmers write code for other humans, not for machines: 'Let us change our traditional attitude to the construction of programs: Instead of imagining that our main task is to instruct a computer what to do, let us concentrate rather on explaining to human beings what we want a computer to do.'[7] In 1984, therefore, he famously formalized the notion of 'literate programming':

> The practitioner of literate programming can be regarded as an essayist, whose main concern is with exposition and excellence of style. Such an author, with thesaurus in hand, chooses the names of variables carefully and explains what each variable means. He or she strives for a program that is comprehensible because its concepts have been introduced in an order that is best for human understanding, using a mixture of formal and informal methods that reinforce each other.[8]

Good code, then, is marked by qualities that go beyond the purely practical; like equations in physics or mathematics, code can aspire to elegance. Knuth remarked about the code of a compiler that it was 'plodding and excruciating to read, because it just didn't possess any wit whatsoever. It got the job done, but its use of the computer was very disappointing.'[9]

To get the job done—a novice may imagine that this is what code is supposed to do. Code is, after all, a series of commands issued to a dumb hunk of metal and silicone and plastic animated by electricity. What more could you want it to do, to be? Knuth answers: code must be 'absolutely beautiful.'[10] He once said about a program called SOAP (Symbolic Optimal Assembly Program) that 'reading it was just like hearing a symphony, because every instruction was sort of doing two things and everything came together gracefully.'[11]

We are now unmistakably in the realm of human perception, taste, and pleasure, and therefore of aesthetics. Can code itself—as opposed to the programs that are constructed with code—be beautiful? Programmers certainly think so. Greg Wilson, the editor of *Beautiful Code*, an anthology of essays by programmers about 'the most beautiful piece of code they knew,'[12] writes in his foreword to that book:

> I got my first job as a programmer in the summer of 1982. Two weeks after I started, one of the system administrators loaned me Kernighan and Plauger's *The Elements of Programming Style* . . . and Wirth's *Algorithms + Data Structures = Programs* . . . [These books] were a revelation—for the first time, I saw that programs could be more than just instructions for computers. They could be as elegant as well-made kitchen cabinets, as graceful as a suspension bridge, or as eloquent as one of George Orwell's essays.[13]

Knuth himself is careful to limit the scope of his aesthetic claims: 'I do think issues of style do come through and make certain programs a genuine pleasure to read. Probably not, however, to the extent that they would give me any transcendental emotions.'[14] But in the many discussions that programmers have about craftsmanship, elegance, and beauty, there is an unmistakable tendency to assert—as Wilson does—that code is as 'eloquent' as literature.

~

'Hackers and Painters' provoked an equally famous takedown titled 'Dabblers and Blowhards' by the painter and programmer Maciej Ceglowski:

> It is true that both painters and programmers make things, just like a pastry chef makes a wedding cake, or a chicken makes an egg. But nothing about what they make, the purposes it serves, or how they go about doing it is in any way similar . . .
>
>   . . . With the exception of art software projects (which I don't believe Graham has in mind here) all computer programs are designed to accomplish some kind of task. Even the most elegant of computer programs, in order to be considered a program, has to compile and run. So just like mechanical engineers and architects, computer programmers create artefacts that have to stand up to an objective reality. No one cares how pretty the code is if the program won't work. The only objective constraint a painter has is making sure the paint physically stays on the canvas (something that has proven surprisingly challenging). Everything beyond that is aesthetics—arranging coloured blobs in a way that best tickles the mind of the viewer.[15]

Paul Graham has been hugely successful as a programmer and venture capitalist, and his essays about technology and business are sometimes thought-provoking and insightful. But his writings about art are full of majestically fatuous statements delivered with oracular certainty: 'One of the reasons Jane Austen's novels are so good is that she read them out loud to her family. That's why she never sinks into self-indulgently arty descriptions of landscapes, or pretentious philosophizing.'[16] And, 'The paintings made between 1430 and 1500 are still unsurpassed.'[17] But for Graham's primary readership of programmers, these pronouncements are the foundational caissons on which his grand art-hacking equivalence rests. Ceglowski the painter is sceptical:

> You can safely replace 'painters'. . . with 'poets', 'composers', 'pastry chefs' or 'auto mechanics' with no loss of meaning or insight . . . The reason Graham's essay isn't entitled 'Hackers and Pastry Chefs' is not because there is something that unites painters and programmers into a secret brotherhood, but because Paul Graham likes to cultivate the arty aura that comes from working in the visual arts.[18]

My first response to Graham's programmers-as-artists manoeuvre was as exasperated as Ceglowski's, but after the initial irritation had passed I began to think about the specific aesthetic claims Graham was making for code, about what kind of beauty code might possess, and why Graham would want to claim the mantle of artistry. Programmers already are famous, rich, influential. Why do they need any other auras? Ceglowski has a theory:

> Great paintings . . . get you laid in a way that great computer programs never do. Even not-so-great paintings—in fact, any slapdash attempt at splashing paint onto a surface—will get you laid more than writing software, especially if you have the

slightest hint of being a tortured, brooding soul about you . . .

Also remark that in painting, many of the women whose pants you are trying to get into aren't even wearing pants to begin with . . . Not even rock musicians have been as successful in reducing the process to its fundamental, exhilarating essence.

It's no surprise, then, that a computer programmer would want to bask in some of the peripheral coolness that comes with painting, especially when he has an axe to grind about his own work being 'mere engineering'.[19]

Ceglowski's evocation of the Picasso swagger natural to artists of course assumes that painters and rock-stars are charismatically male and women are (ideally) pants-less; that programmers are all men is such an obvious assumption that neither he nor Graham feels the need to qualify their assertions with a reference to gender. So it turns out—as always—that formulations of the aesthetic are embedded in specific histories and cultures of power, privilege, gender, and 'cool.' This particular landscape of American programming is one to which I am a foreigner twice over; I am a writer from India, but I've worked professionally as a programmer in the United States. Fiction has been my vocation, and code my obsession.

I came to computers while trying to run away from literature. I first published fiction—a plotty little sci-fi story heavily influenced by Isaac Asimov—when I was twelve, in a student-run magazine at my boarding school in India. Until then, reading stories and telling them (mainly to myself) had been a reliable, profound pleasure and a desperately needed comfort. The shock of seeing my secret life made public, in print, thrilled into my awkward, nerdy soul. I was a stereotypically budding writer, thickly bespectacled, shy, bad at cricket, worse at field hockey. When fellow students—even some of the remote, godlike athletes who were the heroes of my school—stopped me in the corridors to talk about the story and praise it and ask for more, I knew I had found a way to be in the world, to be of it.

So I kept writing. I read and, in various classrooms, imbibed a strange mix of Victorian classics, the great twentieth-century fictions produced by the stalwarts of Hindi literature, and fragments of Sanskrit from the epics. The only American texts we were prescribed were abridged, bowdlerized editions of *Tom Sawyer* and *Huckleberry Finn*. But in our dormitories, in the school-wide trading system for leisure-time reading, the most avidly sought prizes were the now-forgotten Nick Carter novels, featuring an eponymous 'Killmaster' for AXE, 'the smallest and most deadly arm of American global [intelligence].'[1] Nick Carter exuded a particularly American glamour. The riches of America gave him an endless supply of killing devices, to which he gave cool names: 'Hugo,' a pearl-handled stiletto made by Benvenuto

Cellini; 'Pierre,' a minuscule gas bomb; and my favourite, 'Tiny Tim,' a low-yield nuclear grenade. Nick Carter's exploits with beautiful women were lingered over every thirty pages or so, in counterpoint to the killing, with a level of explicit detail that made James Bond seem fusty and prudish and, well, British. And our home-grown spies, who adventured chastely in Hindi on the pulpy grey paper of the *jasoosis* available at railway stations, were too unspeakably Third World-ish and provincial to pay even cursory attention to.

During one long summer vacation at home in Bombay, I dug through the stacks at a commercial lending library. I had already exhausted their stock of thrillers (at a rupee per book), then held off book drought for a couple of weeks with science fiction and westerns, before finding Hemingway at the back of a shelf. I was fourteen, had read some smatterings of what I didn't know then was called 'literary fiction'—Conrad, Heller, Tolstoy—but I wouldn't have bothered with Hemingway if not for the charging lion on the cover of the paperback. That, and the décolletage of a distressed damsel and the very large rifle wielded by a hunter promised excitement, so I paid up and went home and read 'The Short Happy Life of Francis Macomber.' Then 'The Capital of the World.' And 'The Snows of Kilimanjaro.' I felt something extraordinary, the dread and clipped despair of the stories, a complete concentration of my own attention, and somehow also a flowing wonder and delight. I'd known this feeling before, during performances of the Ramayana I'd seen as a child perched on my father's shoulders, in moments of high Hindi-movie drama in darkened theatres, but I was now experiencing concentrated waves which I felt in my mind and my body: prickles on my forearms, a tingling at the back of my neck. I knew, even in that moment, that I didn't understand everything the stories were doing, what they were *about*. I had no idea who this Hemingway was. And yet, here I was at our kitchen table in Bombay, entranced.

Thus began my encounter with American modernists. Through Hemingway, I found Fitzgerald, and Faulkner, and Hurston, and Wharton, and Eliot. After I left my boarding school and joined a college in Bombay, I switched to the 'arts stream' and was able to study English literature, which comprised both British and American traditions. I wrote fiction, seriously and self-consciously, trying to work out what literature was and what it was meant to do. And I knew I wanted to go to America. That was where *Gatsby* had been written, and somehow that meant I needed to go there to be a writer. For my parents, I had more elaborate justifications, reasons that included the sheer ineptitude of many of the teachers who were supposed to be teaching me about literature, and the stupidity of the Indian educational system's obsession with rote learning and exams. But really, at the root of it all was this inchoate love for a literature that was not mine. In those days, from inside the socialist bubble of the Indian economy, America was ineffably far away and glamorous and rich, and many of us wanted to go there. But usually people went as graduate students, and studied engineering or medicine. What I wanted was pretty much unheard of and unaffordable, but because of my parents' astonishing generosity, and happenstance—my corporate-executive father was posted to Hong Kong and was suddenly being paid in dollars instead of rupees—I found myself in the promised land as a sophomore. I was a little dazed and very happy. This was the adventure I had dreamt about. I read, and I wrote.

I successfully avoided the question of how I was going to make a living until the summer after I finished my undergraduate degree (with a major in English, a concentration in creative writing, and a novella for an honours thesis). When I was forced to come up with an answer, it was film school: if I couldn't sell screenplays, at least there was a thriving Indian film industry I could get a job in. I applied to the film department at Columbia University, and showed up a few months later on the fifth floor of Dodge Hall, driven not so much by clarity about what cinema could offer me, but by a profound uneasiness about what was on offer just a floor below in the writing program: a commitment to a life as a writer of fiction. It wasn't just the paucity of money in the profession; I knew most writers had day jobs. But writing was difficult. Gruelling in a different way from making movies, from having to deal with dozens of egos and schedules and weather fluctuations to get a single shot. Making fiction with resonance, with that endless, echoing depth of feeling I had found in Hemingway was very, very hard. Writing sentences felt like construction, and, also, simultaneously, a steady, slow excavation. You put each word in place, brick upon brick, with a shimmery sense of what the whole edifice would look like, the shape of the final thing. But each phrase was also a digging inward, an uncovering. You tunnelled, dug, dug. On good days, you emerged from your labours tired but happy. On bad days you were left quivery, stupefied. There was risk and danger involved in this work. You always got strung out, ground down, strained thin. Ended up a little sad, maybe a little mad. Not a way to spend a life.

So, there I was in 1986, at film school, with the first semester's tuition paid for and 200 dollars in my bank account.

On my second day in New York, I went looking for employment to Columbia's job board and found a listing for 'scribes.' Of course this was providential, I thought. I called from the first payphone I could find, set up an interview, and didn't ask what kind of scrivening they needed. No matter how dead-letterish the situation was, I wasn't going to prefer not to.

The job, it turned out, was not mere copying—the company provided specialized secretarial services for doctors hired by medical insurance companies. We, the scribes, took the handwritten notes from doctors' examinations and typed them up under their letterheads so that they could be submitted as legal statements when insurance claims were taken to court. We deciphered the handwriting, constructed full sentences out of the doctors' telegraphese, inserted a lot of boilerplate text, and sent it off to the respective doctor to review and sign and submit. The work paid well over minimum wage, and I found I could do it in an automated haze which required almost no mental effort.

Three months after I began working, the company acquired its first personal computers (PCs) for us to work on. I had typed my papers and stories on a terminal attached to the huge mainframe computer at college, and had taken a couple of programming classes, which I thought were tepidly interesting—I was good at writing bubble sorts for lists of words, but it all seemed quite abstract, of no immediate practical purpose. The mainframe was controlled by a specialized cadre of tech-heads, and my access to it was distanced and narrow. Now, though, at my scrivener job, I had a computer I could play with.

I blazed through my assigned work (no more worrying about typos and omissions), propped up stacks of paper to signal that I was busy, and dove into the arcane depths of DOS.

Here was a complete world, systems and rules I could discover and control. I could write little batch files to run commands to change directories and copy files. And the software we used to write the reports, WordPerfect, I could control that too, write clever macros to put in the date, to recognize my abbreviations for the medical jargon, to pop in whole paragraphs of text. And now any repetition of effort seemed like an insult. Spend half an hour writing a report that didn't quite fit the standard format? No way. Screw that. I'd rather spend six hours tinkering with if-then-else routines in my report macro so it would support this specialized format too.

Soon I was the de facto tech-support guy for our little office, and was advising on future purchases of hardware and software. I bought computer magazines on the way home, and lusted after the monster PCs in the double-page photo spreads: more speed, bigger memory, huge hard disks. I wanted all these, but even on the decidedly low-end machines I had access to, there was an entire universe to explore. There were mysteries, things I didn't understand, but there were always answers. If I tried hard, there was always a logic to discover, an internal order and consistency that was beautiful. And I could produce these harmonies, test them, see them work. When a program broke, when it did something unexpected, I could step through the code, watch the variables change, discover where I had made unwarranted assumptions, where the user had done something I didn't expect, and then I could change, adapt, and run the code again. And when I fixed the code, when it ran, the victory coursed through my brain and body. I wanted to do it again.

~

I left New York with a taste for this wizardry and an idea for a novel. I'd figured out in fairly short order that the collaborative, cash-intensive business of film-making wasn't a good fit for me. Being around people all day tired me out, not writing fiction made me ferociously cranky, and the ideas I had for screenplays required gargantuan budgets. The novel I wanted to write moved back and forth between the nineteenth and twentieth centuries, featured cavalry battles, a typing monkey, a character dismembering himself, and many other special effects that I could pull off myself, without a crew or funding. So I finally accepted my fate: a lifetime of fiction-making anxiety and possible poverty was what I was built for, and running about on a film set wouldn't rescue me from writers' demons. There was a fortifying relief in knowing this, and I went off to a couple of graduate writing programs to get on with the work. I did a year at the Writing Seminars at Johns Hopkins, and then moved on to the University of Houston.

I wrote my novel and lived the life of the itinerant graduate teaching assistant (TA), which meant many wonderfully tipsy, passionate highbrow conversations in low-end bars during post–pay cheque fortnights and a steady decline in the quality and quantity of food thereafter. I was with my tribe, happy, writing steadily and hard, but clearly my revenue streams needed some new tributaries. Most of my fellow TAs had second teaching jobs, but these were poorly paid, and biweekly confrontations with towering stacks of freshman composition papers had engendered in me a bitter hatred for all students. I looked around for other writing work, and requested information from publishers of porn and romance novels. I was quite willing to do this honest, easy labour, but found that literary-novel-writing apparently exhausted my creative resources, which ran to about four hundred words a day and were subsequently incapable of delivering even formulaically heaving bosoms and thrusting rods.

I was saved by a fellow graduate student who had noticed my burgeoning geekiness. By now I was walking around campus with 800-page computer manuals tucked under my arm and holding forth about the video-game virtues of *Leisure Suit Larry in the Land of the Lounge Lizards* in the grad-student lounge. My friend asked me to help set up her new computer, and I arrived at her house with a painstakingly curated collection of bootlegged programs and freeware utilities and an extra-large bottle of Diet Coke. She just wanted to be able to write short stories and print them out, but one of the pre-eminent signs of computer mania is a fanatical exactitude, a desire to have the system work just so. I tricked out her machine, emptied my bottle of soda, and then gave her my standard lecture about on-site and off-site backups and the importance of regular hard-disk checks and defragging. She looked a bit overwhelmed, but a couple of weeks later she called to ask if I would help a friend of hers, the owner of a local bookstore, with his new computers at the shop. 'They'll pay you,' she said.

Pay me? For letting me play with their new machines, no doubt still boxed and unsullied and ripe for my superior setup skills? This seemed incredible, but I gathered myself and said, 'Sure, sounds good.' This was the beginning of a busy and profitable career as an independent computer consultant, which in short order led to paid programming gigs. As many consultants and programmers do, I learnt on the job—if I didn't know how to do something, Usenet and the technical sections of bookstores pointed me in the general direction of a solution. I was fairly scrupulous about not billing clients for the hours spent educating myself, more from a desire not to overprice my services than moral rectitude. I did provide value—word of mouth gave me a growing list of clients, and I was able to raise my hourly rate steadily.

I set up computers for elegant ladies in River Oaks and gave them word-processing lessons; I went out to factories and offices in the hinterlands of Houston to observe assembly lines and then modelled workflows and production processes. The programming I did was journeyman work; I mostly wrote CRUD applications, menu-driven screens that let the users Create, Retrieve, Update, and Delete records that tracked whatever product or service they provided: precision-engineered drill parts for high-heat applications, workers for the oil industry, reservations at restaurants. Simple stuff, but useful, and I always felt like I was learning, and making good money, sometimes even great money. I could afford biannual trips to India. Programming in America paid for my research and writing. I managed to get through graduate school without taking any loans, finished my novel, found an agent.

After the novel was published, I accepted a university teaching job in creative writing, and finally gave up the professional freelance computer work. It had served me well. Now it was time to write.

I found, soon enough, that although I may have stopped chasing the fat consulting pay cheques, the impulse to program had not left me. The work of making software gave me a little jolt of joy each time a piece of code worked; when something wasn't working, when the problem resisted and made me rotate the contours of the conundrum in my mind, the world fell away, my body vanished, time receded. And three or five hours later, when the pieces of the problem came together just so and clicked into a solution, I surfed a swelling wave of endorphins. On the programming section of Reddit, a popular social news site, a beginner posted a picture of his first working program with the caption, 'For most of you, this is surely child [sic] play, but holy shit, this must be what it feels like to do heroin for the first time.'[2] Even after you are long past your first 'Hello, world!' there is an infinity of things to learn, you are still a child, and—if you aren't burnt out by software delivery deadlines and management-mandated all-nighters—coding is still play. You can slam this pleasure spike into your veins again and again, and you want more, and more, and more. It's mostly a benign addiction, except for the increased risks of weight gain, carpal tunnel syndrome, bad posture, and reckless spending on programming tools you don't really need but absolutely must have.

So I indulged myself and puttered around and made little utilities, and grading systems, and suchlike. I was writing fiction steadily, but I found that the stark determinisms of code were a welcome relief from the ambiguities of literary narrative. By the end of a morning of writing, I was eager for the pleasures of programming. Maybe because I no longer had to deliver finished applications and had time to reflect, I realized that I had no idea what my code actually did. That is, I worked within a certain language and formal system of rules, I knew how the syntax of this language could be arranged to affect changes in a series of metaphors—the 'file system,' the 'desktop,' 'Windows'—but the best understanding I had of what existed under these conceptualizations was a steampunk-ish series of gearwheels taken from illustrations of Charles Babbage's Difference Engine. So now I made an attempt to get closer to the metal, to follow the effects of my code down into the machine.

The seven lines of the 'Hello, world!' code at the beginning of this book—written in Microsoft's C# language—do nothing until they are swallowed and munched by a specialized program called a compiler, which translates them into thirty-odd lines of 'Common Intermediate Language' (CIL) that look like this:

```
{
  .entrypoint
  // Method begins at RVA 0x2050
  // Code size       13 (0xd)
  .maxstack  8
  IL_0000:  /* 00  |                    */ nop
  IL_0001:  /* 72  | (70)000001         */ ldstr
    "Hello, world!" /* 70000001 */
  IL_0006:  /* 28  | (0A)000011         */ call       void
    [mscorlib/*23000001*/]System.Console/*01000013*/::Writ
    eLine(string) /* 0A000011 */
  IL_000b:  /* 00  |                    */ nop
  IL_000c:  /* 2A  |                    */ ret
} // end of method Program::Main
```

Figure 3.1: CIL for 'Hello, world!' program in C#

This, as the name of the language indicates, is a mediating dialect between human and machine. You could write a 'Hello, world!' program in another Microsoft language like Visual Basic and get almost exactly the same listing, which is how the program is stored on disk, ready to run. When you do run it, the CIL is converted yet again, this time into machine code:

21

```
55
8B EC
83 3D 78 81 B0 04 00
74 05
E8 B6 92 A2 65
90
8B 0D 94 3A B0 03
FF 15 C4 70 89 02
90
90
5D
C3
```

Figure 3.2: Machine code for 'Hello, world!' program in C#

Now we're really close to computing something, but not quite yet. Machine code is actually a really low-level programming language which encodes one or more instructions as numbers. The numbers are displayed above in a hexadecimal format, which is easier for humans to read than the binary numbers ('1010101 10001011 . . .') sent to the computer's central processing unit (CPU). This CPU is able to accept these numbers, each of which represents an instruction native to that particular type of CPU; the CPU reacts to each number by tripping its logic gates, which is to say that a lot of physical changes cascade in a purely mechanical fashion through the chips and platters in that box on your desk, and 'Hello, world!' appears on your screen.

But, but—what are 'logic gates'? Before I began my investigation of the mechanics of computing, this phrase evoked some fuzzy images of ones and zeros and intricate circuits, but I had no idea how all of this worked together to produce 'Hello, world!' on my screen. This is true of the vast majority of people in the world. Each year, I ask a classroom of undergraduate students at Berkeley if they can describe how a logic gate works, and usually out of about a hundred-odd juniors and seniors, I get one or two who are able to answer in the affirmative, and typically these are computer science or engineering majors. There are IT professionals who don't know how computers really work; I certainly was one of them, and here is 'Rob P.' on the 'programmers' section of stackexchange.com, a popular question-and-answer site:

> This is almost embarrassing [to] ask . . . I have a degree in Computer Science (and a second one in progress). I've worked as a full-time .NET Developer for nearly five years. I generally seem competent at what I do.
>
> **But I Don't Know How Computers Work!** [Emphasis in the original.]
>
> I know there are components . . . the power supply, the motherboard, ram, CPU, etc . . . and I get the 'general idea' of what they do. But I really don't understand how you go from a line of code like Console.Readline() in .NET (or Java or C++) and have it actually *do* stuff.[1]

How logic gates 'do stuff' is dazzlingly simple. But before we get to their elegant workings, a little primer on terminology: you will remember that the plus sign in mathematical notation (as in '2 + 3') can be referred to as the 'addition operator.' The minus sign is similarly the 'subtraction operator,' the forward slash is the 'division operator,' and so on. Mostly, we non-mathematicians treat the operators as convenient, almost-invisible markers that tell us which particular kindergarten-vintage practice we should apply to the all-important digits on either side of themselves. But there is another way to think about operators: as functions that consume the digits and output a result. Perhaps you could visualize the addition operator as a little machine like this, which accepts inputs on the left and produces the output on the right:

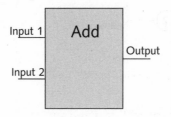

Figure 3.3: Addition operator

So if you give this 'Add' machine the inputs '3' and '2,' it will produce the result '5.'

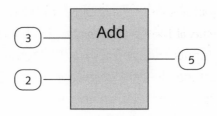

Figure 3.4: Addition operator with inputs '3' and '2'

A 'Subtract' operator might be imagined like this:

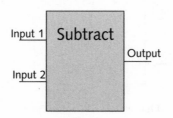

Figure 3.5: Subtraction operator

So, giving this 'Subtract' operator a first input of '4.2' and a second input of '2.2' will cause it to output '2.0.'

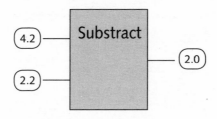

Figure 3.6: Subtraction operator with inputs '4.2' and '2.2'

The mathematical addition and subtraction operators above act on numbers, and only on numbers. In his 1847 monograph, *The Mathematical Analysis of Logic*, George Boole proposed a similar algebra for logic. In 1854, he corrected and extended these ideas about the application of symbolic algebra to logic with a seminal book, *An Investigation of the Laws of Thought, on Which Are Founded the Mathematical Theories of Logic and Probabilities*. In 'Boolean algebra,' the only legal inputs and outputs are the logical values 'true' and 'false'—nothing else, just 'true' and 'false.' The operators which act on these logical inputs are logical functions such as AND (conjunction), OR (disjunction), and NOT (negation). So the logical AND operator might look like this:

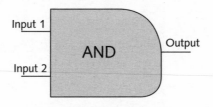

Figure 3.7: AND operator

The AND or conjunction operator, according to Boole, outputs 'true' only when both inputs are 'true.' That is, it works like this:

Input 1	Input 2	Output
false	false	false
false	true	false
true	false	false
true	true	true

If you gave the Boolean operator AND a first input of 'false' and a second input of 'true,' it would output 'false.'

Figure 3.8: AND operator with inputs 'false' and 'true'

The output of '(Teddy can fly) AND (Teddy is a dog)' would therefore be 'false.' But the output of '(Teddy is a dog) AND (Teddy has a keen sense of smell)' would be 'true.'

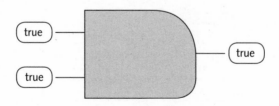

Figure 3.9: AND operator with inputs 'true' and 'true'

Other operators work similarly. The 'truth table' for the Boolean 'OR' operator would look like this:

Input 1	Input 2	Output
false	false	false
false	true	true
true	false	true
true	true	true

So, the output of '(Teddy can fly) OR (Teddy is a dog)' would be 'true.' That is, a first input of 'false' and a second input of 'true' would produce the output 'true.'

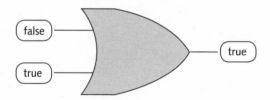

Figure 3.10: OR operator with inputs 'false' and 'true'

If one were to adopt the convention that 'false' was represented by the digit '0' and 'true' by '1,' the functioning of the OR operator could be represented as follows:

Input 1	Input 2	Output
0	0	0
0	1	1
1	0	1
1	1	1

And so we could draw our OR operator example like this:

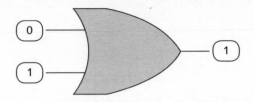

Figure 3.11: OR operator with inputs '0' and '1'

The XOR operator—sometimes referred to as the 'exclusive-OR' operator—is a variation of the OR operator. It outputs 'true' if either, but not both, of the inputs are 'true.'

Input 1	Input 2	Output
0	0	0
0	1	1
1	0	1
1	1	0

You can think of XOR as an 'either-or' operator—it returns 'true' if one of the inputs is true, but returns 'false' if both of the inputs are 'true' or if both of the inputs are 'false.' For example, a future robot-run restaurant might use an XOR operation to test whether your sandwich order was valid: '(With soup) XOR (With salad)'—you could have soup or salad, but not both or nothing. The last line of the truth table for the XOR operator could be drawn like this:

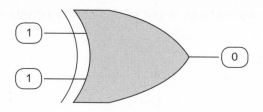

Figure 3.12: XOR operator with inputs '1' and '1'

~

Boolean algebra allows the translation of logical statements into mathematical expressions. By substituting ones and zeros into our soup-XOR-salad statement above, we can get back another number we can use in further operations.

Now here's the magical part: you can build simple physical objects—logic gates—that mechanically reproduce the workings of Boolean operators. Here is an AND logic gate built out of LEGO bricks, cogs, and wheels by Martin Howard, a physicist from the UK:

Figure 3.13: LEGO AND logic gate with inputs '0' and '0'
(Martin Howard)

This is a push–pull logic gate. The two levers on the left are for input: a pushed-in lever represents a value of 'true' or '1,' while a lever in the 'out' position represents a 'false' or '0.' The mechanism of the logic gate—its gears and rods—has been set up so that when you push in the input levers on the left, the output lever on the right *automatically* takes a position (in or out) that follows the workings of the Boolean logical operator AND. In figure 3.14, both input levers have been pushed in (set to 'true' and 'true'), and so the output lever has slid into a position representing 'true' or '1.' Or, in Boolean terms, 'true AND true = true.' Any possible positioning of the input levers will produce the correct positioning of the output lever. The logic gate always follows the truth table for the AND operator.

Figure 3.14: LEGO AND logic gate with inputs '1' and '1'
(Martin Howard)

And here is a push–pull XOR logic gate that mimics the workings of the Boolean XOR operator:

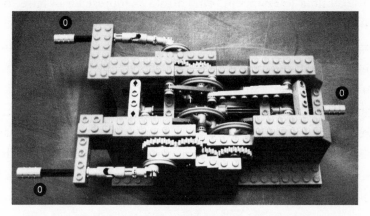

Figure 3.15: LEGO XOR logic gate with inputs '0' and '0'
(Martin Howard)

Figure 3.16: LEGO XOR logic gate with inputs '0' and 'I'
(Martin Howard)

If you're still having trouble visualizing how these Lego logic gates work, you can watch videos at http://www.randomwraith.com/logic.html. A physical logic gate is any device that—through artful construction—can correctly replicate the workings of one of the Boolean logical operators.

You may still be wondering how all of this leads us towards computation, towards calculation. Well, as it happens, you can also represent numbers in a binary fashion, with ones and zeros, or with absence and presence, off states and on states. In binary notation, the decimal number '3' is '11.' How does this work? You'll recall from elementary school that in the decimal system, the position of a digit—from right to left—changes what that digit means. If you write the decimal number '393,' you are putting the digits into columns like this:

Hundreds (10^2)	Tens (10^1)	Ones (10^0)
3	9	3

So what you're representing when you write '393' is something like 'three hundreds, plus nine tens, plus three ones' or '(3 x 10^2) + (9 x 10^1) + (3 x 10^0).' A more precise way to think about the columns in the decimal system is to say each column, from right to left, represents an increase by a factor of ten. The small superscript number—the exponent—tells you how many times to use the number in a multiplication by itself. So, the 'Hundreds' column represents quantities of '10^2' or '10 x 10.' Any number to the power of 1 gives you the number itself, so '10^1' is '10'; and any number to the power of zero is just '1,' so '10^0' is '1.'

In base-2 or binary notation, our column headings would look like this:

256	128	64	32	16	8	4	2	1
(2^8)	(2^7)	(2^6)	(2^5)	(2^4)	(2^3)	(2^2)	(2^1)	(2^0)

And you would write '393' in binary like this:

256	128	64	32	16	8	4	2	1
(2^8)	(2^7)	(2^6)	(2^5)	(2^4)	(2^3)	(2^2)	(2^1)	(2^0)
1	1	0	0	0	1	0	0	1

When you write the binary number '110001001,' you are putting a '1' in every column which you want to include in your reckoning of the quantity you are trying to represent. In a base-2 system, you have only two symbols you can use, '0' and '1' (as opposed to the ten symbols you use in a base-10 system, '0' through '9'). So, with '110001001,' you are representing something like '256, plus 128, plus 8, plus 1' or '(1×2^8) + (1×2^7) + (1×2^3) + (1×2^0)'—which equals decimal '393.'

Decimal '9' is the same as binary '1001,' and decimal '5' is binary '101'—all very baffling to the decimal-using brain, but completely consistent and workable. So if you wanted to add '9' to '5' in binary, it would look like this:

```
      1   0   0   1
  +       1   0   1
  ─────────────────
      1   1   1   0
```

And binary '1110' is of course equivalent to '8 + 4 + 2 + 0' or decimal '14.' From the above, you can deduce the rules of binary addition:

- $0 + 0 = 0$
- $0 + 1 = 1$
- $1 + 0 = 1$
- $1 + 1 = 0$, and carry 1

The last rule may seem a bit mystifying until you recall how addition works in decimal arithmetic. In decimal, you use the digits '0' through '9' to represent numbers; when the sum of the digits in a column exceeds '9' you write the least significant figure ('4' in the number '14') in that column and carry the more significant figure ('1' in the number '14') to the next column on the left. In binary notation, you can only use the digits '1' and '0'—so when you add '1' to '1,' you write '0' in that column and carry '1.'

Now this may begin to remind you of Boolean logic—you're taking inputs of zeros and ones and sending out zeros and ones. In fact, except for the 'carry 1' part of the last rule, this looks very much like the truth table for the XOR logical operator:

Input 1	Input 2	Output
0	0	0
0	1	1
1	0	1
1	1	0

It turns out that if you put together certain logical operators in clever ways, you can completely replicate addition in binary, including the 'carry 1' part. Here is a schematic for a 'half adder'—built by combining an XOR operator and an AND operator—which takes in two single binary digits and outputs a sum and an optional digit to carry.

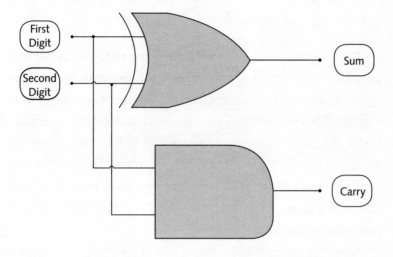

Figure 3.17: Schematic for half adder

So the half adder would function as follows:

First Digit	Second Digit	Sum	Carry
1	1	0	1
1	0	1	0
0	1	1	0
0	0	0	0

And since we can build logic gates—physical objects that replicate logical operations—we should be able to build a physical half adder. And, indeed, here is a LEGO half adder built by Martin Howard.

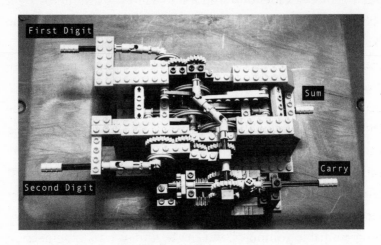

Figure 3.18: LEGO half adder (Martin Howard)

At last we have computation, which is—according to the *Oxford English Dictionary* (OED)—the 'action or process of computing, reckoning, or counting; arithmetical or mathematical calculation.' A 'computer' was originally, as the OED also tells us, a 'person who makes calculations or computations; a calculator, a reckoner; spec. a person employed to make calculations in an observatory, in surveying, etc.' Charles Babbage set out to create a machine that would replace the vast throngs of human computers who worked out logarithmic and trigonometric tables; what we've sketched out above are the beginnings of a mechanism which can do exactly that and more. You can use the output of the half adder as input for other mechanisms, and also continue to add logic gates to it to perform more complex operations. You can hook up two half adders together and add an OR logic gate to make a 'full adder,' which will accept two binary digits and also a carry digit as input, and will output a sum and a carry digit. You can then put together cascades of full adders to add binary numbers eight columns wide, or sixteen, or thirty-two. This adding machine 'knows' nothing; it is just a clever arrangement of physical objects that can go from one state to another, and by doing so cause changes in other physical objects. The revolutionary difference between it and the first device that Charles Babbage built, the Difference Engine, is that it represents data and logic in zeros and ones, in discrete digits—it is 'digital,' as opposed to the earlier 'analog' devices, all the way back through slide rules and astrolabes and the Antikythera mechanism. Babbage's planned second device, the Analytical Engine, would have been a digital, programmable computer, but the technology and engineering of his time was not able to implement what he had imagined.

Once you have objects which can materialize both Boolean algebra and binary numbers, you can connect these components in ways that allow the computation of mathematical functions. Line up sufficiently large numbers of simple on/off mechanisms, and you have a machine that can add, subtract, multiply, and through these mathematical operations format your epic novel in less time than you will take to finish reading this sentence. Computers can only compute, calculate; the poems you write, the pictures of your family, the music you listen to—all these are converted into binary numbers, sequences of ones and zeros, and are thus stored and changed and recreated. Your computer allows you to read, see, and hear by representing binary numbers as letters, images, and sounds. Computers may seem mysteriously active, weirdly alive, but they are mechanical devices like harvesting combines or sewing machines.

You can build logic gates out of any material that can accept inputs and switch between distinct states of output (current or no current, 1 or 0); there is nothing special about the chips inside your laptop that makes them essential to computing. Electrical circuits laid out in silicone just happen to be small, cheap, relatively reliable, and easy to produce in mass quantities. The Digi-Comp II, which was sold as a toy in the sixties, used an inclined wooden plane, plastic cams, and marbles to perform binary mathematical operations. The vast worlds inside online games provide virtual objects that can be made to interact predictably, and some people have used these objects to make computing machines *inside* the games—Jong89, the creator of the 'Dwarven Computer' in the game *Dwarf Fortress*, used '672 [virtual water] pumps, 2000 [faux wooden] logs, 8500 mechanisms and thousands of other assort[ed] bits and knobs like doors and rock blocks' to put together his device, which is a fully functional computer that can perform any calculation that a 'real' computer can.[2] Logic gates have been built out of pneumatic, hydraulic, and optical devices, out of DNA, and flat sticks connected by rivets. Recently, some researchers from Kobe University in Japan announced, 'We demonstrate that swarms of soldier crabs can implement logical gates when placed in a geometrically constrained environment.'[3]

Many years after I stopped working professionally as a programmer, I finally understood this, truly grokked this fact— that you can build a logic gate out of water and pipes and valves, no electricity needed, and from the interaction of these physical objects produce computation. The shock of the revelation turned me into a geek party bore. I arranged toothpicks on dinner tables to lay out logic-gate schematics, and harassed my friends with disquisitions about the life and work of George Boole. And as I tried to explain the mechanisms of digital computation, I realized that it is a process that is fundamentally foreign to our common-sense, everyday understanding. In his masterly book on the subject, *Code: The Hidden Language of Computer Hardware and Software*, Charles Petzold uses telegraphic relay circuits—built out of batteries and wires—to walk the lay reader through the functioning of computing machines. And he points out:

> Samuel Morse had demonstrated his telegraph in 1844—ten years before the publication of Boole's *The Laws of Thought* . . .
>
> But nobody in the nineteenth century made the connection between the ANDs and ORs of Boolean algebra and the wiring of simple switches in series and in parallel. No mathematician, no electrician, no telegraph operator, nobody. Not even that icon of the computer revolution Charles Babbage (1792–1871), who had corresponded with Boole and knew his work, and who struggled for much of his life designing first a Difference Engine and then an Analytical Engine that a century later would be regarded as the precursors to modern computers . . .
>
> . . . Nobody in that century ever realized that Boolean expressions could be directly realized in electrical circuits. This equivalence wasn't discovered until the 1930s, most notably by Claude Elwood Shannon . . . whose famous 1938 M.I.T. master's thesis was entitled 'A Symbolic Analysis of Relay and Switching Circuits.'[4]

After Shannon, early pioneers of modern computing had no choice but to comprehend that you could build Boolean logic and binary numbers into electrical circuits and work directly with this equivalence to produce computation. That is, early computers *required* that you wire the logic of your program into the machine.

If you needed to solve a different problem, you had to build a whole new computer. General programmable computers, capable of receiving instructions to process varying kinds of logic, were first conceived of by Charles Babbage in 1837, and Lady Ada Byron wrote the first-ever computer program—which computed Bernoulli numbers—for this imaginary machine, but the technology of the era was incapable of building a working model.[5] The first electronic programmable computers appeared in the nineteen forties. They required instructions in binary—to talk to a computer, you had to actually understand Boolean logic and binary numbers and the innards of the machine you were driving into action. Since then, decades of effort have constructed layer upon layer of translation between human and machine. The paradox is, quite simply, that modern high-level programming languages hide the internal structures of computers from programmers. This is how Rob P. can acquire an advanced degree in computer science and still be capable of that plaintive, bold-faced cry, **'But I Don't Know How Computers Work!'**[6]

~

Computers have not really changed radically in terms of their underlying architecture over the last half-century; what we think of as advancement or progress is really a slowly growing ease of human use, an amenability to human cognition and manipulation that is completely dependent on vast increases in processing power and storage capabilities. As you can tell from our journey down the stack of languages mentioned earlier, the purpose of each layer is to shield the user from the perplexing complexities of the layer just below, and to allow instructions to be phrased in a syntax that is just a bit closer to everyday, spoken language. All this translation from one dialect to a lower one exacts a fearsome cost in processing cycles, which users are never aware of because the chips which do all the work gain astonishing amounts of computing ability every year; in the famous formulation by Intel co-founder George E. Moore, the number of transistors that can be fitted on to an integrated circuit should double approximately every two years. Moore's Law has held true since 1965. What this means in practical terms is that computers get exponentially more powerful and smaller every decade.

According to computer scientist Jack Ganssle, your iPad 2 has 'about the compute capability of the Cray 2, 1985's leading supercomputer. The Cray cost $35 million more than the iPad. Apple's product runs 10 hours on a charge; the Cray needed 150 KW and liquid Flourinert cooling.'[7] He goes on to describe ENIAC—the Electronic Numerical Integrator and Computer— which was the world's first general-purpose, fully electronic computer capable of being programmed for diverse tasks. It was put into operation in 1945.[8] 'If we built [an iPhone] using the ENIAC's active element technology,' Ganssle writes:

> the phone would be about the size of 170 Vertical Assembly Buildings (the largest single-story building in the world) . . . Weight? 2,500 Nimitz-class aircraft carriers. And what a power hog! Figure over a terawatt, requiring all of the output of 500 of Olkiluoto power plants (the largest nuclear plant in the world). An ENIAC-technology iPhone would run a cool $50 trillion, roughly the GDP of the entire world.[9]

So that smartphone you carry in your pocket is actually a

fully programmable supercomputer; you could break the Enigma code with it, or design nuclear bombs. You can use it to tap out shopping lists because millions of logic gates are churning away to draw that pretty keyboard and all those shadowed checkboxes. And I can write working programs because modern high-level languages like C# protect me from the overwhelming intricacy of the machine as it actually is. When I write code in C#, I work within a regime that has been designed to be 'best for human understanding,' far removed from the alien digital idiom of the machine. Until the early fifties, programmers worked in machine code or one of its close variants. As we've just seen, instructions passed to the computer's CPU have to be encoded as binary numbers ('1010101 10001011 . . .'), which are extremely hard for humans to read and write, or even distinguish from one another. Representing these numbers in a hexadecimal format ('55 8B . . .') makes the code more legible, but only slightly so. So assembly language was created; in assembly, each low-level machine-code instruction is represented by a mnemonic. So our earlier hexadecimal representation of 'Hello, world!' becomes:

```
push      ebp
mov       ebp,esp
cmp       dword ptr ds:[06FF9A78h],0
je        00000011
call      6D2197F0
nop
mov       ecx,dword ptr ds:[03B35718h]
call      dword ptr ds:[02A0CB3Ch]
nop
nop
pop       ebp
ret
```

Figure 3.19: 'Hello, world!' in assembly language

One line of code in assembly language usually translates into one machine-code instruction. Writing code in assembly is more efficient than writing machine code, but is still difficult and error-prone.

In 1954, John Backus and a legendary team of IBM programmers began work on a pioneering high-level programming language, FORTRAN (from FORmula TRANslation), intended for use in scientific and numerical applications. FORTRAN offered not only a more English-like vocabulary and syntax, but also economy—a single line of FORTRAN would be translated into many machine-code instructions. 'Hello, world!' in FORTRAN is:

```
PROGRAM HELLO
PRINT*, 'Hello, World!'
END
```

Figure 3.20: 'Hello, world!' in FORTRAN

All modern high-level languages provide the same ease of use. I work inside an orderly, simplified hallucination, a *maya* that is illusion and not-illusion—the code I write sets off other subterranean incantations which are completely illegible to me, but I can cause objects to move in the real world, and send messages to the other side of the planet.

The American novels I found on the shelves of my lending library in Bombay were dense little packets of information and emotion and culture from across the globe. I consumed them and the values and mythologies they incarnated, and was transformed in some very intimate way. Once I was in America, face-to-face with the foreign, I wrote a novel about another Indian encounter with the Other: about colonialism, about the coming together and clash of cultures. Despite my love for American modernism, it turned out I didn't want to write a modernist novel. I ended up writing a hybrid book, a kind of mongrel construction which used, in one half, the Indian storytelling mode of magical tale-within-tale and all the sacred and profane registers of classical Indian literature; the other half operated more or less within the mode of modern psychological realism. Colonialism exercised its depredations not only within the realms of economics and politics; an essential part of its ideology was the assertion that Indian narrative modes were primitive, or childish, or degenerate, and that Western aesthetic norms were more civilized and sophisticated. History was progress, the colonized were told, and the West was more evolved. The current state of the world was living proof of this developmental teleology. I wanted to write a book that incarnated in its very form a resistance to this Just-So story about culture.

I understood this intention quite clearly as I wrote, but looking back now I see, also, a very young writer finding a form to contain all his various selves. I was moving between cultures, from India to America and back. I was a wanderer between nation states, I negotiated my way through their rigid borders and bureaucracies, and what could be more modern than that? I was surely a postmodern lover of modernist fiction. Yet, in my creative urges, in the deepest parts of myself, I also remained somehow stubbornly premodern. I didn't use those premodern forms only for political and polemical reasons; I wasn't only trying to ironize psychological 'realism' by placing it next to the epic and the mythical, or only to create *lo real maravilloso* as a critique of bourgeois Western imperial notions of the real. No, the impulse was not merely negative. This multiply layered narrative was how I lived within myself, how I knew myself, how I spoke to myself. There was the modern me, and also certain other simultaneous selves who lived on alongside. These 'shadow selves'—to follow sociologist Ashis Nandy— responded passionately and instantly to epic tropes, whether in the Mahabharata or in Hindi films; believed implicitly and stubbornly in reincarnation despite a devotion to Enlightenment positivism; insisted on regarding matter and consciousness as one; and experienced the world and oneself as the habitations of *devatas*, 'deities' who simultaneously represent inner realities and cosmic principles. So my book—to speak in my voice—had to contain these selves too.

This un-modern half of my book tended to confuse my American writing-program peers. In our workshops, the prevailing aesthetic tended towards minimalism; the models were Raymond Carver and Ann Beattie and Bobbie Ann Mason. The winding tales I brought in were judged, at least initially, to be melodramatic, mystical, exotic, strange. I didn't try to explain what I was trying to do mainly because I didn't have a vocabulary in which I could articulate the lived sensation of this shadow-world within me. I wrote on.

My other life as a computer geek was excitingly active and remunerative. As I taught myself about code, I discovered yet another culture on the newsgroups of Usenet and in meetings of the Houston Area League of PC Users (HAL-PC), 'the world's largest PC user group.' Programmers had their own lingo, their own hierarchies of value and respect, their own mythology. Many of these new norms were being created online. By the turn of the twenty-first century, Scott Rosenberg notes, programmers were writing

> personally, intently, and voluminously, pouring out their inspirations and frustrations, their insights and tips and fears and dreams, on Web sites and in blogs. It is a process that began in the earliest days of the Internet, on mailing lists and in newsgroup postings . . . Not all of this writing is consequential, and not all programmers read it. Yet it is changing the field— creating, if not a canon of the great works of software, at least an informal literature around the day-to-day practice of programming. The Web itself has become a distributed version of that vending-machine-lined common room . . . an informal and essential place for coders to share their knowledge and kibitz. It is also an open forum in which they continue to ponder, debate, and redefine the nature of the work they do.[1]

One of the urtexts in this shared folklore of computing is 'The Story of Mel, a Real Programmer.' It first appeared on a Usenet discussion board in May 1983, as a riposte to a recently published article 'devoted to the *macho* side of programming [which] made the bald and unvarnished statement: Real Programmers write in FORTRAN.'[2] Our Usenet storyteller here, like any chronicler of the days of yore, wants to set the quiche-eating, FORTRAN-writing young 'uns straight. He begins:

> Maybe [real programmers] do [use FORTRAN] now, in this decadent era of Lite beer, hand calculators, and 'user-friendly' software but back in the Good Old Days, when the term 'software' sounded funny and Real Computers were made out of drums and vacuum tubes, Real Programmers wrote in machine code. Not FORTRAN. Not RATFOR. Not, even, assembly language. Machine Code. Raw, unadorned, inscrutable hexadecimal numbers. Directly.[3]

This post was originally written in straightforward prose by Ed Nather, an astronomer, but some anonymous coder responded to its rhythms and elegiac tone and converted it into free verse, and so it has existed on the Web ever since:

> Lest a whole new generation of programmers
> grow up in ignorance of this glorious past,
> I feel duty-bound to describe,
> as best I can through the generation gap,
> how a Real Programmer wrote code.
> I'll call him Mel,
> because that was his name.[4]

Mel, the eponymous protagonist of this epic, is the kind of programmer who is already a rarity in 1983: he understands the machine so well that he can program in machine code. The

conveniences afforded by high-level languages like FORTRAN
and its successors—which now all seem primitive—have by
1983 already so cushioned the practitioners of computing from
the metal, from the mechanics of what they do, that they are
hard-pressed to debug Mel's code. Mel's understanding of his
hardware seems uncanny, mystical, a remnant from a bygone
heroic epoch:

> Mel never wrote time-delay loops, either,
> even when the balky Flexowriter
> required a delay between output characters to work right.
> He just located instructions on the drum
> so each successive one was just *past* the read head
> when it was needed;
> the drum had to execute another complete revolution
> to find the next instruction.
> He coined an unforgettable term for this procedure.
> Although 'optimum' is an absolute term,
> like 'unique', it became common verbal practice
> to make it relative:
> 'not quite optimum' or 'less optimum'
> or 'not very optimum'.
> Mel called the maximum time-delay locations
> the 'most pessimum'.
>
> . . .
>
>
> I have often felt that programming is an art form,
> whose real value can only be appreciated
> by another versed in the same arcane art;

there are lovely gems and brilliant coups

hidden from human view and admiration, sometimes forever,

by the very nature of the process.

You can learn a lot about an individual

just by reading through his code,

even in hexadecimal.

Mel was, I think, an unsung genius.[5]

Within the division of Microsoft that produces programming tools, a Mel-like programmer is represented by the persona 'Einstein,' who is an 'expert on both low level bit-twiddling and high-level object oriented architectures.'[6] There is also another persona named 'Elvis,' a 'professional application developer.'[7] As described by Eric Lippert, former senior software engineer at Microsoft, both Einstein and Elvis 'got their jobs by studying computer science and going into development as a career.'[8] And then there is the persona 'Mort,' who is 'an expert on frobnicating [tweaking, adjusting] widgets, [who] one day realizes that his widget-tracking spreadsheets could benefit from a little [Visual Basic for Applications] magic, so he picks up enough VBA to get by.'[9]

The vast majority of programmers in the world today are Morts. Despite my intermittent, fumbling attempts at studying data structures and algorithms—the bricks and mortar of computer science—I most definitely remain on the Mort end of the scale. The ever-receding minority of Mels and Einsteins has observed this democratization of the computer with mixed feelings: on the one hand, the legendary early hackers at MIT and Apple are revered precisely because they took on the bureaucratic priesthood that protected the mainframes, defeated its defences, and made computing available to all; on the other, the millions of Morts who have benefited from the computer revolution produce awful, bloated, buggy software because they don't know how the machine really works, and, what's worse, most Morts don't *want* to know. 'Mort is a very *local* programmer—he wants to make a few changes to one subroutine and be done,' writes Lippert.

> Mort does not want to understand how an entire system works in order to tinker with it. And my goodness, Mort *hates* reading documentation . . . Mort's primary job is to frobnicate widgets—code is just a means to that end—so every second spent making the code more elegant takes him away from his primary job.[10]

Mort lacks 'mechanical sympathy,' that quality possessed by the best race-car drivers, who understand their machines so well that they flow in harmony with them.

To the Morts of the world, and even to the Elvii, Mel the Real Programmer's programming is inscrutable and his mystique dazzling. The narrator of our epic is asked to investigate and change the behaviour of a program that Mel has written. He reads through Mel's code, and is baffled by an 'innocent loop' which doesn't have a test within it—as is usual—to break the loop. Code loops always contain a conditional test of the form 'if numberOfLoops > 4 then break'; without such a construct you are trapped in an endless circling repetition. 'Common sense said that it had to be a closed loop, / where the program would circle, forever, endlessly.'[11] But Mel's program doesn't get stuck in the loop, it flows through, it works. It takes the narrator two weeks to comprehend Mel's uncanny melding of code and machine, which uses the test-less loop and a programmer-forced malfunction in the system's memory to position the next program instruction in the right location; such is the force of this revelation that 'when the light went on it nearly blinded me.' After such knowledge, reverence is the only proper emotion; the narrator tells his Big Boss that he can't fix the error because he can't find it.

I didn't feel comfortable
hacking up the code of a Real Programmer.[12]

~

Despite the allusion above to 'the *macho* side of programming,' the non-geek may not fully grasp that within the culture of programmers, Mel es muy macho. The Real Programmer squints his eyes, does his work, and rides into the horizon to the whistling notes of Ennio Morricone. To you, Steve Wozniak may be that cuddly penguin who was on a few episodes of Dancing with the Stars, and by all accounts, he really is the good, generous man one sees in interviews. But within the imaginations of programmers, Woz is also a hard man, an Original Gangsta: he wired together his television set and a keyboard and a bunch of chips on a circuit board and so created the Apple I computer. Then he realized he needed a programming language for the microprocessor he'd used, and none existed, so Woz—who had never taken a language-design class—read a couple of books, wrote a compiler, and then wrote a programming language called Integer BASIC in machine code. And when we say 'wrote' this programming language we mean that he wrote the assembly code in a paper notebook on the right side of the pages, and then transcribed it into machine code on the left.[13] And he did all this while holding down a full-time job at Hewlett-Packard: 'I designed two computers and cassette tape interfaces and printer interfaces and serial ports and I wrote a Basic and all this application software, I wrote demos, and I did all this moonlighting, all in a year.'[14]

That second computer was the Apple II, the machine that defined personal computing, that is on every list of the greatest computers ever made. Woz designed all the hardware *and* all the circuit boards *and* all the software that went into the Apple II, while the other Steve spewed marketing talk at potential investors and customers on the phone. Every piece and bit and byte of that computer was done by Woz, and not one bug has ever been found, 'not one bug in the hardware, not one bug in the software.'[15] The circuit design of the Apple II is widely considered to be astonishingly beautiful, as close to perfection as one can get in engineering.

Woz did both hardware and software. Woz created a programming language in machine code. Woz is *hardcore*.

~

Working in machine code is very hard, so assembly code was created by adding some mnemonics to machine code. Working in assembly code is still hard; doing anything complex—like making games—in it is insanely hard. On programmers.stackexchange.com, a user going by the nom de guerre 'DFectuoso' asked, 'Are there any famous one-man-army programmers?'[16] During the ensuing discussion about lone coders, one of the participants mentioned Chris Sawyer, who wrote the hugely successful 1999 game, *RollerCoaster Tycoon*: 'He had a little help with music and graphics, but otherwise RollerCoaster Tycoon was all him. Amazing, especially given the physics engine. Last but not least, the entire game was written in assembly language.' And another commenter responded, 'He wrote that in assembly?! Jesus Christ. I think I need to go boil my brain now.'

Sawyer's achievements are indeed brain-boilingly immense, but why and how does a lone Scottish geek toiling obsessively over his virtual roller coasters become a 'one-man-army'? Why do the Einsteins of programming affect—in their online personas and sometimes in person—a blustery *True Grit* swagger? Therein lies one of the tales that Nathan Ensmenger tells in his illuminating social history of computing, *The Computer Boys Take Over: Computers, Programmers, and the Politics of Technical Expertise*. Ensmenger does for computing in North America what historians of science have done for other disciplines: locate the development of knowledge and technology firmly within a messy matrix of human agency and politics; there is no orderly teleological progress from triumph to triumph, only competing interests which struggle over authority, access, and power. The computer boys of Ensmenger's title are the early software-builders, the pioneers; the irony, as Ensmenger shows, is that many of them were women. In fact, the earliest programmers were all women: the 'ENIAC girls' were women recruited by the (male) engineers and managers of the Electronic Numerical Integrator and Computer. The creators of the ENIAC had a clear division of labour in mind: the male scientist or 'planner' would do the hard intellectual work of creating the mathematical algorithms and structures necessary to solve a problem; the female 'coder' would then carry out the 'static' manual labour of entering this plan into the machine by manipulating plugboard wiring and thousands of switches. Numerous wires had to be plugged and switches flipped for each machine instruction; each problem required thousands of instructions, so wiring—which was the programming—would take several days, and checking the wiring would take another few.[17]

Figure 4.1: Programming the ENIAC (US Army photo)

This division of tasks of course echoed the hierarchies already present; men did the thinking and inventing, women were clerks. 'The telephone switchboard-like appearance of the ENIAC programming cable-and-plug panels,' Ensmenger writes, 'reinforced the notion that programmers were mere

Figure 4.2: Programming the ENIAC (US Army photo)

machine operators, that programming was more handicraft than science, more feminine than masculine, more mechanical than intellectual.'[18] The planners considered the coding process so transparently simple that they couldn't imagine that once in the machines, their algorithms might fault and hang, might need to be stopped. One of the ENIAC programmers, Betty Holberton, had to work very hard to convince John von Neumann that programs were complex and therefore fragile:

> But to my astonishment, [Dr von Neumann] never mentioned a stop instruction. So I did coyly say, 'Don't we need a stop instruction in this machine?' He said, 'No we don't need a stop instruction. We have all these empty sockets here that just let it go to bed.' And I went back home and I was really alarmed. After all, we had debugged the machine day and night for months just trying to get jobs on it.

So the next week when I came up with some alterations in the code, I approached him again with the same question. He gave me the same answer. Well I really got red in the face. I was so excited and I really wanted to tell him off. And I said, 'But Dr. von Neumann, we are programmers and we sometimes make mistakes.' He nodded his head and the stop order went in.[19]

Once von Neumann and everyone else involved with computers understood this hitherto unimaginable fact—that programming, translating algorithms into the language of machines, was very difficult—programmers became valuable commodities. A 1959 Price Waterhouse report warned that 'high quality individuals are the key to top grade programming. Why? Purely and simply because much of the work involved is exacting and difficult enough to require real intellectual ability and above average personal characteristics.'[20] Such individuals weren't easy to find, and as corporations looked for competitive advantage by computerizing their business processes, a shortage resulted. Corporations set up training programmes, fly-by-night vocational schools sprang up guaranteeing jobs: 'There's room for everyone. The industry needs people. You've got what it takes.'[21]

In 1967, Cosmopolitan magazine carried an article titled 'The Computer Girls' which emphasized that programming was a field in which there was 'no sex discrimination in hiring'— 'every company that makes or uses computers hires women to program them . . . If a girl is qualified, she's got the job.' Admiral Grace Hopper, programming pioneer, assured the Cosmo readers that programming was 'just like planning a dinner . . . You have to plan ahead and schedule everything so it's ready when you need it. Programming requires patience and the ability to handle detail. Women are "naturals" at computer programming.'[22]

Already, though, the 'masculinization process' of the computing industry was underway. The severe limitations of memory and processing power in the machines of the day demanded Mel the Real Programmer's wizardry; John Backus described programming in the fifties as 'a black art, a private arcane matter . . . [in which] the success of a program depended primarily on the programmer's private techniques and inventions.'[23] The aptitude tests used by the industry to identify potential Mels consisted primarily of mathematical and logical puzzles, which often required a formal education in these disciplines; even *Cosmopolitan* magazine, despite its breezy confidence about the absence of sexism in computing, recognized this as a barrier to entry for its readers. An industry analyst argued that the 'Darwinian selection' of personnel profiling resulted in an influx of programmers who were 'often egocentric, slightly neurotic, and [bordering] upon a limited schizophrenia. The incidence of beards, sandals, and other symptoms of rugged individualism or nonconformity are notably greater among this demographic group.'[24] The Real Programmers that the industry found through these aptitude tests were weird male geeks wielding keyboards.

As Ensmenger puts it:

It is almost certainly the case that these [personality] profiles represented, at best, deeply flawed scientific methodology. But they almost equally certainly created a gender-biased feedback cycle that ultimately selected for programmers with stereotypically masculine characteristics. The primary selection mechanism used by the industry selected for antisocial, mathematically inclined males, and therefore antisocial, mathematically inclined males were overrepresented in the programmer population; this in turn reinforced the popular perception that programmers ought to be antisocial and mathematically inclined (and therefore male), and so on ad infinitum.[25]

The surly male genius, though, was perceived as a threat by corporate managers, especially as the initial enthusiasm over computerization gave way to doubts about actual value being produced for the companies spending the money. A programmer-turned-management-consultant described the long-haired computer wonks as a 'Cosa Nostra' holding management to ransom, and warned that computer geeks were 'at once the most unmanageable and the most poorly managed specialism in our society. Actors and artists pale by comparison.'[26] Managers should 'refuse to embark on grandiose or unworthy schemes, and refuse to let their recalcitrant charges waste skill, money and time on the fashionable idiocies of our [computer] racket.'[27]

The solution that everyone agreed upon was professionalization. Managers liked the idea of standardization, testing, and certification; it would reduce their dependence on arty individuals practising arcana: 'The concept of professionalism affords a business-like answer to the existing and future computer skills market.'[28] Programmers wanted to be recognized as something other than mere technicians— the rewards would be 'status, greater autonomy, improved opportunities for advancement, and better pay.'[29] Within academia, researchers were struggling to establish computer science as a distinct discipline and establish a theoretical foundation for their work. So, 'an activity originally intended to be performed by low-status, clerical—and more often than not, female—[workers],' Ensmenger tells us:

> was gradually and deliberately transformed into a high-status, scientific, and masculine discipline.
>
> . . . As Margaret Rossiter and others have suggested, professionalization nearly always requires the exclusion of women . . .
>
> . . . As computer programmers constructed a professional identity for themselves during the crucial decades of the 1950s and 1960s . . . they also constructed a gender identity. Masculinity was just one of many resources that they drew on to distance their profession from its low-status origins in clerical data processing. The question of 'who made for a good programmer' increasingly involved in its answer the qualifier 'male.'[30]

~

In 1892, a British colonial official named Sir Lepel Griffin wrote:

> The characteristics of women which disqualify them for public life and its responsibilities are inherent in their sex and are worthy of honour, for to be womanly is the highest praise for a woman, as to be masculine is her worst reproach. But when men, as the Bengalis, are disqualified for political enfranchisement by the possession of essentially feminine characteristics, they must expect to be held in such contempt by stronger and braver races, who have fought for such liberties as they have won or retained.[31]

Sir Griffin was certain that Bengalis were unfit for political power because they were effeminate, weak, and it was unthinkable that they might 'represent . . . precede . . . and govern the martial races of India'—that is, certain other ethnic groups within India who were deemed sufficiently warlike by the English. If a Bengali were to demonstrate such aspirations to equality, 'then the English, as the common conqueror and master of all, may justly laugh at his pretensions and order him to take the humbler place which better suits a servile race which has never struck a blow against an enemy.'[32]

The gender politics of the Raj were of course much on my mind while I wrote my first novel in the late eighties and early nineties, as I travelled back and forth between India and America. The British 'Cult of Manliness' had been an essential component of the creed of Empire, which—as above—conflated masculinity, violence, civic virtue, and morality. Even intelligence and intellectual capability were inextricably intertwined with masculinity; women and all others who exhibited symptoms of femininity were fuzzy headed, illogical, and easily overcome by emotion; they were incapable especially of scientific reasoning and therefore self-knowledge and progress. The state of the world—women without power, Englishmen ruling Indians—bore out the truth of these propositions.

By now, I'd read my Edward Said, and I prided myself on being aware of the ideological mechanisms that transformed local contingencies of history and culture into Nature itself. The attractions of Nick Carter, Killmaster, seemed altogether more sinister now that I had listened to many scholarly deconstructions of imperial American masculinity. But at the time, I didn't question much the demographics of programming. The meetings of the special interest groups of HAL-PC devoted to programming were all-male; I think in all my years of consulting work I met one female programmer. This was just the way things were. The male programmers I met were often astonishingly generous with knowledge and technical advice, and yet, the very same men were also abrupt and outright rude. Indians are frequently taken aback by the American virtues of quick intimacy and bluntness, which come across as shockingly bad manners; I knew to discount for this, and understood that our own predilection for face-saving, *izzat*-preserving niceties made us maddeningly opaque and slippery to the average American. Still, these coders were deliberately obnoxious by anyone's standards, especially online. They ad-hominemed, flamed, name-called, dismissed, despised. Not to put too fine a point on it: these guys were assholes. Pre-eminence amongst programmers was often decided by competitions of assholery, a kind of ritual jousting.

This unfortunate condition has only intensified over the decades. The 'masculinization process' that Ensmenger describes has resulted in a contemporary American culture of programming that is overwhelmingly male, as one can see at conferences, on websites and blogs. The metaphors used within this world of one-man armies are very often martial. Teams working against impossible deadlines go on 'death marches.' Finding and fixing defects in software is a painstaking, detail-oriented task, one which Grace Hopper might have compared to housekeeping; but in the parlance of many programming shops, the most proficient bug sweepers are 'bug slayers.'

In March 2011, David Barrett, CEO of Expensify ('Expense Reports That Don't Suck'), blogged about how his start-up wouldn't hire programmers who used Microsoft's very large and elaborate .NET framework, which—according to him—provided ready-made, assembly-line tools that turned these programmers into drudges capable of only mass-producing pre-designed code, the programming equivalent of fast-food burgers. No, he wanted passionate programmers who could write 'everything from assembly to jQuery, on PCs to mobile phones, [and code] hard core computer graphics to high level social networking.'[33] Barrett wanted Einsteins, not Morts—fair enough. But this is how he described his Einsteins:

> As you might know, we're hiring the best programmers in
> the world. Sure, everyone says that. But my coders will beat
> up your coders, any day of the week. For example, Mich is
> barely 5 foot tall, but is a competitive fencer. Witold is a 6'3"
> former professional hockey player. Nate practices knife fighting
> for fun.[34]

Over a few days, I read hundreds of comments and blog posts debating the merits of Barrett's case against .NET programmers; some argued that many great programmers used .NET, and that other frameworks had as many bad or lazy programmers. The discussions were long and nuanced. But nobody seemed to notice his very literal conflation of omnivorous intellectual curiosity with manly combat skills. He extends his fast-food riff—'Programming with .NET is like cooking in a McDonalds kitchen. It is full of amazing tools that automate absolutely everything'—but then turns the metaphor into a paean to programmer-as-blood-soaked-pioneer:

> The sort of person [we are looking for] grew up cooking squirrels over a campfire with sharpened sticks—squirrels they caught and skinned while scavenging in the deep forests for survival. We don't want a short order chef, we want a Lord of the Flies, carried by wolves into civilization and raised in a French kitchen full of copper-bottomed pots and fresh-picked herbs.[35]

'A Lord of the Flies in a French kitchen' neatly catches the geek machismo and extraordinary privilege that are essential ingredients in the cultural paradox that is Silicon Valley. Wages are so high here, Rebecca Solnit reports, that 'you hear tech workers complaining about not having time to spend their money.'[36] Depending on which San Francisco neighbourhood you live in, your rent rose by anywhere from 10 per cent to 135 per cent over 2012, driven up by young techies outbidding each other.[37] In the booming restaurants and cafes, there's a general disdain for government, which is often described as fatally broken, in desperate need of 'disruption,' that condition beloved of programmers and venture capitalists. Workers' unions are regarded as anachronisms that hold back progress. Company founders chafe at any restrictions imposed by local or federal government as leftover mechanisms from a failed system which prevent the markets from working properly.[38]

Given these attitudes, it's easy to conclude that Silicon Valley is a haven for Libertarians. Doing so would be simplistic.

President Obama won his second presidential election by 49 percentage points in the Bay Area, as compared to his 22-point lead in California as a whole. Employees at Google gave 97 per cent of their campaign contributions to Obama, and Apple employees gave 91 per cent.[39] But these denizens of the tech campuses aren't, as we've seen, leftists or progressives of the Berkeley–Oakland ilk either. Rather, this new 'virtual class' of digital overlords combine the social and sexual attitudes of San Francisco bohemianism with a neo-liberal passion for idealized free markets and unchecked profit-making, thus producing a caste orthodoxy for people who might be best described as 'hippie capitalists.'

The media theorists Richard Barbrook and Andy Cameron have usefully described this new faith as 'the Californian Ideology,' which 'promiscuously combines the free-wheeling spirit of the hippies and the entrepreneurial zeal of the yuppies. This amalgamation of opposites has been achieved through a profound faith in the emancipatory potential of the new information technologies.'[40] This high-tech determinism dictates that through the new worldwide amalgamation of hardware and software, a frictionless 'electronic agora' will come into being, allowing the profitable exchange of both goods and ideas. Individuals will be empowered, they will speak to each other across all sorts of borders and come to mutual understanding. The governments of the world—useless as they are—will fade into irrelevance because governance will be provided by the crowd-sourced wisdom of the masses, led of course by the fearless and very cool visionaries who make software and hardware, who found companies, who make billions. If you've 'solved'—for instance—some problems in online social networking, surely you'll be able to disrupt world hunger. Pioneering individuals will focus their skills, their genius, on one domain after another and so transform the world for the better.

Programmers and entrepreneurs tend to believe implicitly in

the liberal ideal of the self-sufficient individual. In American folklore, the nation was built out of a wilderness by free-booting individuals—the trappers, cowboys, preachers, and settlers of the frontier. The American revolution itself was fought to protect the freedoms and property of individuals against oppressive laws and unjust taxes imposed by a foreign monarch. For both the New Left and the New Right, the early years of the American republic provide a potent model for their rival versions of individual freedom.[41]

David Barrett's knife-wielding, Lord-of-the-Flies programmer belongs to this mythology. Despite eating lunch in company-provided kitchens 'full of copper-bottomed pots and fresh-picked herbs,' he is a rugged man of action. He may complain mightily about an 80,000-dollar salary two years out of college, but he is a hunter and killer. A man who leads a magnificent posse of such hardened, hardcore individuals might justly say, 'My coders will beat up your coders, any day of the week.'

This figuring of computing as agon, a geeky arena of competition in which code-warriors prove their mettle against all comers, demands a certain manly style from those who would win and be recognized as victors. Steve Jobs was famed not only for his success but also his aggressive rudeness; his erstwhile partner Woz describes him as a 'real rugged bastard' who found it necessary to 'put people down and make them feel demeaned.'[42] The social ineptitude of the sandal-wearing, long-haired pioneers of the early days has been elevated to a virtue. Shouting at co-workers and employees, abrasive behaviour, indifference to the feelings of others, all these constitute both a privilege earned by skill and a signifier of the programmer's elite status. This is most true, paradoxically, in the open-source movement, within which volunteer programmers collaborate to produce programs (like Firefox and Linux) under licensing schemes that guarantee universal, free access. These volunteers must cooperate to produce viable programs; yet it is within open source that programmers most fiercely pledge allegiance to the legacy of the early neckbeards. And so Linus Torvalds, the 'benevolent dictator' of Linux, dismissed the makers of a rival operating system as 'a bunch of masturbating monkeys'; and so, Eric S. Raymond, author of The New Hacker's Dictionary and The Cathedral and the Bazaar, once told an interviewer proudly, 'I'm an arrogant son of a bitch,' and refused a hapless Microsoft headhunter's form-letter inquiry with an email that ended, 'On that hopefully not too far distant day that I piss on Microsoft's grave, I sincerely hope none of it will splash on you.'[43]

These postures and attitudes are common enough that some programmers have found it necessary to protest against them, as in a recent blog post by Derick Bailey titled 'Dear Open Source Project Leader: Quit Being a Jerk.' Bailey writes about 'open source elite' programmers making fun of inexperienced would-be contributors to their very own projects. 'I've seen people delete their accounts, disappear from the internet, and leave the open source community behind because of jerks that torment and belittle and tear apart the work that they are putting in,' Bailey writes. 'The worst part of this is knowing that some of these "OSS Elite" were the geeks and freaks and nerds in high school, that got picked on by the jocks and other popular kids . . . The victims are becoming the perpetrators.'[44]

The financial systems which support the software industry bring their own models of masculinity into interactions with programmers. Alec Scott, a Canadian journalist who writes about the Valley, was told by a rising young entrepreneur that he was surprised how 'brusque' the venture capitalists were in meetings. 'At first, I was taken aback by how tough they can be, but I learned to roll with it. There's not much time wasted when they shoot you down quickly at least.' Another start-up founder told Scott, 'This is a guy's guy world, and you've gotta be prepared to go *mano a mano* with them. You might go down in flames, and they honour that. You can't apologize. You must be ready for the fight.'[45]

Those who do not participate in this manly roughhousing are regarded as suffering from a fatal incapability which precludes them making good software. The rudeness of elite programmers—the explanation goes—is actually the necessarily blunt, no-bullshit style of problem-solving engineers who value results over feelings. And finally what matters is the quality of the code—which is an objectively definable value—and the nationality or ethnicity of the programmers is irrelevant. Culture is irrelevant. Or, perhaps, in code, culture is absent, non-existent. So if there are no women in programming, it is because they don't or can't code, because they are not interested in the craft. The world of programming is as it should be, as it has to be.

One of the hallmarks of a cultural system that is predominant is that it succeeds, to some degree, in making itself invisible, or at least in presenting itself as the inevitable outcome of environmental processes that exist outside of the realm of culture, within nature. The absence of women within the industry is thus often seen as a hard 'scientific' reality rooted in biology, never mind that the very first algorithm designed for execution by a machine was created by Lady Ada Byron, never mind Grace Hopper's creation of the first compiler, and never mind that the culture of the industry may be foreign or actively hostile to women.

The tech industry prides itself on being populated by rational thinkers, by devotees of the highest ideals of freedom and equality. Human resources departments are rightfully leery of litigation, and try to protect the companies through training and education. Yet, over the last few years, the industry has been beset by controversies sparked by acts of casual sexism—images of bikini-clad women used as backdrops for presentations about software; a Boston start-up which announced a hack-a-thon and as 'Great Perks' offered gym access, food trucks, and women: 'Need another beer? Let one of our friendly (female) staff get it for you.'[46] In the heated discussions that have followed, one of the main rhetorical modes used by defenders of the status quo has been that sexism doesn't really exist in the tech industry because in this perfect meritocracy programmers who write excellent code will rise to the top. Programming is male because men are excellent programmers. As male doctors and lawyers and chefs were once thought to naturally possess certain essential qualities that fitted them for these once universally male professions, male programmers have logic and problem solving written into their DNA, they are *naturals*. A woman who codes is out of her realm; one might say that 'to be masculine is her worst reproach.'

Of course, as Ensmenger shows us, the personalities and

behaviour that one encounters within the world of programming are embedded in a contingent culture constructed by a particular history. Ensmenger's narrative denaturalizes the maleness and machismo of American programming, and as it tells a story that takes place mostly in America, at MIT and in the hallways of American corporations, it allows us to think of other ways it might have happened or will happen in the future.

~

The pre-Independence India my parents grew up in served as a vast source of raw materials and ready market for finished goods produced by the British Empire. 'Before Gandhiji's movement,' my mother told me many times when I was a child, 'you couldn't even find a sewing needle that had been made in India. Everything came from there.' The factories over there— in Glasgow and Manchester—turned iron ore into steel, cotton into cloth, and sold it all back to the Indians, whose poverty was understood as a pre-existent fact that the current regime was attempting to alleviate. The colonial educational system of course reflected this economic imperative in its structure and methods.

'The engineering colleges established by the British in India had a circumscribed role: to prepare Indians to work in subsidiary positions under British rule,' the historian of technology Ross Bassett tells us.[47] 'The British established the engineering [colleges] . . . as a way to produce intermediate-grade engineers for the British Public Works Department, which had control over the schools.'[48] This policy, carefully designed to limit the range of technological advancement in India, meant that students interested in cutting-edge or even just up-to-date engineering education had no option but to look abroad. And so, between 1900 and 1947, roughly a hundred young men made their way to MIT, which was already famous as the foremost institution of its type. Since the colonial government would grant no aid for such students, they depended on private or family funding, which ensured that most of them came from the upper echelons of Indian society. Some of them were from elite 'law, business, and government service' families deeply involved in the movement for Independence, and were therefore connected to leaders like Nehru and Gandhi.[49] As Bassett points out, 'The early twentieth century marked the rise of the *swadeshi* movement in India, in which Indians developed indigenous industries as an act of resistance to British rule and dominance.'[50] The Indians who went to MIT were motivated as much by a nationalist desire to reconstruct the shattered economy of their country as by a thirst for technology. Gandhi himself wrote to Bal Kalelkar, a young erstwhile associate now at MIT:

> I have your beautiful letter. I can understand that western music has claimed you. Does it not mean that you have such a sensitive ear as to appreciate this music? All I wish is that you should have all that is to be gained there and come here when your time is up and be worthy of your country.[51]

By 1944, Indian bureaucrats and politicians were trying to plan for Independence, which everyone knew was coming. That year, the Executive Council of Planning and Development announced 'a plan to send 500 students abroad in 1945 to institutes in the United Kingdom, Canada, and the United States to meet the demands for "urgent needs of post-war development."'[52] How deeply Indians believed that the technological future was to be found at MIT may be judged from the fact that from the 500 who were selected to benefit from this unprecedented funding, 271 applied to this one institution. MIT admitted 16 for the fall semester, and placed 180 on the waiting list, 'implicitly stating that the students were well qualified for MIT but that there was no room for them.'[53]

This 'technological elite' of MIT-trained students played a central role in the development of science and technology in post-Independence India:

> In the first forty years of independence, MIT graduates occupied an astounding number of the highest-level positions in the Indian technical community—more than graduates of any other single school in the United States or the United Kingdom, and quite possibly more than the graduates of any single school in India.[54]

Under Jawaharlal Nehru's leadership, beginning in 1951, the government began setting up the Indian Institutes of Technology (IITs), designed from the start to provide world-class scientific and technological education on a meritocratic, heavily subsidized basis. The institutes were necessarily built with foreign aid, but the manner in which this aid was acquired and used was designed to reflect the country's non-aligned status during the Cold War. After the first institute at Kharagpur, each campus had one national sponsor—the USSR provided support for IIT Bombay, and West Germany, the United States, and the United Kingdom followed with Madras, Kanpur, and Delhi respectively. MIT created and anchored a consortium of nine

Figure 4.3: 'Installing IBM 1620 computer in 1963 when first laboratory building was under construction.' Photographer unknown. *Tech Engineering News*, Vol. XLIX, no. 3, April 1967. Institute Archives and Special Collections, MIT Libraries, Cambridge, MA

American universities that joined the Kanpur Indo-American Program in 1961. It was through this program that the first computer arrived in India: in July 1963, a chartered DC-7 flew an IBM 1620 mainframe to a military airbase in Kanpur.[55]

A photograph of the arrival of the computer on the IIT campus (figure 4.3) has all the solemn symbolism and poignant hope and pathos of a history painting. The computer itself comprises two enormous white cuboid masses that flank a large console panel. The 1620 sits on a wheeled flatbed platform that is pushed by a crowd of dhoti-clad Indian men into a building still wrapped in a framework of rope-hitched bamboo stilts (used by construction workers and painters). An older man in Western clothes—white short-sleeved shirt, dark pants, shoes—hurries from right to left with a rather supervisory air. As always, a gaggle of onlookers watches the proceedings. And at the very edge of the frame, at the bottom right, a boy in shorts—eight years old? Ten?—cups his hand over his face.

The building in the picture is the computer centre of the permanent campus of IIT Kanpur, which was still under construction. 'The centrality of the computer to the plans for IIT Kanpur,' Ross Bassett tells us, 'is indicated by the fact that the delivery of the 1620 was scheduled for the earliest possible date.'[56] So, a small 'technological elite'—the 'suited and booted,' in Indian parlance—led by Nehru, made a visionary decision to pour vast amounts of wealth and skills into institutions aimed at the future and in large part motivated by the recent past, by the knowledge that technological lag in the subcontinent at a crucial historical moment had led to the defeats and depredations of industrialized colonialism, a gigantic plundering which was begun and extended for its first hundred years not by a nation state but by a modern corporation, the Honourable East India Company. The Indian leaders built the institutes and brought computers into a country which had an abundance of cheap labour—those men in dhotis—and a desperate need for development. A half-century later, the questions asked then are still pertinent: Should the nation expend its resources on such institutions while people starve? Do we need computers or tractors? In any drawing room or village square, today, you can hear the rueful lament, 'We can put satellites in orbit but can't get clean drinking water to two hundred and fifty million people.' What became of that boy in the picture? Was his life improved by the creation of the institutes? The consequences—

salutary or otherwise—of the setting up of the institutes are of course embedded in the tangled skein of recent Indian history, intertwined and inseparable from all the myriad, ambiguous narratives of growth, corruption, hope and disappointment that followed Independence.

As a young boy myself, I believed the Institutes would save us; I pinned my hopes on the newly built steel plants, the irrigation projects, the huge hydroelectric dams, the factories that sprang up on the edges of cities. My mother's mother lived in a village which still lacked electricity, but even there you could see signs of change, a tractor or two, a newly built road. I knew the Institutes had computers, but I never saw one until I came to the States. Our 'progress,' our 'development,' was fragmented and piecemeal—some people became very rich, but many remained poor.

What is abundantly, unambiguously clear is that the Nehruvian vision, evangelized outwards from Kanpur and the other institutes, succeeded in its stated aim of producing 'world-class' engineers, so much so that the world tempted them away from Gandhi's country with siren songs of well-stocked laboratories, abundant resources, and wealth. This famous 'brain drain,' which once so irritated some IIT faculty that they refused to write recommendation letters to American universities for their students, has been reimagined as 'brain circulation' with attendant flows of remittances and expertise back to the home country. As Indian geeks have gained prominence and power abroad—especially in Silicon Valley—they have been instrumental in driving and facilitating investments by international companies in India. In the American computer industry, the presence of Indians is impossible to miss—by 2005, Indians had founded 26 per cent of all tech start-ups in the valley. By 2012, this percentage had increased to 33.2 per cent, more than the next nine ethnic groups combined (immigrants from China, the United Kingdom, Canada, Germany, Israel, Russia, Korea, Australia, and the Netherlands).[57] In a 2013 interview, the executive chairman of Google, Eric Schmidt said, 'Forty per cent of the startups in Silicon Valley are headed by India-based entrepreneurs.'[58] And, according to Vinod Khosla, IIT graduate and co-founder of Sun Microsystems, 'Microsoft, Intel, PCs, Sun Microsystems—you name it, I can't imagine a major area where Indian IIT engineers haven't played a leading role.'[59]

The ubiquity of the Indian geek has been recognized even by popular American media in the figure of Raj Koothrappali, a character on the television show *The Big Bang Theory*. Raj is an astrophysicist at Caltech; he is mild, socially awkward, especially around women; he is effeminate by American standards (the other characters frequently suspect him of being gay); his parents try to run his life, so his attempts to live as an independent adult form one of the show's running gags. 'Koothrappali' is a Malayalam last name, or at least 'Koothrappallil' is, so I'm guessing that Raj is supposed to be a south Indian, but he could well be the modern version of Sir Lepel Griffin's hapless Bengali. These broad strokes catch precisely the larger culture's notions of geeky Indianness, which—especially within the machismo of the IT industry—sometimes become a liability for Indians. In his autobiographical book, *Dude, Did I Steal Your Job? Debugging Indian Programmers*, N. Sivakumar recalls the advice he received when he first arrived in the US for a programming gig:

One of my friends advised me to walk smart. He told me that Americans think we are very humble and not smart enough to handle a crisis. He said that the way we walk in the company corridors itself portrays the shabbiness of Indians . . .

. . . Most of the consulting companies and personal advisers tell the Indian programmers to behave smart and bold. They also advise them to be more aggressive, positive, and outspoken, so that Americans will love them. Most Indians lack all of these good qualities. Indians are no match to Americans when it comes to the above skills.[60]

To anyone who has grown up within the Indian educational system, the notion that Indian techies would be regarded as 'very humble' is puzzling. At my high school, we all knew which kids were preparing themselves for scientific or technical careers. We called them 'Brains,' as in, 'That Maitra is a huge Brain, he'll surely get into IIT.' And the Brains were completely aware of their own superiority. Some of them had known at age ten that they were destined for one of the IITs or some similarly elite university; they knew because their families and teachers told them so, and they knew because their marks told them so. Every examination was ranked, and Maitra knew he had been 'standing first' in class since first grade, just as the boy who was ranked 49 out of 50 knew exactly where he stood. Maitra also knew that the direction of his life could be determined by a fraction of a percentage point—if his desired college set its 'cut-off marks' at 92.3 per cent, a score of 92.2 per cent would render him illegible to apply. Maitra started waking up at 4 a.m. when he was thirteen, to attend a pre-school coaching class that prepared him to get into another nationally known coaching class that regularly placed its students into prominent universities. He knew that the names of students who got into nationally known institutions would be publicly announced along with their ranks, that pictures of the 'top rankers' would appear in the newspapers, that they would be interviewed on prime-time television.

This educational process, with its obsessive emphasis on examinations and rankings, produces legions of rote learners, mark grubbers, and cheaters. It causes casualties—7379 students committed suicide in 2010, an increase of 26 per cent over 2005.[61] It also produces fanatically disciplined and motivated competitors who are capable of decades of extraordinary concentration and ceaseless effort. But their competitiveness is couched in a cultural idiom that is not legible to many Americans, and therefore remains invisible or is read as general meekness or 'shabbiness.'

This misreading works in both directions. I suspect I find David Barrett's invocation of the ideal programmer as a 'Lord of the Flies' who 'grew up cooking squirrels over a campfire with sharpened sticks' so bizarre because my own cultural models of pioneering knowledge production come from the Indian scientists and technologists my classmates and I idolized during my childhood: J.C. Bose, S. Chandrasekhar, Homi J. Bhabha, Vikram Sarabhai. Whatever their actual caste or religion or beliefs may have been, these men seemed to embody Brahminical rectitude and austerity; they may have been as arrogant and ruthless and sexist as the American warrior-kings of software, but I'm completely unable to recast these particular Indians as gore-flecked paladins. In my mind, they are indubitably pandits, *gyaanis*, *vidvaans*, *aalims*, *daanishmands*, seekers after eternal knowledge and therefore eternal students; they are all brain, their brawn is irrelevant. Their affect is rabbinical, detached from the humdrum worries of the everyday world. A famous verse describes the five qualities of the ideal scholar: 'Far-seeing as the crow; concentrated as the stalking crane; light-sleeping as the hound; in control of the appetites; unencumbered by desires or a household.'

But within the mythologies of American nationhood and selfhood, from which Nick Carter the Killmaster and his low-yield nuclear grenade were born, innovation is conquest, and great programming makes 'killer apps.' Californian cowboys range over the frontiers of knowledge, triumphing over the natural environment and its native denizens because of their toughness and tough-mindedness, their practicality, and their ability to blow away anything or anyone who stands in their path. Manifest destiny—with its cast of robber barons, tragically doomed natives, labouring Asians and African Americans, grizzled soldiers, and Lone Rangers—still casts its spell over the boardrooms and universities of America, and so the practitioners of some of the most nerdy professions in history (media-making; software-making; lending and borrowing money) develop codes of masculinity that allow them to 'walk smart.'

In September 2011, the programmer Rob Spectre gave a presentation at a conference entirely in character as Chad the Brogrammer, wearing the standard fraternity-bro uniform of popped pink collar and dark glasses. A video of the presentation quickly went viral, and Spectre's lines were suddenly all over the blogosphere: 'In the immortal words of Brosef Stalin, "Dude, I'm way too faded to build this [difficult low-level] shiz. Imma have some other broheims do the grunge work. Totes magotes.'"[62] Spectre was joking, but he had touched on a trend that many had noticed: 'Tech's latest boom,' Businessweek observed in 2012, 'has generated a new, more testosterone-fueled breed of coder,' such as Danilo Stern-Sapad, a twenty-five-year-old who doesn't like being called a geek, who 'wears sunglasses and blasts 2Pac while programming,' who proudly reports that 'we got invited to a party in Malibu where there were naked women in the hot tub. We're the cool programmers.'[63] So, in addition to the nerd machismo of the programmers and the buccaneer strutting of the venture capitalists, there is also now the frat-bro aggressiveness of young men who get into coding because it's a cool-dude way to make stacks of cash.

In a 2012 Globe and Mail story about Canadian programmers in Silicon Valley, Alec Scott quotes a high-level female Canadian executive who's worked with many of the top companies as saying:

> People ask me, would you encourage your daughter to follow you into tech. My answer is no frickin' way. I would tell a woman going in, you're going to be 40 years old pitching a VC in the Valley, and he's going to pinch your bum. I had that happen to me! . . . I got demoted [at a tech company] when I got pregnant. We're not making progress in tech. If anything, it's going the other way.[64]

~

The annual Global Gender Gap Report 2012, released by the World Economic Forum, ranks women's status in countries around the world in four key areas: economic participation and opportunity; educational attainment; health and survival; and political empowerment. The report ranks the United States at 22 out of the 135 countries surveyed. India comes in at a dismal 105.[65] Yet, according to some accounts, the proportion of programmers in India who are women may be higher—at least 30 per cent—than America's 21.1 per cent.[66] This might be dismissed as an anomaly were it not for other trends: the proportion of undergraduate computer-science degrees awarded to women in the US has declined from 37 per cent in 1984 to 18 per cent in 2010. The number of female freshmen who thought they might major in computer science has fallen steadily, from 4.1 per cent in 1982 to 1.5 per cent in 1999, and to 0.3 per cent in 2009.[67]

Meanwhile, in India, the trend has gone in the opposite direction. Until the mid-eighties, according to researcher Roli Varma, the number of women engineers was 'negligible.'[68] But in 2003, 32 per cent of the Bachelor of Engineering degrees in computer science and 55 per cent of the Bachelor of Science degrees in computer science were awarded to women. I've been told, anecdotally, that these percentages have risen since. Varma notes that Indian women took to computer science in spite of lack of early exposure; many Indian families cannot afford computers, and before opting for formal instruction, many of her respondents had only ever used computers in Internet cafes.

The young Indian women, though, came to computing with a confidence in their logical abilities which has been nurtured in their schools and homes. A study

showed that almost all female students [of computer science] interviewed asserted that mathematics was their strongest subject in high school, followed by physics. A little over half of the students also believed that their high school and intermediate college did not prepare them 'well' for the study of CS at the university level, and another one-third felt 'partially' prepared. These female students qualified their responses by stating that their schools either did not expose them to computers or did not teach details, applications, and basic languages of CS. However, they were extremely confident about their mathematical skills and, thus, their logical thinking and analytical abilities. Therefore, even though they found CS a hard, demanding, technical field, female students felt their mathematical training enabled them to do well in CS at the university level . . . no one ever considered changing their field from CS to something else due to difficulties.[69]

The Indian women programmers' notions about the characteristics displayed by a typical programmer were very different from those reported in the US, where 'geeks/hackers/ nerds [were thought to be] predominantly White males, fascinated with technology, [who] sit in front of the computer all day and sleep near it.'[70] In India, however, the study

showed that most female students interviewed believed that the computing field is changing from being dominated by men to increasingly being penetrated by women. Female students believed that the typical computing culture consists of dedicated, hard-working, intelligent, meticulous, and smart students . . . They help those needing assistance and it is pleasant to be around them. They are active in social and cultural events held at their universities, as well as participate in sports. Most importantly, female students believed CS to be a field in which women could excel. According to them, economic rewards for a woman with a CS degree are much higher than with a degree in other [Science and Engineering] fields. Women who study CS are well respected by faculty and peers in the educational arena and by family members, friends, and neighbors in the social arena.[71]

Parents want their daughters to work in computing in particular and scientific disciplines in general, and support and cajole and push towards this end.

In India, the logical nature of work in computing, its abstraction and headiness, is precisely what makes the field a kind of haven from all the indignities and horrific cruelties that subcontinental culture inflicts on women elsewhere:

For Indian women, being indoors in an office in front of a computer means they are protected from the outside environment, which is seen as unfriendly to women. Construction sites and factories are the work sites where a degree in other engineering fields, such as mechanical or civil, are seen as more suited for men.[72]

Sexism of the most ugly and violent kind exists in the environments that these women must negotiate away from the computer, but knowledge itself is not gendered as male:

[Indian] women do not feel that teachers neglect them in mathematics and computing classes. This is one of the reasons that these fields do not emerge as a male domain. From early on, female students are taught to invest in hard work, which is seen to solve scientific and technical problems and, thus, a requirement to succeed in life.[73]

The outlook for these Indian women is not altogether rosy, however. Alok Aggarwal is co-founder and chairman of Evalueserve India, a research and analytics company that employs approximately 2000 people, out of which 30 per cent are women. He told me:

> We believe that currently in most IT companies (IBM India, Accenture India, Infosys, Wipro, TCS, HCL, Cognizant, iGate, etc.), the percentage of women is also 30% [in the category of] 'computer programmers.' However, unfortunately, at the managerial level, both within our company, Evalueserve, and the other IT companies mentioned above, the percentage of women managers drops to approximately 10%.[74]

In terms of the retention of employees, Aggarwal adds, 'Among new joinees, 35% are women but within five years, this number comes down to 25% (because some of the women who get married leave Evalueserve India or the work-force altogether—at least on a temporary basis).'[75] Cultural narratives about domesticity, children, and the exercise of power outside the home are still very much in place.

Still, research in countries as varied as Iran, Hong Kong, Mauritius, Taiwan, and Malaysia has yielded results consistent with those found in studies in India, showing that there is nothing about the field of computing that makes it inherently male. Varma's conclusion is blunt: 'The gender imbalance in the United States seems to be specific to the country; it is not a universal phenomenon, as it has been presented in the scholarly literature.'[76]

~

In her book *Delusions of Gender: How Our Minds, Society, and Neurosexism Create Difference*, Cordelia Fine observes that 'in prosperous countries it is not economic prosperity that tracks sex segregation in degree choices, but differences in adolescent boys' and girls' attitudes toward math and science. In richer countries, the greater the difference between boys' and girls' interest in science and math, the greater the sex segregation.'[77]

Fine also cites studies of the participation of American girls in the prestigious International Math Olympiad (IMO), where profoundly gifted mathematical whizz-kids spend nine hours solving extremely difficult problems:

> If you're Hispanic, African American, or Native American, it matters not whether you have two X chromosomes or one—you might as well give up now on any dreams of sweating for nine hours over some proofs. Then within girls, interesting patterns emerge. Asian American girls are not underrepresented, relative to their numbers in the population. But that doesn't mean that it's even simply a *white girl* problem. Non-Hispanic white girls born in North America are sorely underrepresented: there are about twenty times fewer of them on IMO teams than you'd expect based on their numbers in the population, and they virtually never attend the highly selective MOSP [Mathematical Olympiad Summer Program]. But this isn't the case for non-

Hispanic white girls who were born in Europe, immigrants from countries like Romania, Russia, and the Ukraine, who manage on the whole to keep their end up when it comes to participating in these prestigious competitions and programs. The success of this group of women continues into their careers. These women are *a hundred times more likely* to make it into the math faculty of Harvard, MIT, Princeton, Stanford, or University of California–Berkeley than their native-born white counterparts. They do every bit as well as white males, relative to their numbers in the population.[78]

A hundred times more likely—emphasis doubly mine and in the original—would seem to indicate that within the American idiom of personhood, power, desire, and meaning, there is a figuring of mathematics as male, something that 'Non-Hispanic white girls' should keep away from. Something similar seems to be true of programming in America, which is marked by a particular machismo that idealizes un-socialized, high-school-outcast geekery; coding excellence earned through solitary, singular focus; and adult programmer-bro success signalled by aggression.

So within this American landscape, on this new frontier, how do those who are not 'cool' (or belong to the wrong gender) succeed? N. Sivakumar, the immigrant programmer who was warned about shabbiness, tried to learn coolitude: 'All right, I am going to walk straight and smart as of tomorrow!' But his colleagues now teased him for walking like 'President Bush,' and so he decided, 'I better be me!'[79] But being himself and succeeding required that he work very, very hard, and adopt certain strategies:

Indians learn for survival whereas most Americans tend to choose their career for passion. Indians learn everything . . .

. . . Indian programmers have a habit of saying 'yes' to everything. Again, it's all about survival. They will say 'Yes' to move to North Dakota tomorrow. Say 'Yes' to work for someone who used to work for him. 'Yes' to long hours. 'Yes' to program in a completely new language (which they will starve to learn within days) . . .

Indian programmers are also tolerant enough to do the 'shit' work. That is: going through somebody else's code. This is one of the toughest challenges for any programmer . . .

Almost all the so-called 'software maintenance' projects . . . were handled by Indian programmers . . .

. . . This is what Indian programmers do and are patient enough to handle. Patience—a unique quality of Indians.[80]

N. Sivakumar is careful to qualify his assertions; he's not saying that every Indian programmer is preternaturally patient and a paragon of hard work: 'My comparisons . . . always focus on the average programmer . . . There will always be a good and a bad and an ugly in every bunch.' He adds:

An Indian programmer will most probably stop learning once he gets a job . . . Indian programmers are least likely to learn something new on their own—in their field of interest—to enhance their knowledge if not required. In other words, they lack initiative once they are settled and once they feel safe. [81]

And finally:

Average American programmers are more innovative than their counterparts. I know my Indian and Chinese friends will disagree with me on this, but this is the truth. Although an average American programmer's knowledge is limited to a certain technology or a programming language, they master the hell out of that, and have a higher probability of innovating something new in their area. Average Indian and Chinese programmers, on the other hand, tend to be all over the place and are least likely to innovate something new in their specific area.[82]

In reference to the success of Indians in Silicon Valley, the tech entrepreneur and academic Vivek Wadhwa credits efficient and ceaseless networking:

The first few [company founders] who cracked the glass ceiling had open discussions about the hurdles they had faced.

They agreed that the key to uplifting their community, and fostering more entrepreneurship in general, was to teach and mentor the next generation of entrepreneurs.

They formed networking organizations to teach others about starting businesses, and to bring people together. These organizations helped to mobilize the information, knowhow, skill, and capital needed to start technology companies . . .

The first generation of successful entrepreneurs—people like Sun Microsystems co-founder Vinod Khosla—served as visible, vocal, role models and mentors. They also provided seed funding to members of their community.[83]

These efforts were successful enough that the denizens of Silicon

Valley sometimes refer to these networks, with decidedly mixed admiration and resentment, as the 'Indian Mafia.'[84]

So this is another history of success in Silicon Valley that may be placed beside the more familiar narrative of solitary, pioneering heroes who seem to have sprung from an Ayn Rand novel—in this Indian–American version we have a tenacious patience, learnt in a country with sparse resources and endless competition, a perseverance trained and honed by a thousand endless queues in government offices; a willingness to work at 'shiz' scorned by people conditioned by a less straitened environment; cooperation and mutual help; and a huge, continuing financial investment by a young nation state, despite the paradoxes of unequal development and the flight of intellectual capital. This alternate narrative of technology should remind us that there are always many pasts, some hidden in plain sight.

~

The fictions about history that form the Frontier Myth, the stories that the Gunfighter Nation tells itself, typically present women as dauntless housewives or prostitutes (with the requisite hearts of gold). In either case, they are the backdrop, they inhabit the fragile outposts of civilization (the parlour, the schoolhouse, the saloon) on whose behalf the silent hero enacts his all-important rituals of violence out on the mesa. Men do the thinking and planning, women provide—as it were—the clerical support. Much scholarship since the seventies—the New Western History—has unearthed the complex roles women played on the frontier, their essential and irreplaceable contributions to the logistics and politics of the westward expansion. Notwithstanding revisionist historians and film-makers, the power of the Frontier Myth, its meaning-making about nation and personhood, its celebrations of regeneration through confrontations with savagery and the wilderness—all this remains intact, as one can see on television shows and hear in the speeches of politicians.

The mythology of computing similarly celebrates the victories of its male protagonists and erases women from the record, and not just programmers. The programmer Jaron Lanier tells us that in the early days of Silicon Valley

> there were . . . extraordinary female figures who served as the impresarios of social networking before there was an internet. It still seems wrong to name them, because it isn't clear if I would be talking about their private lives or their public contributions: I don't know how to draw a line.
>
> These irresistible creatures would sometimes date alpha nerds, but mostly brought the act of socialising into a society where it probably would not have occurred otherwise. A handful of them had an extraordinary, often unpaid degree of influence over what research was done, which companies came to be, who worked at them and what products were developed.
>
> That they are usually undescribed in histories of Silicon Valley is just another instance of what a fiction history can be.[85]

Silicon Valley may have in reality needed Lanier's salonnières and the Indian Mafia, but its heroic narrative—from which it draws its ambition, its adventurousness, and its seductiveness—requires lone American cowboys to ride the range.

Towards the end of their critique of the Californian Ideology, Barbrook and Cameron remark in passing, 'Any attempt to develop hypermedia [innovative forms of knowledge and communications] within Europe will need some of the entrepreneurial zeal and can-do attitude championed by the Californian New Right.' But it seems to me that you cannot get the can-do attitude and zeal without the ideology, without the shimmering dream of California, without the furious continent-conquering energy, the guns, the massacres, without the consequences—good *and* bad—of belief. Fictions about history are not just distractions; they move individuals and nations into action, and so they change history itself.

About four years into the writing of my own fiction about history, I travelled to New York over a summer break. I wanted to see friends, to do some computer work for my old scribing company, and also to escape my novel for a few weeks. This was my first book, but by now I had learnt that when you are in the middle of a novel, you cannot escape the writing except through distraction. The story buzzes and hums inside you, and any moment of rest gives it an opportunity to scrabble to the surface and claw at your attention. New York was full of diversions. And being away from my papers and books meant that I couldn't really work, so I could indulge freely.

One evening, a friend told me about a reading by five touring Indian poets at The Museum of Modern Art (MoMA). We went, and I heard the critic and poet A.K. Ramanujan read his translation of a classical Tamil poem:

What could my mother be
to yours? What kin is my father
to yours anyway? And how
did you and I meet ever?
But in love
our hearts have mingled
like red earth and pouring rain.[1]

I felt a shiver of recognition. I had been scribbling titles in my notebooks for years, but now I knew. This was what my book would be called. I went to a library the next day and found Ramanujan's book, *The Interior Landscape*. The poem had been written some time between the first and third centuries CE by a poet known only as Cempulappeyanirar, 'The Poet of the Red Earth and Pouring Rain.' It lost none of its simple, evocative vastness when I read it on a page, and I was grateful, but a title was not the only richness that Ramanujan offered me. In his elegant afterword, he led the reader into the intricacies of the Sangam literature of south India, which flourished from about 300 BCE to 300 CE. 'Sangam' is 'confluence' in Tamil, and refers to the assemblies of scholars and poets who—according to legend—had met for thousands of years in the south. The Sangam poets divided the world into *akam*—Ramanujan's 'interior landscape,' suffused with the pleasures and pains of love, sex, and attachment—and *puram*—the external panorama of politics, heroic striving, social attachment and obligation. In these poems, a complex series of symbolic associations creates mood and meaning; each flower and landscape functions within a convention. So, the desert or drought-ridden land of the *palai* is where lovers part; the *kurinji* flower, which blooms only once every twelve years, gives its name to the landscape of the hills, abundant with water and fruit, alive with desire. 'In their antiquity and in their contemporaneity, there is not much else in any Indian literature equal to these quiet and dramatic Tamil poems,' Ramanujan wrote. 'In their values and stances, they represent a mature classical poetry: passion is balanced by courtesy, transparency by ironies and nuances of design, impersonality by vivid detail, austerity of line by richness of implication.'[2]

Ramanujan's explication of this complex aesthetic gave me

the beginnings of a vocabulary which I could use to speak about what I was trying to do with my book. I was not writing a Sangam fiction, of course, but I now began to investigate the rich traditions of Indian literary theory. There was a peculiar comfort in reading about the structures and operations of literature as understood by these theorists; in their investigations, they explored what literature was and what it did as a system, as a set of interlocking conventions and assumptions. And as I read Ramanujan and others, I had the curious sensation of recognizing myself, of beginning to know why I was moved by a certain kind of narrative construction, why a particular heightened mode of drama struck me as sublime. The fractures induced by colonialism hadn't eradicated these aesthetic preferences from within me or my culture; they remained embedded in practice, in the shapes of temples and in Indian movies and spoken languages and my novel. But a certain silencing had happened, so that what was known couldn't be spoken, so that this longing had no language in which it could be uttered.

I am using the English word 'aesthetic' here, but I should emphasize that there is a very strong tendency in the developmental, evolutionary model of history to limit the possibility of aesthetic thinking and theorizing to the modern, the contemporary. According to the literary scholar Geoffrey Galt Harpham:

No concept is more fundamental to modernity than the aesthetic, that radiant globe of material objects and attitudes ideally independent of politics, rationality, economics, desire, religion, or ethics. For as Shaftesbury, Kant, Alexander Baumgarten, Friedrich Schiller, and their successors have elaborated it, the aesthetic gathers into itself and focuses norms and notions crucial to the self-description of an enlightened culture.

Among these philosophers and thinkers, the general consensus—following Kant—is that the aesthetic can flourish

> only in a certain kind of culture, a 'modern' culture capable of sustaining a 'disinterested' attention to things that have no utilitarian function, no necessary connection to meanings or concepts . . .
>
> The aesthetic is thus . . . an ideological creation, an attribute posited by modernity of itself.[3]

The cult of modernity, in order to demonstrate the newness of modernity, needs to always insist on the chasms that separate modernity from the past. The modernity of colonialism insisted on a corresponding un-modernity in the regions it conquered. It had to, in order to justify its own presence in these areas of darkness. Progress demanded that the premodern—usually characterized as primitive, childish, lesser developed, and, most significantly, as feminine—be brought into the light through judicious, disinterested applications of education and force. Guns, trains, and the telegraph were the blessed tools of this righteous, masculine mission. And it is no coincidence that the first classrooms in which the English novel was studied were located in colonial universities in India. The task of turning Indians into proper modern subjects with the right sort of interiority, reflexivity, and individuality demanded that the most sophisticated technology of selfhood be brought into play, and of course this instrument was the modern novel. But many of the protagonists of my novel were premoderns. One of them, Sanjay, was a poet. How did he imagine the self? And Sanjay might have asked, what makes a poem beautiful? I tried to find out, and to do so I had to find my way into the Sanskrit cosmopolis—so named by the Indologist Sheldon Pollock—into the Sanskrit-speaking and writing ecumene which, at its height, sprawled from Afghanistan to Java, across dozens of kingdoms, languages, and cultures.

~

The earliest available text in Sanskrit is the Rig Veda, dating—according to current scholarly consensus—from around 2000–1700 BCE.[4] The Rig Veda, and the other Vedas that followed—the Sama, Yajur, and Atharva Vedas—were considered to be eternal, uncreated, 'not of human agency' (*apaurseya*), and 'directly revealed' (*shruti*) to the seers; these qualities distinguished them from all other religious texts, which were 'what is remembered,' *smriti*. The language that these Vedic wisdom texts were orally transmitted in—not yet called 'Sanskrit'—was therefore also eternal, uncreated, *devavani*—'the language of the gods.' The truths that the Vedas embodied lay not only in the sense, the verbal meaning, but also in the sounds, the pitch, the tonality, the metre. Therefore it was vitally important to maintain these qualities from generation to generation, to guard against linguistic deterioration and slippage. Among the auxiliary sciences developed as 'limbs of the Veda,' *vedanga*, there were several that ensured faultless reproduction across the years, including phonetics, grammar, etymology, and metre. Accurate preservation of the Vedas earned spiritual merit. Grammar was the 'Veda of Vedas,' the science of sciences; it was called *vyakarana*, simply 'analysis,' and was the foundation of all education. The Brahmins, the priestly caste, were trained rigorously in the cultivation of memory and linguistic expression. The effort was successful; the Vedas are chanted today exactly as they were almost four millennia ago, complete with archaic tones and usages present nowhere in the Sanskrit that followed.

A single text from about 500 BCE, the *Ashtadhyayi* (Eight chapters), is usually credited with forming this later 'classical Sanskrit'; with this one book, the grammarian Panini created the fields of descriptive and generative linguistics. Drawing on the sophisticated regimes already developed, he attempted to create a 'complete, maximally concise, and theoretically consistent analysis of Sanskrit grammatical structure.'[5] His objects of study were both the spoken language of his time, and the language of the Vedas, already a thousand years behind him. He systemized both of these variations by formulating 3976 rules that—over eight chapters—allow the generation of Sanskrit words and sentences from roots, which are in turn derived from phonemes and morphemes.[6] In addition to these rules, he provides a list of all Sanskrit phonemes, along with a metalinguistic scheme that allows him to refer to entire classes of phonological segments with just one syllable; a classified lexicon of about two thousand Sanskrit verbal roots along with markers that encode the properties of these roots; and another classified list of lexical items that are idiosyncratically acted upon by certain rules.

The rules are of four types: (1) rules that function as definitions; (2) metarules—that is, rules that apply to other rules; (3) headings—rules that form the bases for other rules; and (4) operational rules. Some rules are universal while others are context sensitive; the sequence of rule application is clearly defined. Some rules can override others. Rules can call other rules, recursively. The application of one rule to a linguistic form can cause the application of other rules, which may in turn trigger other rules, until no more rules are applicable. The operational rules 'carry out four basic types of operations on strings: replacement, affixation, augmentation, and compounding.'[7]

In addition to ordered rules, Panini also pioneered the use of linguistic 'zero elements' for constituents posited in analysis but omitted in usage, as in the sentence 'Women adore him,' in which the determiner 'the' is assumed to precede 'women.'[8] He also created a metalanguage comprising special technical terms and markers which enabled him to speak precisely and unambiguously about the language he was analysing. [9]

In Sanskrit, word order is not important other than for stylistic purposes; the verb can be placed anywhere in a sentence. So the *Ashtadhyayi* concerns itself mainly with word formation. When it does concern itself with sentence formation

Panini accounts for sentence structure by a set of grammatical categories which allow syntactic relationship to be represented as identity at the appropriate level of abstraction. The pivotal syntactico-semantic categories which do this are roles assigned to nominal expressions in relation to a verbal root, called *karakas*. A sentence is seen as a little drama played out by an Agent and a set of other actors, which may include Goal, Recipient, Instrument, Location, and Source.[10]

The rules of the *Ashtadhyayi* are extremely concise; here are numbers 58 through 77 of the fifth chapter: [11]

५८ संक्यायाच्श्र गुशान्तायाः ५६ समयाच्च यापनायाम्
६० सप्रत्रनिष्पत्त्रादति०यथने ६१ निष्कुलान्निष्कोषसे
६२ सुरवप्रियादानुलोम्ये ६३ दुःरवात्प्रातिलोम्ये ६४
रूलात्पाके ६५ सत्यादरापथे ६६ मद्रात्परिवापसे
६७ समासान्ताः ६८ न पूजनात् ६६ किमः क्षेपे
७० नज्स्तत्पुरुषात् ७१ पथो विभाषा ७२ बहुव्रीहौ
संर०येये डजबहुगसात् ७३ त्ऋक्पूर०धःपथामानक्षे ७४
त्र्यच्प्रत्यन्ववपूर्वात्सामलोम्रः ७५ त्र्यक्षोऽदर्शनात् ७६
त्र्यचतुरविचतुरसुचतुरस्त्रीपुंसधेन्वनदुहक्सामवाङ्नसा—
क्षिभ्रुवदारगवोर्वश्रीवपदश्रीवनत्तंदिवरात्रिंदिवाहर्दिव—
सरजसनिश्श्रेयसपुरुषायुष्द्वथायुष्त्र्यायुषर्ग्यजुषजातोक्ष—
महोक्षवृद्धोक्षोपशुनगोष्ठश्वाः ७७ ब्रह्महस्तिभ्यां वर्चसः

Only a few rules are more than two or three words long, so the entire rule set comprises only 32,000 syllables and fits into about forty pages of printed text. [12] The economy of Panini's prose is such that a recent translation into English ran to over 1300 pages. Panini somehow caught, the saying goes, an ocean in a cow's hoof print. With this very finite analysis, Panini not only comprehensively described the functioning of his language, he also opened it up to infinity. S.D. Joshi points out:

The *Astadhyayi* is not a grammar in [the] general Western sense of the word. It is a device, a derivational word-generating device . . . It derives an infinite number of correct Sanskrit words, even though we lack the means to check whether the words derived form part of actual usage. As later grammarians put it, we are *lakṣaṇaikacakṣuṣka*, solely guided by rules. Correctness is guaranteed by the correct application of rules.[13]

The systematic, deterministic workings of these rules may remind you of the orderly on-and-off workings of logic gates. The *Ashtadhyayi* is, of course, an algorithm, a machine that consumes phonemes and morphemes and produces words and sentences. Panini's machine—which is sometimes compared to the Turing machine—is also the first known instance of the application of algorithmic thinking to a domain outside of logic and mathematics. The influence of the *Ashtadhyayi* was and remains immense. In the Sanskrit ecumene, later grammarians suggested some additions and modifications, and other grammars were written before and after Panini's intervention, but all have been overshadowed by this one 'tersest and yet most complete grammar of any language.'[14]

The West discovered the *Ashtadhyayi* during the great flowering of Orientalist research and translation in the eighteenth and nineteenth centuries. Ferdinand de Saussure, 'the father of structural linguistics,' was a professor of Sanskrit and influenced by Panini and his successor, Bhartrihari; Saussure's notion of the linguistic 'sign' is heavily reminiscent of Bhartrihari's theory of *sphota* (explosion, bursting), which tries to account for the production of meaning from linguistic units.[15] Leonard Bloomfield—the renowned scholar of structural linguistics whose work determined the direction linguistic science would take through the twentieth century, particularly in America— studied Sanskrit as a graduate student at the University of

Wisconsin and later in Germany. As an assistant professor at the University of Illinois, he taught elementary Sanskrit even as he began his own research, 'using Paninian methods . . . and studying Panini.'[16] In his own writing, Bloomfield was unstinting in his praise of Panini's grammar: it was 'a linguistic achievement beyond any it [i.e. European scholarship] had known'; it was 'one of the greatest monuments of human intelligence' and 'an indispensable model for the description of language.'[17] He summarized the impact of Panini's work on modern linguistics as follows:

> Around the beginning of the nineteenth century the Sanskrit grammar of the ancient Hindus became known to European scholars. Hindu grammar described the Sanskrit language completely and in scientific terms, without prepossessions or philosophical intrusions. It was from this model that Western scholars learned, in the course of a few decades, to describe a language in terms of its own structure.[18]

Paul Kiparsky tells us:

> Western grammatical theory has been influenced by [Panini's work] at every stage of its development for the last two centuries. The early nineteenth-century comparativists learned from it the principles of morphological analysis. Bloomfield modelled both his classic Algonquian grammars and the logical-positivist axiomatization of his *Postulates* on it.[19]

Further:

Theoretical linguists of all persuasions are . . . impressed by its remarkable conciseness, and by the rigorous consistency with which it deploys its semi-formalized metalanguage, a grammatically and lexically regimented form of Sanskrit . . . Generative linguists for their part have marveled especially at its ingenious technical devices, and at intricate system of conventions governing rule application and rule interaction that it presupposes, which seem to uncannily anticipate ideas of modern linguistic theory (if only because many of them were originally borrowed from Panini in the first place).[20]

Modern linguistic theory, in its turn, became the seedbed for high-level computer languages. To ease the pain of programming in low-level languages like machine code and assembly, computer scientists were driven to create artificial, formal languages. The efforts of linguists towards understanding language in formal and generative terms led to the work of John Backus, the IBM language designer whose team created FORTRAN, the first widely used high-level programming language. Backus proposed using 'metalinguistic formulae' to describe the working of a programming language in 1959. This method was further simplified by Peter Naur, and the resulting 'Backus–Naur Form' remains the primary method of describing and generating formal computer languages. Backus apparently came up with his ideas knowing nothing of Panini, at least directly, but, as the Sanskritist Murray Emeneau put it, 'Most of the specific features that are taken . . . to distinguish an "American" school of linguistics from others are Bloomfieldian, and . . . many are Paninean.'[21] In 1967 a programmer named Peter Zilahy Ingerman wrote to the *Communications of the ACM*

(Association for Computing Machinery) to argue that 'since it is traditional in professional circles to give credit where credit is due, and since there is clear evidence that Panini was the earlier independent inventor of the notation, may I suggest the name "Panini-Backus Form" as being a more desirable one?'[22]

Panini's analysis and innovations may therefore be seen as the foundation of all high-level programming languages. But the *Ashtadhyayi* also had an indelible effect on Sanskrit, the language he was describing: it gave this spoken tongue the stability of formal languages—like programming languages—in which a set of rules precisely constrains the symbols, syntax and usages. Natural languages have the tendency to change over time, but Sanskrit has remained astonishingly unchanged in the two and a half millennia since Panini. There have been strong trends towards certain usages, such as the use of compound words, but in general 'the stress on refinement and correctness, the overwhelming anxiety to live up to a felt Paninian ideal, kept the language formal for everyone, and channelled creativity towards involution, elaboration, and increasing precision.'[23]

So one of the problems of working with Sanskrit texts is that internal linguistic usages give you very little evidence, if any, of provenance and dating. If you had a pandit in contemporary Varanasi write a letter in Sanskrit and time-machined it back 2000 years, his ancestors would be able to read it with perfect ease. In Sanskrit, therefore, the usual distinction between normal and formal language is collapsed, and the original derivation of the language's name from the root *samskrta*, 'constructed, finished, well or completely formed,' carries precise denotative value. It is only later that 'Sanskrit' comes to suggest refined speech, to refer to the language of the *shishta*, the educated, the superior, the polite.

Then, as now, Indians spoke more than one language in daily use. Sanskrit was the eternal language of the cosmopolis, of the *marga*, the path; the Prakrits were the 'natural, normal, ordinary' regional languages, the languages of *desha*, of place. Because Prakrits were subject to change, the stricter grammarians regarded them as *apabhramsa*, 'degenerate languages' that had sloughed off from the eternal Sanskrit through careless usage. People spoke both Sanskrit and Prakrits, and they were not—as elsewhere in the world—speaking two registers of the same language. They existed in a condition that is better described as 'hyperglossia' than 'diglossia': 'What we encounter is not an internal split (di-) in registers and norms, typically between literary and colloquial usage,' Sheldon Pollock tells us, 'but a relationship of extreme superposition (hyper-) between two languages that local actors knew to be entirely different.'[24]

The *Kamasutra*, a Sanskrit text addressed to urban sophisticates, advises that 'by having one's conversations in the assemblies neither too much in Sanskrit nor too much in the local language a person should become highly esteemed in the world.'[25] Too much eternal language and you revealed yourself as a total *marga* snob; too much Prakrit, on the other hand, marked you as a desi bumpkin. Sanskrit drama reproduced these social dynamics as a convention: the upper-class males—kings, ministers, educated Brahmins—spoke Sanskrit; everyone else spoke Prakrit: merchants and bankers, women (with the exception of courtesans), and of course the lower classes.

Sanskrit—once the language of liturgy—was officially available only to the 'twice-born' of the caste system, to its top three tiers of Brahmins, Kshatriyas (warriors), and Vaishyas (traders). Sudras—the manual labourers, the people who provided services—were forbidden to learn or speak Sanskrit, as were those who fell outside the caste system altogether, such as tribal peoples. Thus those who spoke against the Brahminical system—the Buddha, for instance—often used Prakrit languages because Sanskrit was marked as the language of the elite.

Whatever its social value, Sanskrit's stability and emphasis on precision meant that it was regarded as an ideal language for the sciences and philosophy. Since it was believed to be an eternal language, the fifty phonemes of Sanskrit, the *matrka*, were regarded as the root vibrations from which the universe had emerged, and were sometimes worshipped as the 'little mothers.'[26] Sanskrit phonemes and words therefore had an elemental, essential link to reality that other languages lacked. This view was challenged by Buddhist thinkers who argued that 'the signifier is related to the signified as a matter of pure convention,' but the notion that the truth could only be spoken in Sanskrit, and grammatically correct Sanskrit at that, was immensely persuasive.[27] Two monks were said to have argued that the Buddha's words should be translated into Vedic Sanskrit, since people were corrupting them by repeating them in local dialects. The Buddha himself rebuked them, 'Deluded men! This will not lead to the conversion of the unconverted,' and he commanded all monks, 'You are not to put the Buddha's words into [Vedic-Sanskrit] verse. To do this would be to commit an infraction. I authorize you, monks, to learn the Buddha's words each in his own dialect.'[28] This injunction was obeyed, and Pali, 'a new and parallel sacred language,' was created by

Buddhists, and yet, by the second century CE, 'a vast Buddhist canon in Sanskrit' had been created.[29] The rebels against Vedic authority—the Buddhists, the Jains, the Tantrics—had to speak in Sanskrit after all.

It was perhaps the multitude of viewpoints and ideologies attempting to speak to each other and against each other in Sanskrit that intensified its grammarians' search for even more exactness. Beginning in the fourth century BCE and culminating in the eighteenth century, an effort was made to create a *shastric* or scientific Sanskrit that could 'formulate logical relations with scientific precision.'[30] In this specialized, condensed Sanskrit, the sentence 'Caitra goes to the village' would be rephrased as 'There is an activity which leads to a connection-activity which has as Agent no one other than Caitra, specified by singularity, [which] is taking place in the present and which has as Object something not different from "village".'

The sentence 'Out of friendship, Maitra cooks rice for Devadatta in a pot, over a fire' would be broken down into:

(1) An Agent represented by the person Maitra;
(2) An Object by the 'rice'
(3) An Instrument by the 'fire'
(4) A Recipient by the person Devadatta
(5) A Point of Departure (which includes the causal relationship) by the 'friendship' (which is between Maitra and Devadatta);
(6) The Locality by the 'pot'[31]

The *shastric* version of the original sentence would therefore be something like:

There is an activity conducive to a softening which is a change residing in something not different from rice, and which takes place in the present, and resides in an agent not different from Maitra, who is specified by singularity and has a Recipient not different from Devadatta, an Instrument not different from . . . [32]

and so on.

So the *shastric* thinkers tried to create a low-level version of Sanskrit, a counterpart to assembly code. In fact, Rick Briggs, a NASA specialist in artificial intelligence, points out that this decomposition of natural language is very similar to what computer programmers do when they attempt to represent knowledge in semantic nets, which use 'triples' to embody logical relations: 'cause, event, friendship; friendship, object1, Devadatta; friendship, object2, Maitra; cause, result, cook; cook, agent, Maitra . . .' and so on. Briggs writes:

> It is interesting to speculate as to why the Indians found it worthwhile to pursue studies into unambiguous coding of natural language into semantic elements. It is tempting to think of them as computer scientists without the hardware, but a possible explanation is that a search for clear, unambiguous understanding is inherent in the human being.[33]

The extraordinarily logical nature of Sanskrit, the fact that 'we are *lakṣaṇaikacakṣuṣka*, solely guided by rules,' that 'correctness is guaranteed by the correct application of rules,' that you can generate a grammatically correct word or phrase you need by applying these rules—all this leads to a strong similarity between it and modern programming languages. The *Ashtadhyayi* itself is replete with features that resemble modern programming constructs: recursion; multiple inheritance (a rule based on other rules acquires all the properties of the parent rules); context-sensitive and context-free rules; conflict resolution for rules; string transformations; ordered operations; a metalanguage; and so on.[34] Programmers who know Sanskrit sometimes claim that it would make the perfect programming language, endlessly rigorous and endlessly flexible.[35]

The inheritors of the Paninian tradition were deeply concerned with the relationship between language, meaning, and function: How is meaning transferred? How is it understood? Does language impel action? These questions became particularly urgent when these theorists were confronted by belletrist poetry written in the unchanging formal language of science and scripture. Over the centuries, Sanskrit developed a flourishing culture of *kavya*—poetry—and so the philosophers of language had to engage with beauty. Their investigations took them inescapably towards considerations of aesthetics: How was beauty produced in language? How does beauty affect or influence the reader, the viewer? Like programmers with their discussions of the 'eloquence' of code, the classical Indian theorists tried to think about the effects that flowed from formal-language texts and went beyond the purely functional.

~

Until about the mid-ninth century CE, the thinkers of the Sanskrit cosmopolis who were interested in the nature and epistemology of literary beauty concerned themselves with the formal qualities of texts; they thought of poetry as language made beautiful through the operations of certain constructions: simile, metaphor, metonymy, double entendre or puns, alliteration, sound, rhythm, and so on. These figures were *alamkaras*, ornaments, which beautified language in much the same way that jewellery embellished a body. Some scholars ascribed a more central role to *riti* or 'style,' to *gunas* or 'qualities' such as *ojas*, 'strength' or 'vigour' (achieved, for example, through the use of long compounds in prose); *prasada*, clarity or lucidity; *samata*, the uniformity of diction; *sukumarata*, softness or delicacy; et cetera. These qualities, the adherents of *riti* argued, produced beauty, which was in turn heightened by figures of speech. Whatever specific emphases the Indian aestheticians may have preferred in their writings on beauty, all of these early scholars were formalists; poetics itself was *alamkara-shastra*, the study of ornamentation. Their critical methods were heavily particularistic, and they therefore produced exhaustive catalogues of *alamkaras* and their effects, of the varieties and sub-varieties of linguistic structures used by writers.

The theorist Anandavardhana (820–90 CE) caused an upheaval among these *alamkarikas* with his treatise *Dhvanyaloka* (The light of suggestion). Until Anandavardhana, Indian philosophers of language had accepted two main modes of signification through which language conveyed meaning: *abhidha*, the literal or the denotative, and *lakshana*, the metaphorical and figurative, the connotative. Anandavardhana proposed that poetic language set yet another semantic function into play: suggestion. The stock example used to illustrate the workings of suggestion in mundane language is the simple sentence, 'The sun has set.' An eleventh-century theorist wrote:

The denoted meaning of a word is one and the same for all persons bearing it; so that it is fixed and uniform; the denoted or directly *expressed* meaning of the words 'the sun has set' never varies (is fixed), while its *suggested* meaning varies with the variation in such accessory conditions as the context, the character of the speaker, the character of the person spoken to, and so forth. For instance, the words 'the sun has set' suggests (1) the idea that 'now is the opportunity to attack the enemy' (when they are addressed by the general to the king);—(2) 'that you should set forth to meet your lover' (when addressed by the *confidant* to the girl in love)

and so on until '(10)—"my love has not come even today" (when spoken by an impatient girl waiting for her beloved's return from a journey); thus, in fact, there is no end to the number of suggested meanings.'[36]

Anandavardhana's assertion was that in literature, suggestion or *vyanjana* added layers of meaning to the text that were not apparent in the denotative or figurative content of the language; *vyanjana* is derived from the root *vi* plus *anj*, 'to reveal, manifest'—*vyanjana* therefore manifests a multitude of meanings within the reader. And, Anandavardhana argued, when 'sense or word, subordinating their own meaning, suggest that [suggested] meaning'—that is, when the denoted and figured meaning becomes less important than the manifested, unspoken meaning—that poetry becomes 'the type of poetry which the wise call *dhvani*.'[37] *Dhvani* derives from *dhvan*, 'to reverberate'; *dhvani* poetry therefore causes an endless resonance within the reader—'the suggested sense [flashes] forth in an instant in the minds of intelligent auditors who are averse to the literal sense and in quest of the real meaning.'[38] So the echoes of *dhvani* are available only to those who are capable, who are alert to the possibilities of poetry. *Dhvani* is 'not understood by the mere knowledge of grammar and dictionaries. It is understood only by those who know the true nature of poetic meaning.'[39] *Dhvani* is 'the soul of poetry.'[40]

Anandavardhana does not claim that he is inventing anything new when he speaks of *dhvani*: it is 'found in the works of great poets. It is that which appears as [something] separate from the well-known elements [of poetry].' The reason we call some poets 'great' is because their work is resonant with *dhvani*, which is something that cannot be described or analysed by listing their beautiful figures of speech or pointing at their style; *dhvani* is not accounted for by the then-current theories of *alamkara-shastra*. And yet, *dhvani* is what makes poetry beautiful. So Anandavardhana insists that he is just naming something that already exists, and showing us how to think about it. He shows us different kinds of *dhvani* in verses taken from the epics, from the renowned poets of his era, from famous poems in Sanskrit and Prakrit. For instance:

> O holy monk, wander without fear.
> That little dog was killed today by him—
> that violent lion living in the thickets
> on the banks of the Godāvarī River.[41]

Here the speaker is a woman, and what is being suggested is a *vastu*, a narrative element: the woman wants to keep the wandering monk away from a trysting place where she meets with her lover. So what we have here is *vastu-dhvani*, through which the poet can suggest things, facts, situations, prohibitions, injunctions. In this poem, the denotative meaning is exactly the opposite of what she really wants, what she is really doing; what the reader grasps is beyond *abhidha* and *lakshana*. Here is another famous example of *vastu-dhvani*:

> Mother-in-law sleeps down there, and I here.
> Look while day remains, O traveler.
> Do not, blind in the night,
> lie down in my bed.[42]

The presumed speaker is a lovelorn woman, a familiar type within the conventions; this married woman is extending—or suggesting—an invitation.

Dhvani can also suggest a figure of speech, an *alamkara*. So:

> O lady with tremulous long eyes,
> as your face
> completely fills the directions
> with the radiance of its beauty,
> the ocean now remains calm,
> absolutely still.
> And so I know it is nothing
> but an insentient mass of water.[43]

The ocean is not stirred *now*—as it was a moment ago, when the moon rose—therefore it must be truly insentient. The eyes are tremulous—perhaps from momentary jealousy?—but now the smiling face 'fills the directions.' What is being suggested here is a metaphor, the beautiful face as the moon. This is the second variety of suggestion, *alamkara-dhvani*.

But the most powerful *dhvani* in poetry, the poet's most desired effect, is the suggestion of *rasa*. *Rasa* is a term which, until Anandavardhana, had mostly been used in dramaturgical texts. At some time between 200 BCE and 200 CE, a perhaps-apocryphal sage named Bharata is said to have written the *Natyashastra* (Treatise on the drama). The *Natyashastra* is a theatre professional's handbook: it includes chapters on what a playhouse should look like; on different gaits; the use of local dialects; costumes and make-up; on the factors that lead to the success of a dramatic performance. The sixth and seventh chapters famously analyse the nature of aesthetic pleasure, *rasa*. According to Bharata:

> People who eat prepared food mixed with different condiments and sauces, etc., if they are sensitive, enjoy the different tastes and then feel pleasure (or satisfaction); likewise, sensitive spectators, after enjoying the various emotions expressed by the actors through words, gestures and feelings feel pleasure, etc. This (final) feeling by the spectators is here explained as (various) *rasa*-s of *natya* [drama].[44]

So *rasa*—the word literally means 'taste' or 'juice'—is not emotion (*bhava*); it is the aestheticized satisfaction or 'sentiment' of tasting artificially induced emotions. Generations of thinkers developed the notion of *rasa* along with a notion of the ideal viewer; the locus of *rasa* was this viewer, not the actors or the stage. *Rasa* is what the drama produces in the *sahrdaya*, the sophisticated 'same-hearted' connoisseur who is the playwright's necessary counterpart. The *sahrdaya*—because of education, experience, and temperament—is able to experience *rasa* precisely because he or she does not identify in a personal, egoistic way with the tragedy on the stage. The naive spectator who ascribes some sort of reality to what is happening on the stage and identifies personally with the emotions of the characters is incapable of *rasa*, which is an impersonal, disinterested pleasure. One might say that a certain psychical distance is necessary for *rasa* to be experienced. *Rasa* is sublime.

On stage, the characters and situation and the patterning of events make up the determinants or catalysts, the *vibhavas*; the actors portray the consequent outward manifestations (*anubhavas*) such as speech, bodily posture, and involuntary reactions (such as trembling). In response to the actors' depictions of momentary situations like a waiting lover's anticipation or doubt, the spectator experiences fleeting emotional states (*vyabhicaribhavas*); and all of these various feelings come together—like condiments and sauces—to allow the viewer access to a stable emotion, a dominant mood, a *sthayibhava*, such as grief. Note that this stable emotion is in the viewer; it is a 'permanent emotional state' that is ever present in all human beings as a potential, a latent trace. The actors cannot act out a *sthayibhava*—it really doesn't matter what the actors feel or don't feel; the purpose of their craft is to allow the *sahrdaya* access to his or her own stable emotions.

And, very importantly, the stable emotion is not the *rasa*. If the actors portray a scene that allows access to the stable emotion of grief, *shoka*, what the viewer relishes is the *rasa* of *karuna*, pathos. The *rasa* is in the tasting of grief, in the relishing of grief, in the reflective cognizing of grief. If the actors portray desire, *rati*, the viewer relishes *sringara*, the *rasa* of the erotic. The pleasure of *rasa* comes from the meta-experience of experiencing oneself experience the stable emotions.

Bharata names eight *rasas* in all; so, in addition to *karuna* and *sringara*, the viewer enjoys *hasya*, the comic; *raudra*, the wrathful; *vira*, the heroic; *bhayanaka*, the terrible; *bibhatsa*, the disgusting; and *adhbuta*, the wonderful. A ninth *rasa* was added by later theoreticians: *shanta*, the peaceful, which arises from the stable emotion of *vairagya*, detachment, dispassion, and which is manifested especially by epics like the Mahabharata, which place the specificity of human striving and passion against the vastness of time.

According to Anandavardhana, poetic language can manifest *dhvani* through the operation of *vyanjana*, suggestion, and so offer the reader an opportunity to taste *rasa*. For instance:

> While the divine sage was speaking
> to Pārvatī's father,
> she, eyes downcast,
> counted the petals
> of her toy lotus.[45]

The 'divine sage' has come to propose to Himavata, the king of the Himalayas, that he marry his young daughter Parvati to the god Shiva. Parvati is in love with Shiva, and has performed great austerities to win him, but in this moment, Anandavardhana says, 'the counting of the petals of the lotus subordinates itself and without the help of any verbal operation reveals another matter in the form of a transient state of mind (*vyabhicāribhāva*) [of the emotion love, namely shyness].'[46] In the perception of the reader, the shyness of Parvati suggests desire, love. The reader therefore relishes the *rasa* of the erotic, *sringara*, evoked through *dhvani*.

We can see that the operations of suggestion are heavily dependent on context (as in 'The sun has set'). Whereas the denotative and connotative meanings of a phrase or a text are limited, *vyanjana* is infinite and can never be exhausted. Consider the following verse, in which the speaker is Rama, the hero of the Ramayana; the season is the monsoon, when lovers come together. Rama has lost his kingdom through court intrigue, has been banished to the wilderness, has faced many dangers, and his beloved wife has been kidnapped by the evil Ravana.

> Clouds smear the sky,
> flocks of cranes tremble
> across their viscous blue-black beauty.
> The winds sprinkle rain, the peacocks call
>   their soft cries of joy.
> Let all this be, as it likes. I am Rāma.
>   I am hard-hearted, I can endure all.
> But Vaidehī? How will she survive?
>   Ah alas, my goddess, be strong![47]

Anandavardhana writes, 'In this verse, the [suggestive] word is "Rama." By this word we understand Rama as developed into various suggested qualities, not simply as the possessor of the name.'[48] That is, the reader already knows that the speaker is Rama; no information is added here by the use of the name. But the name evokes, for the reader, all the tragedy and suffering that this man has already experienced and will experience in the future. In a flash, this sudden explosion of light illuminates the past and the future.

A century later, the greatest exponent of *rasa-dhvani* theory, Abhinavagupta, wrote about this verse:

> The suggestions of other properties . . . are endless; for example, his banishment from the kingdom, etc. And since these suggestions are countless, they cannot be conveyed [simultaneously] by means of the denotative functions of words. Even if these innumerable suggested properties were to be conveyed [by denotation] one by one, since they will not be had in one single act of cognition, they will not be the source of a wondrous aesthetic experience and hence they will not give rise to a great beauty. But if these properties are suggested, they will assume countless forms (*kiṃ kiṃ rūpaṃ na sahate*) because in the suggestion their separateness will not be clearly perceived. In this way they will become the source of a strikingly beautiful aesthetic pleasure that is analogous to the flavor of a wonderful drink, or cake, or sweet confection [where the individual ingredients cannot be separately tasted but yet add to the flavour of the final product]. For it has been said already [by Anandavardhana] that a word which is suggestive reveals a beauty 'which cannot be conveyed by another form of expression.'[49]

~

Rasa-dhvani can operate at the level of a word, a sentence, or an entire work. According to Anandavardhana, *rasa* is 'an object on which no words can operate directly,' and therefore *dhvani* is the only way to manifest *rasa*.[50] So Anandavardhana might have said to an aspiring writer: suggest, don't tell. *Dhvani* is literally 'reverberation,' and is often compared to the 'sounding of a bell' or 'a needle falling through a pile of lotus leaves.' If we hear the phrase, 'A village on the Ganga' (in Sanskrit, *gangayam ghoshah*, literally 'a village in the Ganga') we understand that the village cannot literally rest on the water, and that we are talking about a village located on the banks of the Ganga. This would be an example of figurative speech. But Anandavardhana would argue that this phrase about the holy river also carries a suggestion—or causes in the listener the manifestation—of coolness, sanctity. This underlying, affective meaning does not emerge from the denotative or figurative aspects of the phrase. This kind of suggestion functions in all speech, is present even in mundane language, but poets knowingly and intentionally concentrate *vyanjana* to construct a coherent, sustained engagement within the reader, and thus to manifest *dhvani*, and hence *rasa*. Patrick Colm Hogan writes:

> *Rasadhvani*, the 'truest' form of *dhvani*, it is an experience—along the lines of what we would call 'a moment of tenderness' or 'a pang of sadness.' It is, in short, an experience of *rasa* . . . [These *rasas*] are evoked through the clouds of non-denumerable, non-substitutable, non-propositional suggestions which surround these texts.[51]

The very sounds and rhythms of language—which pre-exist meaning—contribute to our experience of *rasa*. Abhinavagupta says that when we hear poetic language without waiting for our understanding of the expressed meaning, [the stylistic qualities] set about building up the *rasas*, giving us a foretaste (*āsvāda*) of them. This is as much to say that as the *rasas* are suggested by style (*saṅghaṭanā*), the ground is laid for the relishing of a *rasa* at the very beginning of the appropriate style before our understanding of the meaning has come into play; and that it is on this account that the *rasa*, even at the later moment, after we have understood the expressed meaning and when the *rasa* has assumed its full flavour, does not appear to have arisen later [than our understanding].[52]

~

Anandavardhana observes, 'When ornamented by even one from among the varieties of *dhvani*, speech acquires a fresh colour, even though it follows a subject matter that has been treated by poets of the past.'[53] Since the properties manifested by *dhvani* are countless, 'poetical material . . . finds no limit . . .

Not even Vacaspati [the god of speech] in a thousand efforts could exhaust it, any more than he could exhaust the nature of the universe.

For just as the nature of the universe, although it has manifested this marvellous proliferation of matter through the succession of past ages, cannot be said now to be worn out and unable to create anything new, just so is the situation in poetry, which, although it has been worked over by the minds of countless poets, is not thereby weakened, but increases with ever new artistic abilities.'[54]

Anandavardhana accepted that there may be poetic texts in which the suggested meaning isn't the dominant pleasure, or even present at all; he rather disdainfully refers to the latter as *chitra kavya*, picture poetry, flashy poetry: 'Poetry which lacks *rasa* or an emotion (*bhāva*) as its final meaning, which is composed only by relying on novelties of literal sense and expression, and which gives the appearance of a picture, is *citra* . . .' Poetry that 'gives the appearance of a picture' refers to very difficult pictorial arrangements in verse, similar to visual pattern poetry and topiary verses in the West—Sanskrit writers wrote stanzas in which interlocking syllables, if connected by drawn lines, revealed the shapes of drums, swords, wheels, and so on.[55] This *chitrabandha* is probably where the more general term *chitra kavya* originates. Anandavardhana continues, '[This poetry also includes] verbal *citra*, such as difficult arrangements, *yamakas* (echo alliterations), and the like. Semantic *citra* . . . may be exemplified by poetic fancy (*utprekṣā*) and such figures . . . It is not real poetry, for it is an imitation of poetry.'[56]

Now that Anandavardhana has shown us how *vyanjana* works in poetry to produce *dhvani* and *rasa*, he tells us, 'Now that instruction is being offered to modern poets in the true principles of poetry, while *citra* may be much used in the efforts of beginners who are seeking practise, it is established for mature poets that *dhvani* alone is poetry.'[57]

~

So *rasa* is what I felt that afternoon I discovered Hemingway at our kitchen table in Bombay, when the bleak undertow of his stories, roiling with unspoken emotion, flung me into an exaltation, a state of delight. Hemingway's famous taut rhythms, the stripped simplicity of his diction, those repetitions of sound that he meticulously builds into his prose, all these enhance the iceberg-sized dhvani of what he leaves unsaid. Every word, every pause, every hesitation makes the dhvani of a story.

Flannery O'Connor writes:

> The meaning of a story has to be embodied in it, has to be made concrete in it. A story is a way to say something that can't be said any other way, and it takes every word in the story to say what the meaning is. You tell a story because a statement would be inadequate. When anybody asks what a story is about, the only proper thing is to tell him to read the story. The meaning of fiction is not abstract meaning but experienced meaning. [58]

The only way to explain to you what I experienced when I first read Hemingway is to tell you to read those stories. And even then, you will read different stories. We may read the same texts, but the dhvani that manifests within you will be unique. Your beauty will be your own. If you reread a story that you read ten years ago, its dhvani within you will be new. Poetry's beauty is infinite.

This is what ugly code looks like:

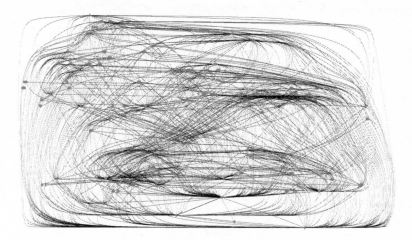

Figure 6.1: Dependency diagram (TheDailyWTF,
www.thedailywtf.com)

This is a dependency diagram—a graphic representation of
interdependence or coupling (the black lines) between software
components (the grey dots) within a program. A high degree
of interdependence means that changing one component
inside the program could lead to cascading changes in all the
other connected components, and in turn to changes in their
dependencies, and so on. Programs with this kind of structure
are brittle, and hard to understand and fix. This dependency
program was submitted anonymously to TheDailyWTF.com,
where working programmers share 'Curious Perversions in
Information Technology' they find as they work. The exhibits

at TheDailyWTF are often embodiments of stupidity, of miasmic dumbness perpetrated by the squadrons of sub-Mort programmers putting together the software that runs businesses across the globe. But, as often, high-flying 'enterprise architects' and consultants put together systems that produce dependency diagrams that look like this renowned TheDailyWTF exhibit. A user commented, 'I found something just like that blocking the drain once.'

If the knot of tangled hair in figure 6.1 provokes disgust, what kind of code garners admiration? In the anthology *Beautiful Code*, the contribution from the creator of the popular programming language Ruby, Yukihiro 'Matz' Matsumoto, is an essay titled 'Treating Code as an Essay.' Matz writes:

> Judging the attributes of computer code is not simply a matter of aesthetics. Instead, computer programs are judged according to how well they execute their intended tasks. In other words, 'beautiful code' is not an abstract virtue that exists independent of its programmers' efforts. Rather, beautiful code is really meant to help the programmer be happy and productive. This is the metric I use to evaluate the beauty of a program.[1]

He goes on to list the virtues of good code: brevity; reusability ('never write the same thing twice'); familiarity (Ruby is an 'extremely conservative programming language' which does not use 'innovative control structures' but 'sticks to traditional control structures programmers are familiar with'); simplicity; flexibility (which Matz defines as 'freedom from enforcement of tools,' so programmers aren't forced to work in a certain way by the tools or languages they use); and, finally, balance:

'No element by itself will ensure a beautiful program. When balanced together and kept in mind from the very beginning, each element will work harmoniously with the others to create beautiful code.'[2]

So, beautiful code is lucid, it is easy to read and understand; its organization, its shape, its architecture reveals intent as much as its declarative syntax does. Each small part is coherent, singular in its purpose, and although all these small sections fit together like the pieces of a complex mosaic, they come apart easily when one element needs to be changed or replaced. All this leads to the happiness of the programmer, who must understand it, change it, extend it. This longing for architectural coherence leads to comparisons of code with music, which is often described as the most mathematical of the arts. There is, in fact, an anecdotal but fairly generalized belief among American programmers that there is a high correlation between coding and music-making, that many coders are musicians. A similar claim is made about mathematicians and music. These connections seem culturally encoded to me, specific to America—I've never heard of Indian programmers or mathematicians having a special affinity for music, apart from some being passionate listeners. Still, the code-and-music analogy is illuminating in that both practices prize harmonious pattern-making and abhor cacophony, a loss of clarity and structure. The snarl in the dependency diagram (figure 6.1) may strike the civilian as a pretty picture, with its swirl of lines and punctuating sparks of grey; to the programmer, it is an abomination because it speaks of incoherence, incomprehensibility, unpredictability, sticky seams of connection that prevent swift diagnosis and make excision and replacement all but impossible.

With his emphasis on programmer happiness, Matz makes explicit his allegiance to Donald Knuth's literate programming. He writes:

> Programs share some attributes with essays. For essays, the most important question readers ask is, 'What is it about?' For programs, the main question is, 'What does it do?' In fact, the purpose should be sufficiently clear that neither question ever needs to be uttered . . . Both essays and lines of code are meant—before all else—to be read and understood by human beings.[3]

The trouble of course is that as software programs grow bigger and more complex, the code they comprise tends to become unreadable and incomprehensible to human beings. Programmers like to point out that if each line of code, or even each logical statement (which may spread to more than one physical line), is understood to be a component, software systems are the most complicated things that humans have ever built: the Lucent 5ESS switch, used in telephone exchanges, derives its functionality from a hundred million lines of code; the 2008 Fedora 9 distribution of Linux comprises over two hundred million lines of code.[4] No temple, no cathedral has ever contained as many moving parts. So if you've ever written code, you understand in your bones the truth of Donald Knuth's assertion, 'Software is hard. It's harder than anything else I've ever had to do.'[5] If you've ever written code, the fact that so much software works so much of the time can seem profoundly miraculous.

~

Software is complicated because it tries to model the irreducible complexity of the world. Even a simple software requirement for a small company that, say, provides secretarial services for the medical insurance industry—'We need an application that makes it easier for our scribes to write up reports from doctors' examinations of insurance claimants'—will always reveal a swirling hodgepodge of exceptions and special cases. Some of the doctors will have two addresses on file, some will have three, and this one was on Broadway until January 22 and in the East Village afterwards. A report will always begin with a summary of the patient's claimed condition, unless it's being written for Company X, which wants a narration of the doctor's exam up front. There are four main types of boilerplate text for the doctor's conclusions, but there needs to be a 'freeform' option, and room for other templates, but creation of new templates needs to be restricted to certain users. And so on, and on, and on.

The program you create in response to these requirements must reduce repetitive labour, automate the work that must be done each time, yet remain flexible enough to allow variation. The business practices that can be formalized into sets of procedures, into Grace Hopper's dinner recipes—first do 'a,' then 'b,' then 'c'—are easy to convert into code. In fact, the software practice that I learnt in the eighties was called 'procedural programming'—you wrote a program as a series of procedures that you called in sequence. Your job as a programmer was to 'chunk' the system you were trying to model into clean, self-contained actions, and then construct more complex parts out of these simple elements. So, if you want to write a new report, what you do is: retrieve the doctor's address, retrieve the patient's information, create a new file. Or, in (pseudo) code: RetrieveDoctorsAddress(), RetrievePatientInfo(), CreateNewFile(). And these procedures would be called from BeginNewReport(). Which might be called from ShowApplicationMainMenu().

To engage in this kind of assemblage of functionality is bracingly logical and orderly; you feel like you are making a perfect little machine, a clean, comprehensible automaton that you have set in motion. But soon, as you adapt your procedural engine for the exceptions, for all the variations that exist in the real world, you find yourself snarled in squirming thickets of if-then-else constructs, each of which contains yet other if-elseif and switch-case monsters, and you find that you have to break out of your beautiful Report-Main-Body loop and backtrack to other reports to retrieve history, and then, inevitably your procedures become more complex and start doing two things instead of one, RetrievePatientInfo() is now doing the retrieving but is also checking for valid addresses, you know that functionality should be somewhere else but you don't have the time to bother, the users ask for a new feature and you patch it in, and of course you mean to come back later and clean everything up, but then, before you know it, you are trapped inside an unwholesome, uncontrollable atrocity, a Big Ball of Mud: '[a] haphazardly structured, sprawling, sloppy, duct-tape and bailing wire, spaghetti code jungle.'[6]

Often, it is not the lack of programming skill that leads to the emergence of a Big Ball of Mud, but something akin to the time-honoured Indian practice of *jugaad*. *Jugaad* is Hindi for a creative workaround, a working improvisation that is built in the absence of resources and under pressure of time (from the Sanskrit *yukti*, trick, combination, concatenation). There can be something heroic about *jugaad*, as in the strange-looking trucks one sees bumping down country roads in rural India, which on closer examination turn out to be carts with diesel irrigation pumps strapped on; or the amphibious bicycles buoyed by improvised air floats and powered by blades taken from ceiling fans. *Jugaad* makes do, it gets work done, it manoeuvres around uncooperative bureaucracies, it hacks. In recent years, *jugaad* has been recognized as down-to-earth creativity, as a prized national resource, and has acquired the dignifying sobriquet of 'frugal engineering.'

In software, repeated applications of excessively frugal engineering by a series of programmers leads to a scheme that has no discernible structure, within which components use each other's functionality promiscuously, so that the logic of the program becomes hard or impossible to follow. In a Big Ball of Mud—and yes, it is a technical term of art—effects flow across boundaries, so that introducing a small change to one piece of code results in unpredictable behaviour in distant parts of the system. Software needs maintenance: bugs need to be fixed, new features are demanded by users. If you are the programmer asked to go into the depths of a Big Ball of Mud, the prospect is terrifying. I mean that quite literally; as you poke and prod into the innards of a badly written program on which users depend, you are often beset by paralysing dread. How can you fix something you can't understand? What if your fix introduces new bugs that reveal themselves in some future disaster which corrupts and loses data? The impulse then is to rewrite the whole program from the bottom up, in accordance with hard-won principles of good program design. But—often there is no budget for a complete rewrite, there is no time, there isn't enough manpower. So maybe you patch a bit here, work in a clumsy kludge there—*jugaad*! Hundreds of programmers may have worked on such a program over the years, each contributing a little to the mess. So you add your handful of mud to the Big Ball, or maybe you just back away carefully and leave the damn thing alone. There are some areas of code in running programs that may as well be marked *Here Be Dragons*, and there are some programs that have run for decades—at universities, corporations, banks—that cannot be efficiently maintained or enhanced because nobody completely understands how they work.

For instance: the US Pentagon's Defense Finance and Accounting Service (DFAS) is known to make 'widespread' errors in paying solders' salaries, and is slow to correct these mistakes when challenged. The software that the Pentagon uses for payroll and accounting comprises about seven million lines of COBOL code, mostly written in the sixties. The system hasn't been updated in more than a dozen years, and significant portions of the code have been 'corrupted'—long-running systems can suffer from 'software entropy' or 'code rot,' a slow deterioration in functionality because of the changing hardware or software environments they run within. A retired Pentagon employee reported that the system is 'nearly impossible' to update because its documentation disappeared long ago: 'It's hard to make a change to a program if you don't know what's in there.'[7]

When a situation like this becomes desperate enough, the powers-that-be may employ skilled 'code archaeologists' to spelunk into the depths. Or pony up for a complete rewrite. Mostly, managers prefer to plug up the holes and leave the Big Balls of Mud to roll on. COBOL, a language first introduced in

1959 by Grace Hopper ('Grandma COBOL'), still processes 90 per cent of the planet's financial transactions, and 75 per cent of all business data.[8] You can make a comfortable living maintaining code in languages like COBOL, the computing equivalents of Mesopotamian cuneiform dialects. These ancient applications—too expensive to replace, sometimes too tangled to fix or improve—run on, serving up the data that appears on the chromed-up surface of your browser, which gives you the illusion that your bank and your local utility companies live on the technological cutting edge. But as always, the past lives on under the shiny surface of the present, and often, it is too densely tangled to comprehend.

~

The International Obfuscated C Code Contest annually awards recognition to the writer of 'the most Obscure/Obfuscated C program'—that is, to the person who can produce the most incomprehensible working code in the language C.[9] The stated pedagogical aim of the contest is 'to show the importance of programming style, in an ironic way.'[10] But it has always seemed to me that confronting unfathomable code is the programming equivalent of staring at the abject, of slowing down to peer into the carnage of a car wreck. This is the reason that programmers expend time and effort in designing esoteric, purposely difficult computer languages like the infamous 'brainfuck'—that really is its official name, with the lowercase 'b'—which was created as an exercise in writing the smallest possible compiler (240 bytes) that could run on the Amiga operating system. 'Hello, world' in brainfuck is:

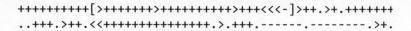

```
++++++++++[>+++++++>++++++++++>+++<<<-]>++.>+.+++++++
..+++.>++.<<+++++++++++++++.>.+++.------.--------.>+.
```

Figure 6.2: 'Hello, world' in brainfuck

brainfuck is a 'Turing tarpit,' which is to say it is a very small language in which you can write any program that you could write in C or Java; but attempting to do so would, well, fuck your brain, and therefore the delectable frisson of terror the code above induces in discerning code cognoscenti. brainfuck is venerable and famous, but my favourite esoteric language is Malbolge, which was designed solely to be the most outrageously difficult language to program in. It is named, appropriately, after the eighth circle of hell in Dante's Inferno, Malebolge ('Evil ditches,' reserved for frauds). In the language Malbolge, the result of any instruction depends on where it is located in memory, which effectively means that what specific code does changes with every run. Code and data are very hard to reuse, and the constructs to control program flow are almost non-existent.[11] Malbolge inverts the sacred commandments of literate programming, and is so impenetrable that it took two years after the language was first released for the first working program to appear, and that program was not written by a human, but generated by a computerized search program that examined the space of all possible Malbolge programs and winnowed out one possibility. 'Hello, world' in Malbolge is:

```
(=<`$9]7<5YXz7wT.3,+0/o'K%$H"'~D|#z@b=`{^Lx8%$Xmrkpohm-
kNi;gsedcba`_^]\[ZYXWVUTSRQPONMLKJIHGFEDCBA@?>=<;:9876543s+O<oLm
```

Figure 6.3: 'Hello, world' in Malbolge

And yet, this snippet doesn't convey the true, titillating evil of Malbolge, which changes and quakes like quicksand. To contemplate Malbolge is to stare into the abyss in which machines speak their own tongues, indifferent to the human gaze; the programmer thereafter knows the pathos of her situation, and recognizes the costs of sacrilege. The coder's quest is for functionality—'all computer programs are designed to accomplish some kind of task'—and the extension and maintenance of that functionality demands clarity and legibility. Illegibility, incomprehensibility—that way madness lies.

~

The desire for lucidity as well as power, and therefore the maximization of productivity and happiness among programmers, has—according to some accounts—created more than eight thousand computer languages over the last half-century.[12] Each of these artificial, formal languages embodies a philosophy of human–computer interaction; whole family trees of dialects have evolved from the hacker's eternal desire to improve, to implement better. Adherents of one language will criticize another's choice with the fierce religiosity of those who are convinced that they are completely rational. The computer scientist Edsger Dijkstra, for instance, didn't hold back his feelings in a famous 1975 memo: FORTRAN was an 'infantile disorder'; PL/I was a 'fatal disease'; programmers exposed to BASIC were 'mentally mutilated beyond hope of recognition'; use of COBOL 'cripples the mind, its teaching should, therefore, be regarded as a criminal offence'; APL was a 'mistake, carried through to perfection.'[13]

In any given year, there are a couple of languages that are cool—at the time of this writing, all the really hip kids are learning Clojure. And there are certain languages that smell of terminal un-coolness: users of Microsoft's Visual Basic are regarded by many as the dorks of the computing world, the most Mort-ish of the Morts. Like all its predecessors in the long 'Basic' lineage of languages, which goes back to 1964, Visual Basic has an English-like syntax. With its first release in 1991, Visual Basic provided a relatively easy way for non-experts to build programs for Windows; precisely for these reasons, it has attracted the contempt of the math-inclined Einsteins, who despise its verbosity and blame its accessibility for the plague of terrible programs that still afflicts Windows.

The evolution of computer languages also reflects the development of computer science and the craft of programming. Procedural programming called for the decomposition of complexity into simpler procedures which were then called sequentially. But this method was clearly inadequate: Big Balls of Mud were being built everywhere, software projects overshot budgets and failed at an alarming rate, there was an ever-present air of crisis. In the mid-eighties, a newly popular method, 'Object Oriented Programming,' offered salvation. OOP—first conceived in the nineteen sixties—uses 'objects,' code constructions that contain both data (attributes that describe the object) and behaviour (methods or procedures that you can call to effect changes); objects interact by passing messages to each other. In procedural programming, information and functionality were scattered all over the place; a doctor's addresses might be in a database, the knowledge of how to use these addresses in a procedure somewhere, and the ability to create new addresses in yet another procedure elsewhere. With OOP, the promise was that you could neatly encapsulate both data and behaviour inside objects, and then use these objects to faithfully model the stuff of the real world, which of course is full of objects. Using OOP, you could write code like this to create an object representing a new doctor and store his phone number:

```
Doctor drKumar = new Doctor();
drKumar.PhoneNumber = "5105550568";
```

Here, 'drKumar' is an object of the type 'Doctor'; one of the data fields of this object is 'PhoneNumber.' You may have another type called 'Patient,' which might have a data field called 'Diagnosis.' So with objects, when you needed the good Dr Kumar's address, you didn't have to go searching through a master list of addresses. You could just retrieve the drKumar object and write something like the following to assign Dr Kumar's address to the 'MailingAddress' field of the report the user wanted to print:

```
report.MailingAddress = drKumar.Address;
```

The dawn of OOP was a heady time. I imagined shiny metallic objects rising out of the primal Big Ball of Mud, pristine and clean, shooting messages at each other like bolts of energy. The rest of the programming world seemed equally excited: hundreds of books were written, OOP conferences were held, some programmers became superstar OOP gurus who charged large sums to teach the secrets of the OOP way of thinking.

Every prominent programming language now acquired object orientation, if only as a possible method among others. And really, programming in this new idiom made it possible to solve certain problems with ease and a degree of elegance.

Yet—Big Balls of Mud continued to be born, to grow. Software projects continued to crash and burn, ruining budgets and careers. If OOP managed to avoid the inevitable snarls of procedural programming, it introduced new kinds of complexity. Even small systems now divided functionality into hundreds and thousands of objects. Thinking about all these pieces and layers and their interactions became increasingly difficult; subtle bugs arose from what felt like spooky action at a distance—entanglements between objects emerged from their whirling dance. In defence, programmers codified best practices into a smorgasbord of easily abbreviated rubrics: Separation of Concerns, Single Responsibility Principle, Don't Repeat Yourself, Liskov Substitution Principle. Automated testing of each independent section of code became more crucial than ever, first to ensure that the code was actually doing what you wanted, and later to be sure that it was still doing what you wanted after you made changes in some other section of code—effects sometimes flowed unpredictably from one region to another.

In fact, adherents of Test-Driven Design (TDD) would have you write the tests before you ever write the code—that is, you write DoesMyAddTwoNumbersFunctionReallyReturnTheRightSum() before you write AddTwoNumbers(), thus forcing you to design AddTwoNumbers() to be easily testable. Usually, you write several tests for each section of code, checking for correct behaviour under varying conditions, and so the lines of test code can easily outnumber the lines of program code by orders of magnitude. The open-source database SQLite, at the time of this writing, has 1177 times the amount of test code as it does program code.[14] Most non-programmers have never heard of SQLite, but it is the most widely deployed database in the world.[15] SQLite is a tiny program. It runs within your Firefox browser, storing your bookmarks; it is used widely within the Mac operating system; it runs within each copy of Skype; it runs on your smartphone, storing contacts and appointments. SQLite's vast suite of tests is an attempt to prevent bugs from creeping into a program that has become an essential, foundational component of the working memory of humanity.

~

Programmers work doggedly towards correctness, but the sheer size and complexity of software ensures that bugs lurk within. A bug is, of course, a flaw or fault in a program that produces unexpected results. In 1986, the award-winning researcher and academic Jon Bentley published a book that is now widely regarded as a classic, *Programming Pearls*. One of the algorithms he implemented was for binary search, a method of finding a value in a sorted array, which was first published in 1946. In 2006, decades after the publication of Bentley's book—by which time his particular implementation had been copied and used many thousands of times—one of his erstwhile students, Joshua Bloch, discovered that under certain conditions this technique could manifest a bug.[16] Bloch published his finding under a justly panic-raising headline, 'Extra, Extra—Read All About It: Nearly All Binary Searches and Mergesorts are Broken.' He wrote:

The general lesson that I take away from this bug is humility: It is hard to write even the smallest piece of code correctly, and our whole world runs on big, complex pieces of code.

... Careful design is great. Testing is great. Formal methods are great. Code reviews are great. Static analysis is great. But none of these things alone are sufficient to eliminate bugs: They will always be with us. A bug can exist for half a century despite our best efforts to exterminate it.[17]

That software algorithms are now running our whole world means that software faults or errors can send us down the wrong highway, injure or kill people, and cause disasters. Every programmer is familiar with the most infamous bugs: the French Ariane 5 rocket that went off course and self-destructed forty seconds after lift-off because of an error in converting between representations of number values; the Therac-25 radiation therapy machine that reacted to a combination of operator input and a 'counter overflow' by delivering doses of radiation a hundred times more intense than required, resulting in the agonizing deaths of five people and injuries to many others; the 'Flash Crash' of 2010, when the Dow Jones suddenly plunged a thousand points and recovered just as suddenly, apparently as a result of automatic trading programs reacting to a single large trade.

These are the notorious bugs, but there are bugs in every piece of software that you use today. A professional 'cyber warrior,' whose job it is to find and exploit bugs for the US government, recently estimated that 'most of the software written in the world has a bug every three to five lines of code.'[18] These bugs may not kill you, but they cause your system to freeze, they corrupt your data, and they expose your computers to hackers. The next great hope for more stable, bug-free software is functional programming, which is actually the oldest paradigm in computing—it uses the algebraic techniques of function evaluation used by the creators of the first computers. In functional programming, all computation is expressed as the evaluation of expressions; the radical simplicity of thinking about programming as only giving input to functions that produce outputs promotes legibility and predictability. There is again the same fervent proselytizing about functional programming that I remember from the early days of OOP, the same conviction that this time we've discovered the magic key to the kingdom. Functional languages like Clojure conjure up the clean symmetries of mathematics, and hold forth the promise of escape from all the *jugaadu* workarounds that turn so much code into a gunky, biological-seeming mess. In general, though, programmers are now sceptical of the notion that there's any silver bullet for complexity. The programmer and popular blogger Steve Yegge, in his foreword to a book called *The Joy of Clojure*, describes the language as a 'minor miracle' and 'an astoundingly high-quality language . . . the best I've ever seen,' but he also notes that it is 'fashionable,' and that

> our industry, the global programming community, is fashion-driven to a degree that would embarrass haute couture designers from New York to Paris . . . Fashion dictates the programming languages people study in school, the languages employers hire for, the languages that get to be in books on shelves. A naive outsider might wonder if the quality of a language matters a little, just a teeny bit at least, but in the real world fashion trumps all.[19]

In respect to programming languages and techniques, the programming industry has now been through many cycles of faith and disillusionment, and many of its members have acquired a sharp, necessary cynicism. 'Hype Cycle'—a phrase coined by the analysts at Gartner, Inc.—adroitly captures the up-and-down fortunes of many a tech fad. [20]

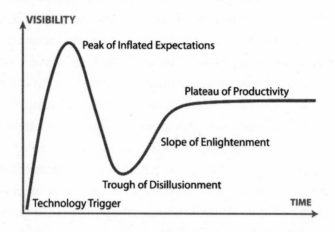

Figure 6.4: Gartner, Inc.'s Hype Cycle (Jeremy Kemp, Wikimedia Commons)

~

The tools and processes used to manage all this complexity engender another layer of complexity. All but the simplest programs must be written by teams of programmers, each working on a small portion of the system. Of course these people must be managed, housed, provided with equipment, but also their product—the code itself—must be distributed, shared, saved from overwriting or deletion, integrated, and tested.

Entire industries have grown around these necessities.

Software tools for building software—particularly 'Integrated Development Environments,' applications used to write applications—are some of the most complex programs being built today. They make the programmer's job easier, but the programmer must learn how to use them, must educate herself in their idiosyncrasies and the workarounds for their faults. This is not a trivial task. For example, every programmer needs to use a revision control system to track changes and easily branch and merge versions of code. The best-regarded revision control system today is Git, created by Linus Torvalds (and named, incidentally, after his famous cantankerousness).[21] Git's interface is command-line driven and famously UNIX-y and complex, and for the newbie its inner workings are mysterious. In response to a blog post titled 'Git is Simpler Than You Think,' an irritated Reddit commenter remarked, 'Yes, also a nuclear submarine is simpler than you think . . . once you learn how it works.'[22] I myself made three separate attempts to learn how Git worked, gave up, was frustrated enough by other revision control systems to return, and finally had to read a 265-page book to acquire enough competence to use the thing. Git is immensely powerful and nimble, and I enjoy using it, but manoeuvring it felt—at least initially—like a life achievement of sorts.

You may have to use a dozen tools and websites to handle the various logistical aspects of software development, and soon the triumph starts to wear a little thin. Add another dozen software libraries and frameworks that you may use internally in your programs—again, each one comes bristling with its own eccentricities, bugs, and books—and weariness sets in. Each tool and pre-constructed library solves a problem that you must otherwise solve yourself, but each solution is a separate body of knowledge you must maintain. A user named jdietrich wrote in a discussion on Hacker News:

> My biggest gripe with modern programming is the sheer volume of arbitrary stuff I need to know. My current project has so far required me to know about Python, Django, Google App Engine and its datastore, XHTML, CSS, JQuery, Javascript, JSON, and a clutch of XML schema, APIs and the like . . .
>
> Back in ye olden days, most programming tasks I performed felt quite natural and painless, just a quiet little chat between me and the compiler. Sometimes longwinded, sometimes repetitive, but I just sat and thought and typed and software happened. The work I do these days feels more like being a dogsbody at the tower of babel. I just don't seem to feel fluent in anything much any more.[23]

And every year, the new technologies arrive in a cloud of acronyms and cute names: MongoDB, HTML5, PaaS, CoffeeScript, TPL, Rx. One must keep up. On programmers.stackexchange.com, one hapless coder wrote:

> I was humbled at a job interview yesterday almost to the point of a beat-down and realized that although I know what I know, my skills are pretty old and I'm getting to where I don't know what I don't know, which for a tech guy is a bad thing.
>
> . . . I don't know if I can keep current just doing my day to day job, so I need to make sure I at least know what's out there.
>
> . . . Are there well known blogs I should be keeping up with for software development?[24]

The best—or at least the most ambitious—programmers read blogs and books, attend conferences to keep up with the state of the art, learn a new language every year or two. When you begin programming, one of the attractions is the certainty that you will never run out of things to learn. But after a few years of working in a corporate cubicle under exploitive managers, after one deadline too many, after family and age and a tiring body, learning the ins and outs of the latest library can feel like another desperate sprint on a non-stop treadmill. There is a reigning cult of overwork in the industry—the legend of the rock-star programmer usually has him coding sixteen hours a day, while simultaneously contributing to open-source projects, blogging, conferencing, and somehow managing to run a start-up—and this ideal has led many an aspirant to burnout, complete with techie thousand-yard-stare, clinical depression, outbursts of anger, and total disinterest in programming. This trough of disillusionment is so deep that for many, the only way to emerge from it is to leave the industry altogether, which rewards a few with fame and dazzling amounts of money, but treats the many as disposable cogs in its software production machine. The endless cycle of idea and action, endless invention, endless experiment, all this knowledge of motion takes its toll, leaves behind a trail of casualties.

∼

Butler Lampson's hope that millions of ordinary people would write 'non-trivial programs' and thus become poets of logic has proved elusive. From the sixties onwards, numerous technologists have promised that their new programming languages would make programmers redundant, that 'managers [could] now do their own programming; engineers [could] now do their own programming.'[25] Advertisements touted the magical abilities of 'automatic programming systems.' But Knuth's 'Software is hard' dictum still remains true, and business users have found that getting custom software out of IT departments requires large budgets and lots of patience. This is because programmers—at their best—try to build software out of elegant code that is modular, secure, and legible, which takes time and money. Instead of waiting, mere mortals often hack something together in the programs they already have available on their machines. This is why, according to the economics blogger James Kwak, 'Microsoft Excel is one of the greatest, most powerful, most important software applications of all time.'[26] Much of the planet's business data is stored in Excel, and its intuitive interface allows non-programmers access to some very powerful capabilities. Executives and marketers and secretaries write formulae and macros to extract information when they need it, and are therefore able to take action in a timely fashion. The trouble is that in Excel there

> is no way to trace where your data come from, there's no audit trail (so you can overtype numbers and not know it), and there's no easy way to test spreadsheets . . . The biggest problem is that anyone can create Excel spreadsheets—badly. Because it's so easy to use, the creation of even important spreadsheets is not restricted to people who understand programming and do it in a methodical, well-documented way.[27]

Sloppy Excel-wrangling can lead to some very bad decisions, as in the 'London Whale' trading disaster of 2012, which caused the financial services firm JPMorgan Chase a loss of approximately six billion dollars; the company's internal investigation listed as one of the contributing factors a financial modelling process which required cutting and pasting data through a series of spreadsheets. One of these spreadsheets contained a formula dividing by the sum of some numbers instead of their average.[28]

~

The day that millions will dash off beautiful programs—as easily as with a pencil—still remains distant. The 'lovely gems and brilliant coups' of coding remain hidden and largely incomprehensible to outsiders. But the beauty that programmers pursue leads to their own happiness, and—not incidentally—to the robustness of the systems they create, so the aesthetics of code impact your life more than you know.

For example, one of the problems that have always plagued programmers is the 'maintenance of state.' Suppose you have a hospital that sends out invoices for services provided, accepts payments, and also sends out reminders for overdue payments. On Tuesday evening, Ted creates an invoice for a patient, but then leaves the office for an early dinner; there is now an 'Invoice' object in the system. This object has its 'InvoiceNumber' field set to 56847, and its 'Status' field set to 'Created.' All of these current settings together constitute this invoice's 'state.' The next morning, Ted comes in and adds a couple of line items to this invoice. Those inserted line items and a new 'Status' setting of 'Edited' along with all the other data fields are now the invoice's state. After a coffee break, Ted deletes the second line-item and adds two more. He has changed the invoice's state again. Notice that we've already lost some information—from now on, we can't ever work out that Ted once inserted and deleted a line item. If you wanted to track historical changes to the invoice, you would have to build a whole complex system to store various versions.

Things get even more complicated in our brave new world of networked systems. Ted and his colleagues can't keep up with the work, so an offshored staff is hired to help, and the invoice records are now stored on a central server in Idaho. On Thursday afternoon, Ted begins to add more line items to invoice 56847, but then is called away by a supervisor. Now Ramesh in Hyderabad signs on and begins to work on the same invoice. How should the program deal with this? Should it allow Ramesh to make changes to invoice 56847? But maybe he'll put in duplicate line items that Ted has already begun working on. He may overwrite information—change the 'Status' field to 'Sent'—and thereby introduce inconsistencies into the system. You could lock the entire invoice record for 56847 on a first come, first served basis, and tell Ramesh he can't access this invoice because someone else is editing it. But what if Ted decides to go to lunch, leaving 56847 open on his terminal? Do you maintain the lock for two hours?

Guarding against inconsistencies, deadlocks of resources by multiple users, and information loss has traditionally required reams of extremely complex code. If you've ever had a program or a website lose or mangle your data, there's a good likelihood that object state was mismanaged somewhere in the code. A blogger named Jonathan Oliver describes working on a large system:

It was crazy—crazy big, crazy hard to debug, and crazy hard to figure out what was happening through the rat's nest of dependencies. And this wasn't even legacy code—we were in the middle of the project. Crazy. We were fighting an uphill battle and in a very real danger of losing despite us being a bunch of really smart guys.[29]

The solution that Oliver finally came to was event sourcing. With this technique, you never store the state of an object, only events that have happened to the object. So when Ted first creates invoice 56847 and leaves the office, what the program sends to CentralServer in Idaho are the events 'InvoiceCreated' (which contains the new invoice number) and 'InvoiceStatusChanged' (which contains the new status). When Ted comes back the next morning and wants to continue working on the invoice, the system will retrieve the events related to this invoice from CentralServer and do something like:

```
Invoice newInvoice = new Invoice();
foreach( singleEvent in listOfEventsFromCentralServer )
    {
        newInvoice.Replay( singleEvent );
    }
```

That is, you reconstitute the state of an object by creating a new object and then 'replaying' events over it. Ted now has the most current version of invoice 56847, conjured up through a kind of temporally shifted rerun of events that have already happened. In this new system, history is never lost; when Ted adds a line item, a 'LineItemAdded' event will be generated, and when he deletes one, a 'LineItemDeleted' event will be stored. If, at some point in the future, you wanted to know what the invoice looked like on Wednesday morning, you would just fire off your 'Replay' routine and tell it to cease replaying events once it got past 9 a.m. on Wednesday morning. You can stop locking resources: because events can be generated at a very fine granular level, it becomes much easier to write code that will cause CentralServer to reject events that would introduce inconsistencies, to resolve conflicts, and—if necessary—pop up messages on Ted and Ramesh's screens. Events are typically small objects, inexpensive to transfer over the wire and store, and server space grows cheaper every day, so you don't incur any substantial added costs by creating all these events.

Oliver writes that when he discovered event sourcing

> it was as if a light went on. I could literally see how adoption of event sourcing could shed a massive amount of incidental and technical complexity from my project . . . Fast forward to today. [I] now have a number of systems in production with several more that are only weeks away and I literally could not be happier. I have significantly more confidence in my software than I had in the past. The code is dramatically cleaner and infinitely more explicit than it would have been otherwise. But that's only the starting point. Our ability to expand, adapt, and scale—to be agile from a business perspective—is infinitely greater than it ever has been, even with each application being significantly larger and each associated domain exponentially more complex than before—all with a smaller team.[30]

'Dramatically cleaner and infinitely more explicit' code is beautiful, and here, enhanced function follows from form. But letting go of object state and embracing events requires some effort and imagination. During another blog discussion about event-sourcing code, a user more familiar with the old-style methods of storing current state remarked, 'Yes, this code is beautiful, really beautiful. And my . . . brain almost blew up when I tried to understand the process.'[31]

As I learnt about the beauty of event sourcing, I was reminded of other discussions of identity-over-time that had bent my mind. The Buddhists of the Yogachara school (fourth century CE) were among the proponents of the doctrine of 'no-self,' arguing: 'What appears to be a continuous motion or action of a single body or agent is nothing but the successive emergence of distinct entities in distinct yet contiguous places.'[32] There is no enduring object state, there are only events. To this, Abhinavagupta—whom we've already seen commenting on Anandavardhana's *Dhvanyaloka*—responded with the assertion that there could be no connection between sequential cognitive states if there were not a stable connector to synthesize these states across time and place.[33] There may be no persistent object state, but there needs to be an event-sourcing system to integrate events into current state. For Abhinavagupta, memory is the pre-eminent faculty of the self: 'It is in the power of remembering that the self's ultimate freedom consists. I am free because I remember.'[34]

And, according to Abhinavagupta, it is memory from which literature derives its powers.

The most prominent of Anandavardhana's successors in the field of *rasa-dhvani* theory was the towering polymath Abhinavagupta (literary critic, aesthetic philosopher, metaphysical philosopher, theologian, poet, musician, and—according to his late-tenth-century contemporaries—a realized yogic master). In his commentaries on the *Natyashastra* and Anandavardhana's *Dhvanyaloka*, Abhinavagupta explored the role of memory in the psychology of *rasa*. Just as Anandavardhana had claimed a distinctiveness in the way *vyanjana* or suggestion worked in poetic language, Abhinavagupta claimed that the commonplace workings of memory, when directed by the poet, gave literature a power that was unique, an ability that was available nowhere else.

Abhinavagupta asserted that all minds contain infinite layers of *samskaras* and *vasanas*—'latent impressions' left by one's experience and past lives; it is these impressions that are brought alive or manifested by *dhvani*. The aesthetic experience allows the viewer, this cognizing subject, to set these latent impressions in motion within itself, to conjure them up out of sub- or unconsciousness and render them active; the subject becomes a participant in the fictional event, it feels, it relives. Yet, according to Abhinavagupta, this event and its evoked emotions are, for the participating subject, free of all ego-driven considerations: 'I am afraid, he—my enemy, my friend, anybody—is afraid.'[1] The viewer or reader, then, is able to engage with the specifics of the art in a way that is profoundly felt and is yet—paradoxically—removed.

So, to a playgoer who hears some lines about a hunted deer

> there appears, immediately after the perception of their literal sense, a perception of a different order, an inner [mānasī] perception, consisting in a direct experience [sākṣātkāra] which completely eliminates the temporal distinction, etc., assumed by these sentences. Besides, the young deer . . . which appears in this perception is devoid of its particularity (viśeṣa), and at the same time the actor, who [playing the role of the deer] frightens [the spectators by appearing to] be afraid, is unreal (apāramārthika). As a result, what there appears is simply and solely fear—fear in itself, uncircumscribed by time, space, etc. This perception of fear is of a different order from the ordinary perceptions . . . for these are necessarily affected by the appearance of fresh mental movements . . . consisting of [personal, egoistic] pleasure, pain, etc., and just for this reason are full of obstacles (vighna). The sensation of the fear above mentioned, on the contrary, is the matter of cognition by a perception devoid of obstacles (nirvighna) and may be said to enter directly into our hearts, to dance (viparivṛt) before our eyes: this is the terrible rasa. In such a fear, one's own self is neither completely immersed (tiraskṛ), nor in a state of particular emergence (ullikh). . . . As a result of this, the state of generality involved is not limited (parimita), but extended (vitata).[2]

This generalization, this trans-personalization, sadharanikarana, is the essential basis of the aesthetic experience. The framing of an object as art produces this necessary detachment from the limited ego. For a viewer, 'the tasting of pleasures, pains, etc., inhering in his own [limited] person' prevents the relishing of rasa.[3] The attachment to limited self prevents universalization; if you are grieving over your own long-lost mother, you are not relishing the rasa of the tragic death scene in the movie you are watching.

> The means of eliminating this obstacle are the so called theatrical conventions (nāṭyadharmi), which include a number of things not found in ordinary life, as, for instance, the zones (kakṣyā) dividing the pavilion (maṇḍapa), the stage (raṅgapīṭha); and . . . also the different dress of the actors—the headwear, etc.—by which they hide their true identity.[4]

It is the very artificiality and conventionality of the aesthetic experience, therefore, that makes the unique experience of rasa possible. Abhinavagupta observes:

> In the theatrical performance there is on one hand the negation of the real being of the actor, and on the other—since the spectator's consciousness does not rest entirely on the represented images—there is no rest on the real being of the superimposed personage; so that, as a result of all this, there is eventually just a negation both of the real being of the actor and of the real being of the character he is playing.[5]

And yet the spectator experiences the full panoply of emotion and thought induced by the action of the play, and simultaneously, the spectator's perception of the aesthetic objects (the story, the actors, the stage) and of his or her own reactions is marked by wonder, chamatkara, and a willingness, an openness toward these perceptions. The result is pleasure that exists 'through the suppression of our [usual] thick pall of mental stupor and blindness' as we encounter the aesthetic object. This pleasure consists of 'the states of fluidity, enlargement, and expansion, and is also called "tasting," and is of a non-ordinary [alaukika] nature.'[6] So, rasa is a supra-mundane mental state that is 'not a form of ordinary cognition, nor is it erroneous, nor ineffable, nor like ordinary perception, nor does it consist of a super-imposition.'[7] Rasa differs from 'both memory, inference and any form of ordinary self-consciousness.'[8]

During the experience of rasa, according to Abhinavagupta, 'what is enjoyed is consciousness itself.'[9] That is, the aesthetic object, through the process of generalization, allows us to experience the emotional and cognitive fluctuations within ourselves without attachment, without obstacles, with a harmonious density (ekaghana) that we cannot find in the chaos of ordinary life. When we watch characters experiencing grief, for instance, we have

a thought-trend that fits with the vibhāvas and anubhāvas of this grief, [which] if it is relished (literally, if it is chewed over and over), becomes a rasa and so from its aptitude [toward this end] one speaks of [any] basic emotion as becoming a rasa. For the basic emotion is put to use in the process of relishing: through a succession of memory-elements it adds together a thought-trend which one has already experienced in one's own life to one which one infers in another's life, and so establishes a correspondence in one's heart.[10]

Daniel H.H. Ingalls, Sr, points out that this reflective, mirroring response of the heart, this hrdaya-samvada, is differently understood by Abhinavagupta than a viewer's 'empathy' in the West ('I feel Hamlet's emotions as my own'); here, one's own latent and personal memories of grief are liberated into 'a universal, impersonal flavour.'[11] It is precisely this impersonality, this ego-less emotion, experienced in tanmayi-bhava, total absorption, which is desirable—the sahrdaya wants the state of objectivity, not increased subjectivity. He doesn't want to experience grief at a personal level, he wants to relish the stable emotion of grief within himself, made available to him because of his heart's concordance with the suffering of the characters. 'The feelings of delight, sorrow, etc., [produced by the representation] deep within our spirit,' Abhinavagupta says, 'have only one function, to vary it, and the representation's function is to awaken them.'[12]

The aesthete rests in rasa in a kind of meditation, tasting the waves of emotions within consciousness, and the bliss he or she experiences is the same as the yogi's beatitude. The difference is that the sahrdaya's limited self is not 'completely immersed' or vanished; the accomplished yogi, on the other hand, goes beyond the self altogether, and exists in a state of complete transcendence which is nirvikalpa, 'without support'—without object, without subject, without ideation and verbalization. This does not mean the yogi's experience is necessarily 'better'—the relishing of beauty cannot happen when there is no subject and no object, and there is a harshness often associated with the yogi's effort, with the sheer enormity of the exertion. But within the aesthetic experience, 'This rasa is poured forth spontaneously by the word which is like a cow, for love of her children; for this reason it is different from that which is (laboriously) milked by yogin.'[13]

~

One of the protagonists in *Red Earth and Pouring Rain* participates in an event usually referred to as 'The First Indian War of Independence' (by Indians) or as 'The Great Mutiny of 1857' (by the English). The memory of an entire culture includes certain events that become shared *samskaras* or latent traces, and these too can be mobilized by the poet. As I wrote about the 1857 war, there was both a sense of great power from resurrecting iconic events, and a feeling of unease from the still-palpable pain of that long-ago trauma.

Jacques Lacan broke from the psychoanalytic establishment with his famous manifesto 'The Function and Field of Speech and Language in Psychoanalysis,' and in this speech he refers directly to Abhinavagupta and *dhvani* theory, invoking 'the teaching of Abhinavagupta' to elaborate upon 'the property of speech by which it communicates what it does not actually say.'[14] Lacan argued that the unconscious 'does not *express* itself in speech; it *reveals* itself through suggestion,' and that the analyst should deploy the power of *dhvani* 'in a carefully calculated fashion in the semantic resonances of his remarks.'[15]

According to Lalita Pandit, through *dhvani*, 'poetic language reaches the condition of silence. It functions like a meta-language, generating many meanings by deploying collective and individual memory banks, latent impressions, mental associations.'[16]

Like the Lacanian analyst, the poet can direct *dhvani* at the depths of what a culture leaves unsaid, and thus manifest in the *sahradaya*'s consciousness the echoes of those great silences.

~

Great art is distinguished by its resonance, by the depth of its *dhvani*. But the *rasa* that the viewer will experience also depends crucially on his own capability and openness: 'The word *sahṛdaya* (lit. 'having their hearts with it') denotes persons who are capable of identifying with the subject matter,' Abhinavagupta writes, 'as the mirror of their hearts has been polished by the constant study and practise of poetry, and who respond to it sympathetically in their own hearts.'[17] The *sahrdaya*'s education and erudition has not made his heart or *hrdaya* impervious, it is able to 'melt' in response to art; this is in contrast with the 'scholar' whose heart 'has become hardened and encrusted by his readings of dry texts on metaphysics.'[18]

Abhinavagupta insists that *rasa* cannot be 'caused.' That is, mimesis—of things, of events, of people—offers us an opportunity for savouring, and this gustation is not a fixed or 'frozen' mental state, a simple matter of stimulus and response, such as the joy one might feel in response to the words, 'A daughter is born to you.' The sensitive viewer or reader inhabits the imitated action through an act of concentrated sympathy, and so

> the relishing of beauty arises in us from our memory bank (*saṃskāra*) of mental states which are suitable to the *vibhāvas* and *anubhāvas* of those basic emotions [that are being portrayed in the characters of a literary work] . . .

So what is born here is a *rasyamāṇatā* (a being tasted, a gustation, of beauty), that is, a savouring that eclipses such worldly mental states as the joy that might be produced by reunion with a constant stream of old friends. And for this reason [viz., because of its super-normal character], the savouring serves to manifest something, not to inform one of something, as might be done by an established means of knowledge (*pramāṇa*). It is not a production such as results from the working of a cause.[19]

The poet's *pratibha* or intuitive genius—which harnesses craft and training—therefore depends on the *sahrdaya*'s intuitive receptivity—which is polished by learning—to become complete. It is for this reason that Abhinavagupta begins his commentary on the *Dhvanyaloka* with an evocation of 'the Muse's double heart, the poet and the relisher of art.' The coming together of the poet and the reader is what creates 'brave new worlds from naught and even stones to flowing sap has brought.' Beauty is imparted by the 'successive flow of genius and of speech' from the poet to the *sahrdaya*.[20]

~

Since *rasa* cannot be 'caused' in a deterministic manner, you cannot produce art through test-driven development; your true *sahrdaya* may be born a hundred years after you die.

There are other qualities of poetic language that make verification difficult or impossible. The speech of the poet can be effective even when it doesn't obey the rules of everyday language. According to Abhinavagupta, even denotative and connotative meanings are only aids to the production of *rasa*, unessential props which can sometimes be discarded: 'Even alliterations of harsh or soft sounds can be suggestive of [*rasa*], though they are of no use as to meaning. Here, then, there is not even the shadow of the metaphor.'[21] So music alone, without lyrics, can be the occasion of *rasa*. Even when language is used to construct an aesthetic object, when meaning and metaphor are necessarily present, to want the object—the poem, the story, the play—to convey coherent, verifiable information about the real world, as a treatise might, is to fall into a category error. Poetry's meaning does not need any external referentiality or validation to produce pleasure. '[In poetry] the savouring . . . arises like a magical flower, having its essence at that very moment, and not connected with earlier or later times.'[22]

Abhinavagupta goes even further, arguing that even at the level of syntactic units or the basic building blocks of a language, poetry is not always bound to the principles of coherence, meaning, and verification. 'Poetic sentences,' for instance, 'do not require validity so as to motivate [hearers] by communicating a true meaning . . . because they culminate only in pleasure.'[23] So even language that does not cohere or produce mundane meaning may produce *rasa*. This is true, for instance, in language or sound poetry. Illegibility has its own pleasures, incomprehensibility may exalt. It is at the end of denotation that *rasa* manifests, as in Hindustani and Carnatic music, where the repetition of a single phrase by the singer—sometimes for hours—so empties the words that finally nothing is left but the fullness of the emotion, that which lies beyond words.

~

The grammarians of Sanskrit—the eternal, formal language—were, as one might expect, obsessed with correctness, precision, clarity. The proponents of the *rasa-dhvani* theory—from Anandavardhana onwards—faced fierce opposition from the orthodox on the grounds that there was no need to introduce a new semantic power to account for the suggestive functioning of art. Connotation, context, the speaker's intent, and inference, the argument went, already accommodated this functionality. A ninth-century logician summarily dismissed Anandavardhana's arguments and added, 'In any case, this discussion with poets is not appropriate; even learned people become confused in this difficult path of sentence meaning.'[24]

Our logician was understandably annoyed by the fuzzing up of the difficult but clean lines of sentence-meaning, least of all by poets, who—it must be admitted—can tend to be somewhat unlearned in logic. Nevertheless, what Anandavardhana tries to achieve in his analysis is completely in keeping with his intellectual tradition, which modelled all knowledge after Panini's grammar: he tries to provide a systematic, algorithmic understanding of literary beauty and its effects. At the end of the *Dhvanyaloka*, he quotes a critic who declares, 'We may speak of *dhvani* whenever an ineffable beauty of certain words and certain meanings is perceptible only to special cognizors, just as the rarity of certain gems [is known only to special experts].' Anandavardhana says bluntly that this critic is wrong, and argues that the

> special [virtues] of words and meanings can be explained and
> have been explained in many ways [by himself]. To imagine
> that there is some ineffable virtue over and above these is

to admit that one's power of analysis has ceased. . . As for the definition sometimes given of ineffability, that it is the appearance of a thing [viz., of a unique particular] which cannot be referred to by a word for a mental construct (*vikalpa*) which is based on . . . the general or universal, this can no more apply to the special virtues of poetry than it can to the special virtues of gems. For the virtues of the former have been analysed by literary critics, while no estimate can be made of the value of a gem by reference merely to the general or universal. It is true, however, in both cases that these special virtues are recognizable only by experts. For only jewellers are knowers of gems and only sensitive critics (*sahṛdaya*) are knowers of the *rasa* of poetry. On this point no one will argue.[25]

Perhaps the logician would have agreed, but I can't help thinking that what also irritated him about Anandavardhana's investigation was what it made of poets. In response to Anandavardhana's assertion that *dhvani* provided endless freshness to language, Abhinavagupta observes that there are a limited number of things worthy of description

but by the multiplicity [of *dhvani*] . . . these same things become limitless; hence there arises an infinity of poetic imagination taking them at its object . . . This can come about only if the poetic imagination is endless, and that only if the objects to describe endless; and that only because of the variety of *dhvani*.[26]

Ingalls writes:

What is notable here is that the variety of suggestiveness is placed outside the human mind; it is the cause, not the result of poetic imagination. It is as though our authors thought of the objects of the world as existing in a pattern which rendered them amenable to mutual suggestions when viewed by a great poet. The poet's imagination, in this view, would be the medium, not the primary cause, of the creation of new worlds. The worlds would already be there through the magic which underlies *dhvani*. Such a view is in harmony with the origin of the Sanskrit word for poet, *kavi*. A *kavi* is a seer, a revealer.[27]

~

'No being (animal or deity) exists with which man has no affinity of nature,' Abhinavagupta writes.

> The *saṃsāra* (world) is beginningless, and every man, before that which he actually is, has been all the other beings as well. The consciousness of the spectator thus possesses (in other words, is varied by . . .) the latent impressions of all the possible beings and he is therefore susceptible of identifying himself with each of them.[28]

Abhinavagupta's assertion that 'everybody's mind is indeed characterized by the most various latent impressions' is elsewhere more amenable to a purely materialist interpretation which requires no belief in rebirth; but, always, memory— selves which have been forgotten, experiences suffered and cherished and half-buried—is the limitless pool on which the reverberating *dhvani* of art enacts its surges and churns out *rasa*.[29]

This susceptibility towards identification with the other, this conjuring up of beings from the endless depths of the self, is what makes

> the educative effect (vyutpādana) [of poetry] . . . different from that which comes from scripture through its mandates and from history through its narrations. For in addition to the analogy which it furnishes that we should behave like Rama [and not like Ravana], it produces in the final result an expansion of one's imagination which serves as the means of tasting the rasas.'[30]

This expansion of the self is available only through the pleasure of rasa, and so 'the end of poetry is pleasure, for it is only by pleasure, in the form of an otherworldly delight, that it can serve to instruct us.'[31]

Poetry as moral instruction gets scant attention from the theorists of rasa-dhvani; when Abhinavagupta does discuss the issue in passing, it is to assure us that

> of instruction and joy, joy is the chief goal. Otherwise, what basic difference would there be between one means of instruction, viz., poetry, which instructs after the fashion of a wife, and other means of instruction, such as the Vedas which instruct after the fashion of a master, or history which instructs after the fashion of a friend? That is why bliss is said to be the chief goal. In comparison with [poetry's] instruction even in all four aims of human life, the bliss which it renders is a far more important goal.[32]

~

To the objection that there was no way to know if *rasa* really existed, Abhinavagupta replied, 'Wrong. It is proved by our own self-awareness, because savouring is a form of knowledge.'[33]

～

The urge to savour is universal, but its expression is culturally shaped. Indian movies mix emotions and formal devices in a manner quite foreign to Western filmgoers; Indian tragedies accommodate comedic scenes, and soldiers in gritty war movies can break into song. According to Anandavardhana:

> While it is well known that larger works contain a variety of *rasas*, a poet who seeks the excellence [of his works] will make just one of them predominant . . .
>
> [But there is] no obstruction to a single *rasa* by its being mixed with others . . . Readers with a ready sense of discrimination, who are attentive and intelligent, will rather take a higher degree of pleasure in such a work.[34]

To which Abhinavagupta adds:

> If the *rasa* that has been taken in hand extends throughout the whole plot and is fitted for predominance by this extensiveness, its predominance will not be harmed by the introduction, by the filling in, of other *rasas* brought in by the needs of the plot and running through only limited sections of the narrative. Rather than being injured, the predominance of the *rasa* which appears as an abiding factor throughout the plot will be strengthened. In other words, the subsidiary *rasas*, although they attain a degree of charm by being fully developed each at

its own stage by its own set of *vibhāvas* and the like, still do not attain such a charm that our apprehension will rest on them; rather, it will be carried on to some further delight.[35]

A song in an Indian film is an interlude which exists outside of story-logic and story-time, but within the emotional palette of the film; its function is to provide subsidiary *rasas* that will strengthen the predominant *rasa* of the whole. The first Indian talkie, *Alam Ara* (The ornament of the world, 1931) featured seven songs. The newspaper advertisements touted an 'all-Star-Cast Production' which was 'All Talking/Singing/Dancing.'

This is why the Aristotelian unities of British and American films seemed so alien to me when I watched them as a child. But this emotional monotone was also—implicitly—modern and grown-up, as opposed to the premodern and childish sentiment-mixing of our own movies. So, self-consciously serious film-makers in India have tended to eschew the traditional forms beloved of commercial cinema, and have signalled their noble artistic and political intentions by hewing to conventions native to more 'developed' countries.

~

Anandavardhana gives an example of mixing *rasas* from the Mahabharata; a wife searches for the body of her warrior-husband upon a bloody battlefield, and finds his severed arm:

> This is the hand that took off my girdle,
> that fondled my full breasts,
> that caressed my navel, my thighs, my loins,
> and loosened my skirt.[36]

Here, the stable emotion of grief is made sharper and more profound by the tasted memory of the erotic. And this provides, for the reader, the savouring of *karuna-rasa*, pathos.

~

When I inflict butcheries on the characters in my fictions, I sometimes think about how strange it is that we can savour, even, the horror of battlefields on which entire races die. This is monstrous. We are monstrous.

But savouring is a form of knowledge. And what is most delicious on my palate is a medley of tastes that come together to reveal a dominant *rasa*. Longer works of fiction that insist on a monotony of emotion always seem awkward to me, incomplete, even if they are elegantly written. But it is not just that the sweet tastes sweetest when placed next to the salty. If savouring is a form of knowledge, then a complexity of affect affords the most to know. I am given pause, I linger, I relish, and I am brought to *chamatkara*—wonder, self-expansion, awe. When I love a book, a film, a poem, a sentence in a novel, when I am absolutely ravished by it, I always find that my delight is overdetermined, has 'more determining factors than the minimum necessary' (as the OED puts it). Where does that '(final) feeling' come from— from the plot, the pace, the words themselves, all those fading memories of the peripheral characters, from the undertones of emotion that I hardly remember? From all of those, at once. From knowing all of those, together.

~

The theorists of *rasa-dhvani* gave me a way to think about writer, text, and *sahrdaya*. I also gained from them a way to think about literary convention—if in poetry 'the savouring . . . arises like a magical flower, having its essence at that very moment, and not connected with earlier or later times,' and also 'the feelings of delight, sorrow, etc., [produced by the representation] deep within our spirit have only one function, to vary it, and the representation's function is to awaken them,' then the claims made for one particular set of conventions—often rather ambitiously called 'realism'—are not only epistemically questionable, they are just irrelevant. There are many ways to manifest *dhvani*, I told my realist writer-friends. Choose the ones that work for you and your *sahrdaya*, and leave off with the proselytizing and pronouncements of your virtuous artistic rigour, of your deeper connection to what-really-is.

All this was satisfying enough, but *dhvani*—or at least resonance, reverberation—was crucial to the structure of the novel I was writing. The book's shape followed what contemporary literary theorists call a 'ring composition,' in which the ending of the narrative somehow joins up with the beginning, forming a circle. A ring composition is often used as a frame, within which further rings are embedded. Elements within a ring often reflect back on each other to form a chiastic structure, A-B-B-A, or A-B-C-B-A. Often, language or tropes or events are repeated, each time somehow changed. 'In ring composition repetitions are markers of structure,' the anthropologist Mary Douglas writes.[37] Ring composition is a structure used all over the world, in narratives as varied as the Bible and mediaeval Chinese novels, she tells us, 'so it is a worldwide method of writing.'[38] She adds that 'ring composition is extremely difficult for Westerners to recognize. To me this is mysterious.'[39]

In India, ring composition is a standard architecture, found prominently in epics like the Ramayana and the Mahabharata, in poems, in the Rig Veda, and in Panini's grammar.[40] When I was writing my first book, I had never heard the phrase 'ring composition,' but the method and its specific implications and techniques came readily to hand because—of course—I had seen and heard it everywhere. What I wanted within the nested circles or chakras of my novel was a mutual interaction between various elements in the structure. That is, for one chapter to act as the transformed reflection of another, for a nested story to act as an echo for another story nested within itself, and so on. Each of these connections would—I hoped—act as a vibration, a *spanda*, and all of them would come together in a reverberation, a *dhvani*—perhaps not quite in the sense that Anandavardhana used the word, but a *dhvani* nevertheless—a hum that would be alive and full and endless.

I didn't exactly plan this architecture, sketch it all out before I began. I knew the general outline, and groped and felt my way into the specifics. I didn't plan it because I couldn't have; the unfolding of the story, all the stories, comes from the tension between intention and discovery. There are unbelievably delicious moments when you feel the pieces falling into place, when you find harmonies and felicities and symmetries that you can't remember constructing, and at those times you cannot help becoming a mystic, believing that you are after all a little bit of a *kavi*, a seer of some sort.

~

'We see,' David Shulman writes:

> reflections almost everywhere we look in South Asia, in all
> artistic media and, perhaps above all, in ritual forms . . .
> One level—verbal, rhythmic, sonar, or semantic—may be
> superimposed, with varying degrees of completeness and
> precision, on another. In effect, two relatively independent
> relational systems may thus coincide . . . Correspondence and
> coincidence of this sort [stem from] the impulse to reconnect
> and recompose[41]

Shulman is an American who teaches in Jerusalem, one of
those many astonishingly knowledgeable non-Indian Indologists
through whom I've learnt much about my tradition. The
global engine of academia is—for the moment—dominated by
Western money and scholars, and Indians can get very prickly
about being once more subjected to powerful foreign gazes.
Tempers have flared over interpretations of Indian history,
religion, and metaphysics. But vigorous debate has always been
the preferred Indian mode of discovery, and perhaps these
arguments too are a kind of mirroring, a reconnection. The
world is a web, a net, as is each human being nested within the
world, holding other worlds within.

Shulman writes that in India, reiterations and ring
compositions

> speak to a notion of reality, in varying intensities and degrees
> of integrity, as resonance, reflection, or modular repetition
> understood as eruption or manifestation (*āvirbhāva*) from a

deeper reservoir of existence, a restless domain driven by the undying urge to speak (*vivakṣā*).[42]

Language itself wants to speak. In speaking, there is pleasure, and by speaking, knowledge is created, and thus the world we know. 'Language cuts forms in the ocean of reality,' the Rig Veda tells us.[43] This is why grammar—*vyakarana*—is the science of sciences.

~

At the beginning of *Red Earth and Pouring Rain*, a young man picks up a rifle and shoots a monkey. The monkey lives, and when he regains consciousness he finds a typewriter and begins typing. He reveals that in a past life he was a poet who abandoned poetry for revolution. Now he tells—or types—the story of this long-ago life.

The monkey will live as long as his audience finds pleasure in his stories. He transforms memory into story, and gives delight so that he may live.

~

Abhinavagupta tells us that his teacher said, '*Rasa* is delight; delight is the drama; and the drama is the Veda,' the goal of wisdom.[44]

The privileging of pleasure as a mode of knowledge has an ancient pedigree in India, particularly within the many streams of Tantra. 'Tantra' derives from the root *tan*, to expand or stretch, and literally means 'extension' or 'warp on a loom.' At its simplest, the word can just mean 'handbook' or 'guide,' and so not all texts with 'Tantra' in the title are Tantric—the *Panchatantra* is a collection of animal fables. There is no one practice or ideology or cosmology that we can identify as 'Tantric'—there are monist Tantrics and there are dualist Tantrics. There is Hindu Tantrism, Buddhist Tantrism, even Jain Tantrism. So what is Tantrism? Attempts at definition have resulted in expanding lists of typical characteristics; one scholar notes six identifiers, another eighteen. At the very minimum, one would note that Tantric lineages, transmitted through gurus, use ritual practices, bodily disciplines, and social norms that deviate from Vedic orthodoxy, all in the service of ultimate spiritual liberation and worldly attainment. And, as Sanjukta Gupta puts it, 'Tantric *sādhāna* (practise, discipline) is a purely individual way to release accessible to all people, women as well as men (at least in theory), householders as well as ascetics.'[1]

Most scholars would date the rise of Tantric systems to the middle of the first millennium of the Common Era.[2] There is much evidence of the commingling of elements taken from Vedic philosophies and desi rural or tribal traditions. Hugh B. Urban says about the Tantra centred on the *shakta-pitha* or 'Seat of Shakti' at the Kamakhya temple:

The Assamese tradition is by no means a simple veneer of Hinduism slapped onto a deeper tribal substratum. Instead, it is the result of a far more complex negotiation between the many indigenous traditions of the northeast and the Sanskritic, brahmanic traditions coming from north India that resulted in what is among the oldest and most powerful forms of Tantra in South Asia.[3]

The eponymous Shakti worshipped at Kamakhya is the Renowned Goddess of Desire. Inside the temple, 'Kamakhya is represented not by any human image, but by a sheet of stone that slopes downwards from both sides, meeting in a yoni-like depression.'[4] The yoni is the vulva; the goddess is believed to menstruate three days a year, during which time the temple is closed. 'On the fourth day after her menstruation, the temple doors are reopened, and red pieces of cloth representing the bloody menstrual flow are distributed to the thousands of pilgrims who thereby receive the power and grace of the goddess.'[5] A majority of these pilgrims are women.

It would be a mistake to reduce this worship of Shakti to only an acknowledgement of biological reproductive power, or of genital sexuality. Urban very correctly argues that

> the Indian concept of kama contains a vast range of meanings that include, but far exceed, the level of sexual desire that has so long preoccupied modern observers. So too, the concept of shakti contains yet far transcends mere political power, also embracing the vital energy that pervades the cosmos, social order, and human body alike.[6]

In the Tantras, descriptions of sexual practices comprise a tiny fraction of the whole, which usually includes wide-ranging discussions of rituals, metaphysical speculations, and enumerations of deities and the powers they represent; people who have been told that Tantra is 'exotic sex' are usually bored witless when they actually try to read one of these texts. Mediaeval Indians wouldn't have found the sex, qua sex, especially titillating; *kama* was one of the legitimate aims of life, and sex within the constraints of dharma or ethical conduct was often depicted quite frankly. For instance, the *Girvanavanmanjari*, a seventeenth-century 'Easy Sanskrit' primer, is set up as a dialogue between a husband and a wife, which swiftly turns into a teasing erotic game in which each partner accuses the other of being too bashful; the book ends 'in the climax of *śṛṅgāra*, with the happy union of the Brāhmana householder and his wife.'[7]

The deviance of the Tantric systems has more to do with their cosmology and their soteriology. Many of the Tantric lineages are *shakta*—they worship the goddess as the ultimate reality—and many of them regard *kama* not as something to be avoided or discarded on the road to salvation, but as an essential motive force in the human quest for the ultimate reality. So, in these systems, pleasure is good—the joys of the body and mind are not distractions or illusions. According to the *Kularnava Tantra*,

[In other systems] the *yogi* cannot be a *bhogi* [enjoyer, epicure], and a *bhogi* cannot be a knower of Yoga. However, O Beloved [Goddess], [the path of the] Kaula [lineage], which is superior to all other systems, is of the essence of *bhoga* [enjoyment] and *yoga*. O Mistress of the *kula* [family]! In the *kula* teaching, *bhoga* becomes *yoga*, and the world becomes a state of liberation.[8]

The Tantric who belongs to one of these lineages uses all experience, even that which may be socially prohibited or psychologically forbidding and therefore inhibiting of self-recognition. And so the followers of these 'left-handed' paths sought spiritual advancement through transgression, through ritual disruptions of the rules of purity and social order. For the advanced practitioner or initiate, the secret and dangerous rites of left-handed Tantra—always approached under the guidance of a guru—were a means of shattering the norms of the normal so that one could know the true, undifferentiated self; this is why these ceremonies included the ritualized consumption of meat and wine, and socially unsanctioned sex—all anathema to Brahminic notions of purity. That which was outside the bounds of purity was to be shut out, according to Vedic norms, but the Tantrics recognized that what was expelled was also tremendously powerful; the Kamakhya temple is shut when the goddess is menstruating because she is then 'impure,' but her menstrual flow brings life force to the earth. There is a

> profound ambivalence [about] the goddess' blood and the power that it embodies, a power that is tied to impurity and to the dangerous potency of sexual fluids . . . The goddess' menstrual blood is the very essence of this contaminating, chaotic but creative force [from which the world emerges].[9]

Some Tantrics sought extreme versions of this antinomian contact with the impure—the Kapalikas carried skulls as begging bowls, smeared themselves with the ashes from cremation grounds, offered blood, meat, alcohol, and sexual fluids to their deities and consumed them as well; they were reputed to practise human sacrifice and ritual ingestion of human flesh. The discipline of the Kapalikas was intended to induce a purposeful derangement from all prescribed norms and notions of otherness and distinction; the Kapalika saw all creation as one.

Members of the orthodox mainstream were fascinated and horrified by such practitioners. Kapalikas were reputed to have fearsome magical powers, and they show up as sinister villains in many narratives. Tantrics of various hues also are depicted as dissemblers and charlatans. In a play by Rajashekhara, a late-ninth-century poet and critic, a Tantric gleefully proclaims:

> I don't know mantra from tantra,
> Nor meditation or anything about a teacher's grace.
> Instead, I drink cheap booze and enjoy some woman.
> But I sure am going on to liberation, since I got the [Tantric]
> Kula path.
> *What's more,*
> I took some horny slut and consecrated her my 'holy wife.'
> Sucking up booze and wolfing down red meat,
> My 'holy alms' are whatever I like to eat,
> My bed is but a piece of human skin.
> Say, who wouldn't declare this Kaula Religion
> Just about the most fun you can have? [10]

But there were also Tantric traditions more attractive to the householder, the person living within society. Abhinavagupta was the most famous and influential member of one such lineage, the Trika branch of a collection of philosophical doctrines and theologies that are sometimes referred to as 'Kashmir Shaivism.' In his magnum opus *Tantraloka* (Light of the Tantras),

Abhinavagupta provides a widespread survey and synthesis of all these strands, and an exposition of how all these traditions are subsumed into the 'most excellent' form of Shaivism, the Trika ('Triad,' for the many triples in its cosmology, including its trio of iconic *shakti*s representing the transcendent; the transcendent within the material; and the material).[11] In the *Tantraloka* and later works, Abhinavagupta marries the mystical rituals and esoteric sexual practices of an existing left-handed tradition, the Kaula (from *kula*, group or family), to the sophisticated metaphysical speculations of *Pratyabhijna*, 'The Doctrine of Recognition.'

According to the *Pratyabhijna* philosophers, the absolute origin of all that exists, the *anuttara*—that beyond which there is nothing—is a singular infinite, primordial, undivided consciousness, Chiti, which exists before time and space. The first step or *spanda*—vibration—towards the unfolding of the phenomenal universe is the foregrounding of the *prakasha* of this consciousness, of its self-illuminating fullness. The next state is a negation of this fullness, a void that is *vimarsha*, self-referential awareness, consciousness as energy. The *spanda* or vibration between *prakasha* and *vimarsha*, the throb of *kama* between fullness and void, between 1 and 0, overflows as a completely free, blissful creative energy, *ananda shakti*. This creative dynamism, which is totally free (*svatantrya*), sets in motion a complex series of further developments which result in the projections of subject and object, materiality, individuality—in other words, all that we know and experience. 'Through her own will power, Citi unfolds the universe on a portion of herself.'[12]

So the entire universe is within Chiti, and is an *abhasa*—usually translated as 'appearance,' but I think better understood here as something like 'simulation.' We are inside a giant Holodeck of

Consciousness, and what we think of as our own subjectivity is a wilfully contracted portion of Chiti herself. This does not mean we are 'unreal,' or that the phenomenal world is somehow illusory or false; within the simulation, the laws of physics are very real and absolute. That brick over there does really exist outside of me, and if you throw it at my head, I will bleed, and my pain will be as real as the brick and you. The universe and you and I and the brick are all epistemically real. But what has been veiled from my mundane consciousness is that the brick, you, myself, and my qualia are all Chiti herself; my experience of my own subjectivity, my *vimarsha*, is a contraction of Chiti's principle of self-reflexivity, her dynamic *Shakti-tattva* or *idam*, which 'gives rise to self-awareness, will, knowledge, and action.'[13] *Pratyabhijna* is therefore sometimes understood as a supreme monism that subsumes dualism; it is a 'Transcendental Realism' that does not deny at all the reality of multiplicity, but locates under that multiplicity a substrate of Chiti, consciousness.

So, why does transcendent Chiti blossom into immanent reality? Because, as Harsha Dehejia puts it, '*vimarśa* acts spontaneously and with freedom, it possesses not an act of will but play, not the expression of a lack, but the display of fullness, its action termed *kriyā* or *spanda* or *svāntantrya*, meaning spontaneous and free action rather than *karma* or volitional action.'[14] All creation is *krida*, the spontaneous play of delight, a game. For pleasure, Chiti hides herself and reveals herself.

One of the ways in which we know Chiti every day is in our recognition of the reality of other people's individual subjectivities. Because we are aware of our own freedom (*svatantrya*) as subjects, because we are aware of our own self-awareness, we make a guess (*uha*) about the freedom inherent in other subjects, outside of one's own individuality.[15] And this theory of mind, this 'awareness of the others' existence is already a partial recognition of the universal Self.' The reality of Chiti also accounts for intersubjectivity: 'If several subjects appear to share a single object of perception,' Isabelle Ratié explains,

> it is not because this object would have an independent existence outside of consciousness, as the externalists contend; nor is it because of a perpetual accidental correspondence between various particular illusions belonging to each cognitive series, as [the Buddhist] Dharmakīrti explains . . . rather, it is due to the absolute freedom of the single infinite consciousness, which is able both to present itself as scattered into a multiplicity of limited subjects, and to manifest its fundamental unity in these various subjects by making them one with respect to one particular object.[16]

The task of the seeker after truth, then, is merely one of recognition: recognition of the nature of the limited self and of that universal self, and recognition that the individual self is Chiti, the macrocosm. You already know you are Chiti, but you have forgotten: 'I am free because I remember.' All aesthetic and ritual practices move towards this recognition, which is not merely conceptual but deeply experiential. *Rasa* is a recognition, a re-cognition of what you have forgotten, that you are blissful consciousness itself.

~

The Trika-Kaula lineage is infamous for its *chakra puja*, the circle rite in which a group of male and female initiates engaged in sex with non-spousal partners. Ritualized sex can move one past the limited self, but what is desired is very different than an 'intimacy' with a specific other person. Abhinavagupta says in the *Tantraloka*:

Consciousness, which is composed of all things, enters into a state of contraction due to the differences generated by separate bodies, but it returns to a state of oneness, to a state of expansion, when all of its components are able to reflect back on each other. The totality of our own rays of consciousness are reflected back one on the other when, overflowing in the individual consciousness of all present as if in so many mirrors, and without any effort whatsoever in an intense fashion, it becomes universal. For this reason, when a group of people gather together during the performance of a dance or of song, etc., there will be true enjoyment when they are concentrated and immersed in the spectacle all together and not one by one . . . but if even one of those present is not concentrated and absorbed, then consciousness remains offended as at the touch of a surface full of depressions and protuberances because he stands out there as a heterogeneous element. This is the reason why during the rites of adoration of the circle (*cakra*) one must remain attentive and not allow anyone to enter whose consciousness is in a dispersed state and not concentrated and absorbed, because he will be a source of contraction. In the practice of the circle (*cakra*) one must adore all the bodies of all those present . . . since they have all penetrated [into] the fullness of consciousness . . . they are in reality as if they were our own body.[17]

The paradox is that once this recognition of self as the vast, primal creative consciousness takes place, nothing changes materially. Multiplicity does not disappear: the universe is not an illusion, it is the manifest form of Chiti, and it is as it is. There is no other better place to go to, no heaven. There is nothing to attain that is not already yours. There is nothing to avoid. In liberation, nothing has been gained and nothing has been lost. You have just remembered something, recognized what you have always been. The only thing that has changed is your awareness of your own fullness, your bliss. In *Pratyabhijna*, 'the primal existential fact is not that of suffering, but that of bliss.' And, as Ratié remarks:

> compassion is not primarily *the acknowledgement of the others' pain*—which is to say, according to an equivalence drawn by these [*Pratyabhijñā*] philosophers themselves, the acknowledgement of the others' incompleteness (*apūrṇatva*)—as it is in Buddhism; on the contrary, it is primarily *the awareness of one's own completeness or fullness—of one's own bliss*. Helping the others is no longer an attempt to fill whatever incompleteness afflicts the others: it is a joyful activity that is not determined by any lack or need and has no other cause besides one's own fullness, because there can be no selfless activity without the blissful consciousness of one's own completeness, and because this blissful consciousness necessarily results in an action aiming at the others' interest.[18]

The person who has realized an identity with the Absolute,

Abhinavagupta says, 'by virtue of which he is full and perfect, has clearly only this left to do, namely—attend to the well-being of the world.'

~

In Abhinavagupta's cosmology, the one supreme consciousness is a 'She.' As Anuttara, she is figured as the Solitary Heroine; as Kali, she absorbs and transcends time.[19] And during the *chakra puja*, within the circle, there was supposed to be no caste or social differentiation, and the women were worshipped as goddesses. Tantric knowledge and ritual—unlike the Vedic texts and practices—were available to all, regardless of status.

How much actual freedom or equality these philosophical systems brought to the underclasses and women is a matter of debate. One reading of the history suggests that low-caste and female Tantrics merely became instruments through which upper- and middle-caste men, now organized into yet another secretive elite, indulged in narcissistic self-exploration and hedonism; all the other participants were mere objects. It has even been alleged that all the women involved in the rituals were prostitutes. And there is a palpable machismo in some of the Tantric texts; the male hero practises Extreme Tantra, he fears nothing, he seeks out powerful and terrifying feminine forces and subjugates them with the power of his mantras, all human women are attracted to him and are susceptible to his charms. His tantric practice gives him tremendous magical force, and he is feared and revered.

But to regard myriads upon myriads of Tantric practitioners as mere tools of the privileged would be—I think—an error.

Abhinavagupta insists that we become aware of others as independent subjects when they resist our attempts to objectify them, to read them inferentially as purely the product of deterministic systems—that is, we know they are subjects when we sense in them the same freedom (*svatantrya*) that we are aware of within ourselves. To say that 'X is a subject' is finally

> nothing but the assertion that X is a free, self-luminous entity, and although this entity is still associated with objective features such as its body, its recognition cannot be reduced to an objectification, for it does not consist in a mere identification of the other's consciousness with the other's body, but precisely in the realization that this entity transcends objective features such as its body insofar as it is self-luminous.[20]

The question, then, is—what was in it for the people who may have been objectified by some upper-class Tantrics, or who we read as objects across the gap of centuries? We are stumped, of course, by the famous silence of the subaltern. The Tantric texts are written from a male viewpoint, and no doubt by the well heeled and comfortable. Or at least this is partly true—some of the revealed Tantric texts are in a strange Sanskrit sprinkled with grammatical errors, archaic styles, and Prakrit derivations, which suggests they 'may have been written by non-brāhmins or brāhmins far from the Sanskritic heartland.'[21] Faced with this discomfiting problem, other scholastically inclined Tantrics engaged in exegesis argued that the gods are allowed to make grammatical mistakes, or indulge in linguistic crookedness for pleasure.

But we can be certain from history and the present that

kings were not the only ones to practise Tantra. The great and mighty and rich of course loved Tantra—since the rites brought power and potency to the practitioner, allowed him or her to dominate and possess, the mediaeval royals built numerous temples for Tantric gods and goddesses, and either openly or in secret worshipped, sacrificed, and believed. Several dynasties built temples at Kamakhya, the most powerful Tantric site of all. But we know that then as now, the worshippers at Kamakhya, the practitioners who conduct their rituals inside and outside these imperial constructions, come from every caste, every class.

Similarly, Hugh Urban's work on the Kartabhajas, a modern sect particularly active in the nineteenth century, shows how the poor can mobilize esoteric belief, secrecy, and rituals—including *parakiya* or extramarital sex—to find autonomy and self-respect. According to their own tradition, they were founded by a wandering fakir, Aulchand, who sometimes proclaimed himself a madman; their members came from the 'lower orders, mainly from the depressed castes, untouchables, Muslim peasants and artisans.' According to a nineteenth-century report, 'Very secretly this movement has become powerful . . . The majority [of the Kartabhajas] are lower class and female.'[22] All of these people practised a kind of equalizing meta-religion which appeared precisely at the onset of colonialism, as the East India Company began to impose land reforms that displaced millions of peasants to the cities. These new members of the urban proletariat hijacked the language of markets and mercantilism to construct a *sandhabhasha*, a cryptic 'intentional language' in which they both mocked the powerful and celebrated themselves:

I will tell you a funny story,
some news about a king.
In his city,
rows and rows of merchants
crowd the roads.
In the Central Market,
in that great landmark,
they import, they export,
they buy, they sell,
all twelve months long.
And in the warehouse
they wheel and deal
over tares great and small.

. . .

[The king] takes no taxes,
no tariffs, no gifts,
and so the traders worship him.
The goods pile up from the sea-trade,
but he excuses all duties
and gathers respect instead.
Listen, listen,
I'll tell you more—
Here there is no brokerage,
no greedy commission-mongering,
no forced labour.
The moon is his companion,
and this king is Kalki
the Avatar.[23]

The Kartabhajas disregarded caste and creed. A journalist attended one of their melas or fairs in 1848 and reported, 'We were amazed. For Brahmins, Sudras, and non-Hindu classes make no distinctions regarding their own food, and eat and drink here together: nowhere before had I seen or heard such a thing!'[24]

The upper classes of the time were engaged in their own movement to eradicate caste, to reform Indian culture according to Western notions of progress and rationality, and the Kartabhajas caused much debate amongst them. The Kartabhajas were sometimes admired, but as often they aroused shame and fear. Their insistence that the body was sacred and their practice of ritual sex outside of marriage provoked rage and disgust. There was a tendency to dismiss them as a degenerate Tantric cult—a famous upper-class poet described the Kartabhaja lineage as 'a ghost in a field strewn with rotten carcasses; an ugly old whore in a place full of rubbish and dung.'[25]

But the Kartabhajas sang, 'Tell the madman that people have become mad; tell the madman that they do not sell rice in the market . . . and tell the madman this is what the madman has said.'[26]

A considered madness, too, can be a form of autonomy, of *svatantrya*. Across the centuries in India, Tantra in its various guises has served as an alternative framework for self-understanding and self-construction, as a very visible counterpoint to the Vedic mainstream. In a culture obsessed with purity and correctness, the secrecy associated with Tantric practice offered a refuge. The dominant model of Brahmin masculinity demanded a constant self-policing and a guarding against pollution. Alexis Sanderson writes:

The Brahman could maintain his privileged position at the summit of the hierarchy of nature only by conformity to his dharma, to the conduct prescribed for him in accordance with his caste and stage of life . . . His greatest enemy was the spontaneity of the senses and his highest virtue immunity to emotion in unwavering self-control.[27]

Given this external reality, the Brahmin as much as the peasant might pay heed to the old dictum, 'When in public, be a Vaishnava. When among friends, be a Shaiva. But in private, always be a Shakta.'

But Tantra has also been practised very much in the open, as at Kamakhya and thousands of other sites across the subcontinent. The colonial attack on Indian culture, often centred on sexual practices, gave rise to a reconstruction of history and the present, a kind of Vedic reformation that attempted to eradicate embarrassing traces of Tantrism and all that it represented. Yet, the past does not vanish so easily, it just hides itself. The mantras that priests chant in temples across India may be Vedic, but the rituals these priests conduct, the manner in which they worship the deities, the goddesses themselves, and the shapes of the temples—all these a mediaeval practitioner like Abhinavagupta would recognize as profoundly Tantric.

~

Within literary practice—that other arena for pleasure and self-understanding and self-construction—Indian women seem curiously absent from the record as we currently know it. There are poems by women in the anthologies and commentaries, but they are far fewer than those written by men. Classical Indian literature—or at least our current canonical version of it—seems quite male. Given the state of gender relations in India today, it is easy to conclude that Abhinavagupta's sister died suppressed, mute, and inglorious. This is especially easy to believe when we read songs like the one written by Sumangalamata, a Buddhist nun from the sixth century BCE:

A woman well set free! How free I am,
How wonderfully free, from kitchen drudgery,
free from the harsh grip of hunger,
And from empty cooking pots,
Free too of that unscrupulous man.[28]

But there is evidence that women participated avidly in the production of *belle lettres*. In his *Kavyamimamsa* (Investigation of poetry), a sort of manual for aspiring poets, Rajashekhara devotes part of the tenth chapter to describing how a poet should utilize the quarters of a day: (1) study all branches of knowledge; (2) write poetry; (3) participate in a 'stimulating talk' about poetry and aesthetics with other poets; (4) workshop the poetry written in the morning. He describes various types of poets and then he writes:

Women can be as good poets as men. Poetic power is born of *saṃskāra* (traces or impressions). These impressions are a part of the inner soul. Thus there need be no discrimination between men and women. There are any number of princesses, daughters of ministers and performing artistes who are endowed with ability born of knowledge of the *śāstras* [sciences] and with the ability to compose poetry.[29]

Rajashekhara's wife, Avantisundari, was a renowned poet, learned critic and rhetorician; he quotes her in his book repeatedly, and she is mentioned in other texts of the period.

So if there was any number, some number, of women with the education, leisure, and inclination to write poetry, where is their work? Susie Tharu and K. Lalita, editors of the invaluable anthology *Women Writing in India*, write in their preface, 'When we began work we were repeatedly warned, often by reputed scholars, that we would find few significant women writers in Marathi or Kannada or Urdu literature . . . We began, therefore, somewhat tentatively—hopeful, but uncertain.' As they researched, reading 'social histories, biographies, and autobiographies,' they found 'debates in which women had intervened . . . wives, companions, and mothers who "also" wrote . . . rebel medieval poets, sixteenth-century court historians, and many unknown women poets, novelists, and polemical writers.'[30] But locating manuscripts for some of the texts required much labour; one of the editors found handwritten copies of a nineteenth-century devotional poet's poems in her own aunt's prayer room: 'Though Venkamamba's work had found no place in public systems of distribution, it had been kept alive in an alternative mode, as it was handed across from woman to woman.'[31]

One story that Tharu and Lalita tell may stand as emblematic of how public systems of distribution can shape our sense of the past: the courtesan Muddupalani was famous for her poetry during the reign of Pratapasimha, who ruled the southern kingdom of Thanjavur from 1739 to 1763. 'Music, dance, and literature flourished as did painting and sculpture,' and Muddupalani was one of the luminaries of this 'Golden Age of Telugu Literature.'[32] She was honoured by the king for her poetry and her learning in Telugu and Sanskrit literature; she was praised by contemporary critics; literary works were dedicated to her. In her own work, she proudly proclaims her literary heritage—her mother, her grandmother, her paternal aunt, all poets—and tells the reader that she herself is 'incomparable . . . among her kind.'[33]

Thanjavur was annexed by the British in 1855, and as elsewhere, entire classes of people who depended on traditional patronage—courtesans, artists, writers, artisans—disappeared into penury and obscurity. A great restructuring of values followed, and much of this process was articulated through the Western-style novels written by members of the new middle class. Particularly prominent debates raged over proper masculinity and femininity, over sexuality, over what it meant to be 'civilized.'

One of the main British accusations against Indian culture was that it was sexually degenerate, that Indians were promiscuous and perverse. The narrative of history developed by Western historians posited a very distant past when Indian civilization had been great; from those properly classical, chaste Vedic heights India had undergone a long descent into depravity, into the darkness of moral confusion and unspeakable Oriental vices and societal decay. Tantra was prime evidence of this degeneration; it was 'nonsensical extravagance and crude gesticulation' (H.H. Wilson); it was 'Hinduism arrived at its last and worst stage of medieval development' (Sir Monier-Williams); it was 'black art of the crudest and filthiest kind' (D.L. Barnett); and it was politically subversive: 'The unnatural depravity represented in the form of erotomania is certainly more common among

Hindu political fanatics' (V. Chirol).[34] The British, who were the rational, ethical post-Renaissance inheritors of their own classical past, were obliged to take power in order to restore order, cleanliness, and moral hygiene. The Indian reformers who responded to this narrative often understood modernization to comprise a suppression of aspects of Indian culture which were now understood to be uncivilized, primitive, embarrassing, Oriental, as well as a restructuring of chaotic Indian traditions to remake them in the image of coherent, unitary Western intellectual and religious systems. A new nationalistic Hinduism was invented; this creed mirrored the monotheism of the Abrahamic religions and insisted on a uniformity of practice and interpretation across the subcontinent. Old stories were reinterpreted—for instance, one of the most famous and alluring episodes of Krishna's life, his erotic dalliances during his youth with the rustic women of his village, was now to be understood to be purely metaphorical. No *actual* sex happened, you see; the dances and embraces were only symbolic representations of the soul's yearning for union with the Lord. The stories were spiritual, not sexual; they couldn't—or shouldn't—be both.

Tharu and Lalita tell us:

Increasingly over the nineteenth century the respectability of women from the emerging middle classes was being defined in counterpoint to the 'crude and licentious' behaviour of lower-class women. Decent (middle-class) women were warned . . . against the corrupting influence of the wandering women singers and dancers whose performances were laced with [bawdiness] and a healthy disrespect for authority . . . Artists, such as Muddupalani, who had been acceptable figures in royal courts came to be regarded as debauched and their art as corrupting.[35]

By the early twentieth century, Muddupalani's work had vanished. A woman named Bangalore Nagarathnamma—a distinguished patron of the arts, historian, and descendant of courtesans herself—found a mention of Muddupalani's poetry in an old commentary on Telugu literature. The critic described Muddupalani as a 'great poet' and quoted some lines from her poem *Radhika Santwanam* (Appeasing Radhika). Nagarathnamma managed to find a copy of the poem only with great difficulty, and when she did she remarked, 'However often I read this book, I feel like reading it all over again.' She decided to publish the work herself, 'since this poem, brimming with *rasa*, was not only written by a woman, but by one who was born into our [courtesan] community.'[36]

But the eponymous heroine of the text, Radhika or Radha, was not the sort of woman who would be allowed unchecked into modern India. Radha is Krishna's lover, who crosses all social and worldly barriers for her passion. The Radha of Muddupalani's poem is sexually aggressive, forthright in her pursuit of her own pleasure. In Krishna's words:

> If I ask her not to get too close
> for it is not decorous,
>
>   she swears at me loudly.

> If I tell her of my vow not
> to have a woman in my bed,
>
>   she hops on
>   and begins the game of love.

Appreciative,
she lets me drink from her lips,
fondles me, talks on,
making love again and again.
How could I stay away
from her company?[37]

The publication of *Radhika Santwanam* caused furious
controversy. A famous novelist who was the doyen of the social
reform movement in the region dismissed Muddupalani as
'one who claims to be an expert in music, classical poetry and
dance.' He declared:

> This Muddupalani is an adultress . . . Many parts of the book
> are such that they should never be heard by a woman, let
> alone emerge from a woman's mouth. Using *sringara* [erotic]
> *rasa* as an excuse, she shamelessly fills her poems with crude
> descriptions of sex . . .
>
> [This is not surprising because] she is born into a community
> of prostitutes and does not have the modesty natural to
> women.[38]

The colonial government banned the book. The publishers
and various scholars protested, pointing out that by these
standards you'd have to ban many, many works of premodern
Indian literature. Nagarathnamma observed that many
premodern 'great men have written even more "crudely" about
sex.'[39] The petitions were dismissed and all copies of the book
were destroyed. After Independence, the ban was repealed and a
new edition was published in 1952. But the norms about what

was natural to women persisted. In the late eighties, Tharu and Lalita's curiosity was aroused by

> the harsh dismissals of Muddupalani's work in almost every contemporary history . . . Critic after critic assured us that her work was obscene and simply not worth reading, though many of them had never seen the text. Students of Telugu literature, even ones sympathetic to women, echoed their judgement.[40]

Premodern India was by no means a utopia of gender parity and sexual freedom, but many beliefs and practices we may firmly believe to be 'traditional' and 'eternal' are in fact of very recent manufacture. And modernity is infused with its own virulent strains of misogyny and fear of women's sexuality. Muddupalani's 'book was no longer banned, but *Radhika Santwanam* had been decreed out of existence ideologically.'[41] After much searching, the editors of *Women Writing in India* were able to find copies of the printed editions of *Radhika Santwanam*; they were never able to locate a palm-leaf manuscript. Muddupalani and her poetry came close to not existing, at least in contemporary awareness. Like women in many other domains across the world, she had been erased; the recovery of Muddupalani was effected, as always, through active efforts towards investigation and reconstruction, through the writing of new histories.

~

There is a vastness of material that remains to be investigated, an ocean of rivers of stories that remain latent, that need to be reactivated and brought into the present. The corpus of pre-print Indian manuscripts is mind-bogglingly vast and still mostly unexplored. The scholar Dominik Wujastyk writes:

> The National Mission for Manuscripts in New Delhi works with a conservative figure of seven million manuscripts, and its database is approaching two million records. The late Prof. David Pingree, basing his count on a lifetime of academic engagement with Indian manuscripts, estimated that there were thirty million manuscripts, if one counted both those in public and government libraries, and those in private collections. For anyone coming to Indian studies from another field, these gargantuan figures are scarcely credible. But after some acquaintance with the subject, and visits to manuscript libraries in India, it becomes clear that these very large figures are wholly justified.[42]

The library at Koba in Gujarat, for example, has about 2,50,000 manuscripts. The Sarasvati Bhavan Library in Varanasi has more than 1,00,000 manuscripts. 'A one-year pilot field-survey by the National Mission for Manuscripts in Delhi, during 2004-2005, documented 650,000 manuscripts distributed across 35,000 repositories in the states of Orissa, Bihar and Uttar Pradesh, and field participants in that project report that they only scratched the surface.'[43] For scale, one may compare the collection of the Bibliothèque nationale de France, one of the biggest repositories in Europe, which contains about 40,000 mediaeval manuscripts in Latin and Romance languages.[44]

The Indian manuscripts are not fragments; they are full works 'typically consisting of scores or hundreds of closely written folios, most often in Sanskrit, and containing works of classical learning on logic, theology, philosophy, medicine, grammar, law, mathematics, yoga, Tantra, alchemy, religion, poetry, drama, epic, and a host of other themes.'[45] A very small fraction of the manuscripts have been catalogued—I have heard numbers ranging from 5 to 7 per cent, but nobody really knows because there is no reliable count of the total; a rough calculation by Wujastyk shows 'half a million catalogued manuscripts out of a minimum total of 7,000,000.'[46] There is an urgency to this Big Data problem. Palm leaf—the most common material—can last more than a thousand years under ideal conditions, but it does deteriorate. The ancient and mediaeval texts have survived because the manuscripts have been copied and recopied, but this practice has died out over the last two centuries. 'The future survival of this Indian literary and intellectual heritage today depends on the discovery, conservation, preservation and reproduction by digital means of the last generation of Indian manuscripts,' Wujastyk writes. 'A back-of-an-envelope calculation based on estimated figures and attrition rates suggests that several hundred Sanskrit manuscripts are being destroyed or becoming illegible every week.'[47]

~

The poet Vidya lived in the seventh century CE. Rajashekhara called her the 'Saraswati of Kanara' (a district in South India). We have thirty of her poems in Sanskrit. This is one of them, in Andrew Schelling's translation:

Black swollen clouds
drench the far
forests with rain.
Scarlet *kadamba* petals toss on the storm.
In the foothills peacocks cry out
and make love and none of it
touches me.
It's when the lightning
flings her bright
veils like a rival woman—
a flood of
grief surges through.[48]

And also:

'To Her Daughter'

As children we crave
little boys
pubescent we hunger for youths
old we take elderly men.
It is a family custom.
But you like a penitent
pursue a whole
life with one husband.
Never, my daughter,
has chastity
so stained our clan.[49]

And—Shilabhattarika lived in the ninth century CE, or perhaps the eleventh. She was perhaps an intimate of the poet-philosopher-king Bhoja, who built a temple to poetry and learning. We have only six of Shilabhattarika's poems. One of them is among the most famous lyrics in the Sanskrit tradition:

Nights of jasmine & thunder,
torn petals,
wind in the tangled *kadamba* trees—
nothing has changed.
Spring comes again and we've
simply grown older.
In the cane groves of Narmada River
he deflowered my
girlhood before we were
married.
And I grieve for those far-away nights
we played at love
by the water.[50]

To think that tomorrow, or perhaps yesterday, a manuscript will disintegrate, has disintegrated, taking with it one more poem by Vidya, one more poem by Shilabhattarika—this is maddening.

~

Shakti is female, Shiva is male. As Ardhanarishvara, they come together in one androgynous, half-female, half-male form, to signal that the primordial reality is beyond gender. But for the most part, gender seems inescapable, a lens through which we always interpret the world and ourselves. Entire races and nations can be gendered. Sir Lepel Griffin thought that Bengalis were 'disqualified for political enfranchisement by the possession of essentially feminine characteristics.' The Indian subcontinent itself has often been figured as female by the West. 'The masculine science of the West,' wrote an American in 1930, 'has found out and wooed and loved or scourged this sleepy maiden of mysticism.'[51] Another observer pointed to the common belief that India's irrationality required 'a stern man who will impose on her the discipline she is too feckless to impose on herself.'[52] In Indian editorial cartoons, the United States often shows up as a gun-toting cowboy or large-stepping Uncle Sam (sometimes appropriately sinister, with his halo of drones).

Memory too can be gendered. If the past is a foreign country, in modernity's view it is a feminine one. In that essential text of literary modernism, *Heart of Darkness*, as Marlow steers his boat up the river, he goes backwards into the past and into a teeming, liquid fertility that is enormously dangerous and seductive. The figure most emblematic of this womb-like wilderness is the 'wild-eyed and magnificent' woman who guards Kurtz, 'the barbarous and superb woman' who stands 'looking at us without a stir, and like the wilderness itself, with an air of brooding over an inscrutable purpose.'[53] Of course, in Conrad's story, she does not get to speak. Chinua Achebe pointed out that Conrad does not give Africans the faculty of speech, they make 'a violent babble of uncouth sounds,' and even among themselves they communicate with 'short grunting phrases.'[54]

So we are at a point of origin, a state of lesser development. The irony here is that apart from the African languages that

Conrad reduces to 'babble,' the frightening 'throb of drums' that Conrad refers to several times contains a sophisticated artificial language rich in metaphor and poetry. The drummers carried on conversations with each other, made announcements, broadcast messages. James Gleick tells us that this language of the drums metamorphosed tonal African languages into 'tone and only tone. It was a language of a single pair of phonemes, a language composed entirely of pitch contours.' The drum language let go of the consonants and vowels of spoken speech and made up for this information loss by adding on additional phrases to each word. '*Songe*, the moon, is rendered as *songe li tange la manga*—"the moon looks down at the earth."'[55] Listeners would hear entire phrases; the drum language dropped information but 'allocated extra bits for disambiguation and error correction.'[56] 'Come back home' would be rendered as:

> Make your feet come back the way they went,
> make your legs come back the way they went,
> plant your feet and your legs below,
> in the village which belongs to us.[57]

The past and the present speak to us in languages we refuse to hear.

An injured monkey regains consciousness, and begins typing the story of his past life.

The past retelling itself in the present—it seems like an obvious enough image, but the image came to me first, not its suggestiveness. Did I create the image, or did the dhvani make it and I find it? Writers are full of themselves, and therefore ask these kinds of annoyingly mystical questions, but they are also full of echoes of what is not in themselves. On my good days I feel like I can hear and catch these fleeting reverberations. Bind them into language before they disappear.

Sometimes the sheer vastness of what I want to put into fiction terrifies me. I survive by not thinking about the whole. I write my 400 words this day, and then another 400 words the next. I find my way by feeling, by intuition, by the sounds of the words, by the characters' passions, by trekking on to the next day, the next horizon, and then the next. I pay attention to the tracks of narratives I leave behind, and I look for openings ahead. I make shapes and I find shapes. I retrace my steps, go over draft after draft, trying to find something, I am not sure what until I begin to see it. I am trying to make an object, a model, a receptacle. What I am making will not be complete until I let go of it.

~

When I write fiction, I create an object that I hope will be savoured by an imagined someone, somewhere. I show my ongoing work to my wife, my friends, my family, but my real collaborators are always the *sahrdayas* of the future, the same-hearted ones who will allow my words to reverberate within them. And each person who reads my story will inevitably read a different story, or rather, will create a different story. Anandavardhana insists that

> In this boundless *saṃsāra* of poetry,
> the poet is the only creator god.
> . . .
> A good poet can transform insentient things
> into sentient,
> and sentient into the insentient, as he likes.
> In poetry the poet is free.[1]

But I am only half a god.

Perhaps this is why I have always turned to coding with such relief: I can see cause and effect immediately. Write some code, and it either works or it doesn't. If it doesn't, re-factor—change it, rewrite it, throw it away, and write new code. It either works or it doesn't.

Poetry has no success or failure. Poetry waits to manifest.

~

And then there is language itself, malleable, slippery, all-powerful and yet always inadequate. Or perhaps it is my craft that is incapable of manifesting completely the reality of the worlds inside me. I am always translating, always bringing from one realm to another, and always there is something left out, something that drifts outside my reach.

I write in English. The language of the conquerors is the language of my *marga*, and it is one of the languages of my interior. English—sprinkled with Hindi, Tamil, Punjabi, Gujarati—is what my schoolmates and I spoke to each other during recess, what we used to call out to each other, to curse and to cajole. Some of our great-grandfathers learnt Persian, perhaps, in their *pathshalas*. And before that, their ancestors chanted Sanskrit.

And so, in *Red Earth and Pouring Rain*, my poet tries to speak in English:

Sanjay moved his head, shut his eye, tried to speak but found his throat blocked tightly by something as hard as metal; he did not know what it was he wanted to say but knew that he couldn't say it, what was possible to say he couldn't say in English, how can in English one say roses, doomed love, chaste passion, my father my mother, their love which never spoke, pride, honour, what a man can live for and what a woman should die for, can you in English say the cows' slow distant tinkle at sunset, the green weight of the trees after monsoon, dust of winnowing and women's songs, elegant shadow of a minar creeping across white marble, the patient goodness of people met at wayside, the enfolding trust of aunts and uncles and cousins, winter bonfires and fresh chapattis, in English all this, the true shape and contour of a nation's heart, all this is left unsaid and unspeakable and invisible, and so all Sanjay could say after all was: 'Not.'

And yet, even if 'Neti, neti' is enough for philosophers, a poet cannot only say 'Not this, not this.' A poet must say, 'This, this, and also this.' And by speaking, make English say things it cannot say.

~

I grew up in a Brahmin family, but without Sanskrit. During the second millennium CE, many of the Sanskrit-speaking Hindu regimes that patronized scholarship and poetry were replaced by Muslim kingdoms that used Persian as a court language. This did not necessarily mean neglect—many of these new rulers continued to sponsor poets, schools, and translations; the immense prestige of the language and its role in the sanctification of kingship and power were attractive to the new establishments. Muslims wrote scientific and poetical works in Sanskrit. Many of the Prakrits developed their own thriving literary and critical cultures, but these regional flowerings in the *desha* were engaged in a vital and mutually revivifying conversation with the *marga*. During this 'vernacular millennium,' Yigal Bronner and David Shulman write:

> the peculiar expressive power of Sanskrit [is] still vital and available . . . True, Sanskrit is now but one of several literary options. But it brings with it unique assets such as the direct verbal and thematic continuities that transcend local contexts and that, for that very reason, enable a powerful articulation of the regional in its true fullness . . . Interacting with these vernaculars, Sanskrit is itself continuously changing, stretching the boundaries of the sayable, thinking new thoughts, searching for ways to formulate this newness.[2]

So on the eve of colonialism in the early eighteenth century, there was still a thriving—if diminished—cosmopolis. Sheldon Pollock writes:

> The two centuries before European colonialism decisively established itself in the subcontinent around 1750 constitute one of the most innovative epochs of Sanskrit systematic thought (in language analysis, logic, hermeneutics, moral-legal philosophy, and the rest). Thinkers produced new formulations of old problems, in entirely new discursive idioms, in what were often new scholarly genres employing often a new historicist framework; some even called themselves (or, more often, their enemies) 'the new' scholars (navya).[3]

This ancient, widespread transmission was finally fractured by the establishment of English as the language of colonial politics and commerce, and the institutionalization of new dispensations of morality, knowledge, and power. The upper castes—especially the Brahmins—devoted themselves energetically to adapting to the new networks of wealth and meaning, to converting their social capital into economic capital. Many in the colonial legislative systems thought that Indian knowledge was flawed materially and morally, and that the only 'cure' for the ills of the culture was the enforcement of change through European education. The early awe with which the eighteenth-century Orientalist scholars regarded Indian thought and art gave way, Vasudha Dalmia tells us:

> to a marginalization of this knowledge and the degradation of the bearers of it to native informants. The Pandits had to deliver the raw material so to speak, the end products were

to be finally manufactured by the superior techniques developed in Europe. In other words, their knowledge became valuable only once it had gone through the filter of European knowledge . . . The loss of authority . . . was not due to the intrinsic worth of either system, it was occasioned by the weightage awarded to Western scholarship by the political power it commanded.[4]

Great works in the sciences and arts continued to be written well into the nineteenth century, but the Indian intellectual tradition was almost wholly removed from the educational system.[5] After Independence, the new Indian state's official policy of 'technology-centric modernization' resulted in the entire native scholastic heritage being described 'as "traditional" in opposition to "modern" and, therefore, understood as retrogressive and an obstruction in the path of progress and development which had been given a totally materialistic definition.'[6] In my early childhood, I heard Sanskrit only in temples or at weddings; in both cases, Pandits chanted verses that the majority of us— children and adults—couldn't understand. In sixth grade, I began to learn Sanskrit as a compulsory subject at school, and a vast, stifling boredom engulfed me immediately. It wasn't just the endless rote learning of verb conjugations and vocabulary lists; Sanskrit came to us surrounded by a thick cloud of piety and supposed cultural virtue. Immediately after Independence, a passionate national debate took place over the institution of a national language for the Indian nation state. English was of course a foreign tongue, but southern speakers of Tamil and Malayalam objected to Hindi as the national language because it would put them at a disadvantage in the competition for jobs and advancement. In this context, the eternal language of the cosmopolis was presented as a good choice by some because it now was equally alien to everyone, because it was nobody's 'mother tongue': 'I offer you a language which is the grandest and the greatest,' said Naziruddin Ahmad during a debate in the Constituent Assembly, 'and it is impartially difficult, equally difficult for all to learn.'[7]

Others insisted that Sanskrit was a source of moral virtue, that its verses

> breathe a high moral tone and display a precious note of what might be called High and Serious Enlightenment. Persons who are attuned to this spirit through an acquaintance from early childhood with verses of this type . . . have a balanced and cultured outlook upon life . . . The message of Sanskrit read or chanted is that of *sursum corda*, 'lift up your hearts.'[8]

Eventually, Hindi was installed as the national language, but Sanskrit was accorded official status by the Constitution and taught in school. Our Sanskrit lessons were replete with High and Serious Enlightenment; the characters in our readers were pompous prigs of every age and gender who went on and on about Right Action and Proper Behaviour. The vast irony was that every Indian child of my generation and after has voraciously consumed the brightly coloured pages of the *Amar Chitra Katha* comic books, which recreate 'Immortal Picture Stories' from India's vast storehouse of narrative. In these comics, much is taken from Sanskrit literature, and in them, muscled epic heroes behave badly, lop off limbs and heads, tangle with monsters, and go on quests; queens launch intricate intrigues; beautiful women and men fall in love and have sex; goddesses bless and create havoc; great sages spy on voluptuous apsaras and inadvertently 'spill their seed' and thereby cause dynastic upheavals and great wars. In short, the beloved *Amar Chitra Katha* comics contain all the gore and romance dear to a twelve-year-old's heart, but we could read them only in Hindi or Tamil or English, never in Sanskrit.

And of course nobody ever told us about Tantric Sanskrit, or Buddhist Sanskrit, or Jain Sanskrit. By the beginning of the second millennium CE, Sanskrit had 'long ceased to be a Brahmanical preserve,' but it was always presented to us as the great language of the Vedas.[9] Sanskrit—as it was taught in the classroom—smelt to me of hypocrisy, of religious obscurantism, of the khaki-knickered obsessions of the Hindu far-Right, and worst, of an oppression that went back thousands of years. As far as I knew, in all its centuries, Sanskrit had been a language available only to the 'twice-born' of the caste system, and was therefore an inescapable aspect of orthodoxy. At twelve, I had disappointed my grandparents by refusing to undergo the ritual of *upanayana*, the ceremonial investiture of the sacred string which would signal my second birth into official Brahmin manhood. This was not out of some thought-out ethical position, but from an instinctive repulsion at the sheer, blatant unfairness of a ceremony and a system predicated on the randomness of birth. Now Sanskrit was being forced on me, with all its attendant casteism, its outdated and hidebound and chant-y ponderousness. As soon as I was offered a choice—a chance to learn another contemporary language to fulfil requirements—I fled from Sanskrit and never looked back, until I had to ask, for the premodern poet in my novel: What makes a poem beautiful?

~

The poet Kshemendra—Abhinavagupta's student—left this advice:

A poet should learn with his eyes
the forms of leaves
he should know how to make
people laugh when they are together
he should get to see
what they are really like
he should know about oceans and mountains
in themselves
and the sun and the moon and the stars
his mind should enter into the seasons
he should go
among many people
in many places
and learn their languages[10]

I have a sabbatical coming up. My plan is: (1) write fiction; (2) learn a functional programming language; and (3) learn Sanskrit.

~

In *Red Earth and Pouring Rain* one of the characters builds a gigantic knot. 'I made the knot,' he says.

I made it of twine, string, leather thongs, strands of fibrous materials from plants, pieces of cloth, the guts of animals, lengths of steel and copper, fine meshes of gold, silver beaten thin into filament, cords from distant cities, women's hair, goats' beards; I used butter and oil; I slid things around each other and entangled them, I pressed them together until they knew each other so intimately that they forgot they were ever separate, and I tightened them against each other until they squealed and groaned in agony; and finally, when I had finished, I sat cross-legged next to the knot, sprinkled water in a circle around me and whispered the spells that make things enigmatic, the chants of profundity and intricacy.

When I wrote that book, when I write now, I want a certain density that encourages savouring. I want to slide warp over woof, I want to make knots. I want entanglement, unexpected connections, reverberations, the weight of pouring rain on red earth. Mud is where life begins.

~

Like palm-leaf manuscripts, the worlds the writer creates will finally be destroyed, become illegible. At least until they are re-excavated and become alive again within the consciousness of a future reader. I don't worry too much about whose work will 'last,' and if mine won't. I do think endlessly about the shapes of stories, about the tones and tastes that will overlay each other within the contours. I don't much like perfect symmetry, which always seems inert to me. The form of art rises from impurity, from dangerous chaos. When I can find perfection and then discover the perfect way to mar that perfection, I am happy. As a creator, I want to bend and twist the grammar of my world-making, I want crookedness and deformation, I want to introduce errors that explode into the pleasure of surprise. In art, a regularity of form is essential, but determinism is boring. When I am the spectator, the caressing of my expectations, and then their defeat, feels like the vibration of freedom, the pulse of life itself.

~

Abhinavagupta's assertions about *rasa-dhvani* may remind Western readers of T.S. Eliot's objective correlative:

> The only way of expressing emotion in the form of art is by finding . . . a set of objects, a situation, a chain of events which shall be the formula of that *particular* emotion; such that when the external facts, which must terminate in sensory experience, are given, the emotion is immediately evoked.[11]

This may not be simply a case of two thinkers separated by centuries coming independently to similar conclusions; Indians like to point out that Eliot read substantially in classical Indian philosophy and metaphysics during his time at Harvard, certainly enough to have encountered *rasa* and *dhvani*. In 1933, Eliot wrote:

> Two years spent in the study of Sanskrit under Charles Lanman, and a year in the mazes of Patanjali's metaphysics under the guidance of James Woods, left me in a state of enlightened mystification. A good half of the effort of understanding what the Indian philosophers were after—and their subtleties make most of the great European philosophers look like schoolboys—

lay in trying to erase from my mind all the categories and kinds of distinction common to European philosophy from the time of the Greeks. My previous and concomitant study of European philosophy was hardly better than an obstacle. And I came to the conclusion . . .

. . . that my only hope of really penetrating to the heart of that mystery would lie in forgetting how to think and feel as an American or a European: which, for practical as well as sentimental reasons, I did not wish to do.[12]

Eliot's reluctance—or inability—to 'think and feel' across a cultural divide, even as he borrowed certain idioms and ideas ('*Datta. Dayadhvam. Damyata.* / *Shantih shantih shantih*') was rooted in his recognition that this would require self-transformation at an elemental level, a departure from comfortable, familiar certainties. To someone raised in the tradition of Western analytical philosophy, encountering the goddess in philosophical texts might indeed induce terror, especially if you think all mysteries can be penetrated to the heart; it is no coincidence that Anuttara is sometimes pictured as a 'hideous, emaciated destroyer who embodies the Absolute as the ultimate Self which the "I" cannot enter and survive, an insatiable void in the heart of consciousness.'[13] The terrible goddesses demand that you sacrifice, that you eat foreign substances, that you let the impure and chaotic penetrate you. The *ishta-devata* or personal deity that you worship will shatter you and remake you.

And yet, when the thunder speaks, we all come away reading a message into the *sphota*, the explosion of sound. Eliot heard what he needed to, and used it in his art and thought. Programmers create elegant techniques like event-sourcing, they make beauty in code, but many—like Paul Graham—use the language of aesthetics and art to describe their work without engaging with the difference of artistic practice, without acknowledging that the culture of art-making may in fact be foreign to them. Eliot was aware that there was a mystery that he wanted to avoid; programmers, on the other hand, often seem convinced that they already know everything worth knowing about art, and if indeed there is something left for them to comprehend, they are equipped—with all their intelligence and hyper-rationalism—to figure it out in short order. After all, if you decompose an operation into its constituent pieces, you can understand the algorithms that make it work. And then you can hack it. Therefore, to make art, you don't have to *become* an artist—that, anyhow, is only a pose—you just analyse how art is produced, you understand its domain, and then you code art. And, conversely, when you are writing code using the formal languages of computing, you are making something that aspires to elegance and beauty, and therefore you are making art.

Abhinavagupta's description of poetic language and its functions reveals the hapless wrong-headedness of these kinds of facile cross-cultural equivalencies: code is denotative, poetic language is centrally concerned with *dhvani*, that which is not spoken; the end purpose of code is to process and produce logic, and any feeling this code arouses in an immediate sense is a side effect, whereas poetic language is at its very inception concerned with affect. *Rasa* arises from the fluctuations of feeling produced by manifestation, so to be aesthetically satisfying, even a play about a meeting between a physicist and his mentor must imbue the theories of physics with personal and emotional ballast, must make the equations resonate with memory. And so on: code may flirt with illegibility, but it must finally cohere logically or it will not work; the language of art can fracture grammar and syntax, can fail to transmit meaning but still cause emotion, and therefore successfully produce *rasa*.

The 'hackers are artists' manifestos and blog posts gloss over these differences, and also remain quite silent about the processes that produce these culminations. For my own part, as a fiction writer who has programmed, thinking and feeling as an artist is a state of being utterly unlike that which arises when one is coding. Programming is very hard, and doing it requires a deep concentration in which I become quite unaware of my surroundings and myself. When I am trying to follow a bug, to understand its origins, time collapses. I type, compile, run, decipher a stack trace, type again, compile, run, and I look up and an hour and a half has gone by. I am thirsty, my wrists are aching, I should get up and stretch, but I am on the verge of discovery, there is one more variation I could try. I type again, and another half hour is gone. There is the machine, and there is me, but I am vanished into the ludic haze of the puzzle. The programmer Tom Christiansen put it succinctly: 'The computer is the game.'[14]

And the poet Robert Hass once said, 'It's hell writing, but it's hell not writing. The only tolerable state is just having written.'[15] That writing is hell is a well-established commonplace among writers. In a series of published letters titled *Writing Is My Life*, Thomas Wolfe wrote:

> I am back at work now. It is going to be another very long
> hard pull. I am already beginning to be haunted by nightmares
> at night. I am probably in for several thousand hours of hell

and anguish, of almost losing hope, utterly, and swearing I'll never write another word and so on, but it seems to have to be done in this way, and I have never found any way of avoiding it . . . Sometimes I am appalled by my own undertaking, and doubt that I can do it.[16]

And of the not-writing, Wolfe said:

> I would say that almost the worst time in a writer's life are those periods between work—periods when he is too exhausted and feels too empty to attempt a new piece of work, or when a new piece of work is still cloudily formulating itself in his mind. It is really hell, or worse than hell, because writing itself is hell, and this period of waiting is limbo—floating around in the cloudy upper geographies of hell trying to get attached to something.[17]

Most certainly there are writers in the world (Bradbury, Borowski?) who smile while they work, who create fiction and poetry in an ecstatic flow. I've never met a single one. Mostly, as far as I can tell, writing is not pleasurable. An interviewer once asked William Styron, 'Do you enjoy writing?' and the great man said, 'I certainly don't. I get a fine warm feeling when I'm doing well, but that pleasure is pretty much negated by the pain of getting started every day. Let's face it, writing is hell.'[18]

Georges Simenon was of the opinion that 'writing is not a profession but a vocation of unhappiness. I don't think an artist can ever be happy.'[19] Anthony Burgess was asked if he thought that Simenon was right, and he answered:

My eight-year-old son said the other day: 'Dad, why don't you write for fun?' Even he divined that the process as I practise it is prone to irritability and despair . . . The anxiety involved is intolerable . . . The financial rewards just don't make up for the expenditure of energy, the damage to health caused by stimulants and narcotics, the fear that one's work isn't good enough. I think, if I had enough money, I'd give up writing tomorrow.[20]

Here's Abe Kobo on the subject: 'The most enjoyable time is when I suddenly get the idea for my work. But when I start writing it is very, very painful . . . To write or commit suicide. Which will it be?'[21] Joan Acocella: 'Writing is a nerve-flaying job . . . Clichés come to mind much more than anything fresh or exact. To hack one's way past them requires a huge, bleeding effort.'[22] Norman Mailer: 'I think nobody knows how much damage a book does to you except another writer. It's hell writing a novel; you really poison your body doing it . . . it is self-destruction, it's quiet self-destruction, civilized self-destruction.'[23]

Malcolm Cowley referred to the writing-is-hell whiners as 'bleeders,' and thought that their suffering stemmed from their slow, overly self-critical method: '[They] write one sentence at a time, and can't write it until the sentence before has been revised.'[24] This is an attractive hypothesis, but it rather breaks down in the case of writers like Wolfe, who 'habitually wrote for long hours, wrote rapidly, and turned huge manuscripts over to his publishers.'[25]

I'm a slow writer, but I'm quite content to leave sentences unrevised until the second or third draft, and I know quite well that my first draft will lack architectural coherence and shapeliness. And yet as I write, something grates and scrapes in my chest. I'm never quite in hell, but in a low-level purgatory that I've put myself in.

There is the effort of shaping the words, of fighting through the thickets of cliché, as Joan Acocella noted. And there is often that self-doubt alluded to by Cowley. Effort and self-doubt are certainly present in other areas of my life—programming, for instance—but I am never ever in this particular agony except when I write.

'It must be lonely being a writer,' people have said to me. But I like being alone, at least for a goodly sized portion of every day. And working by myself on other things—programming, for instance—is never painful. There is something else altogether that is peculiar to the process of fiction writing, a grinding discomfort that emerges from the act itself: it feels, to me, like a split in the self, a fracture that leaves raw edges exposed.

The premodern Indian tradition investigates the reception of literature thoroughly but remains strangely silent about the actual workings of the creative process. Abhinavagupta, for example, writes that 'The poet's genius [*pratibhā*] is not inferred by the audience, but shines forth with immediacy because of his inspiration with *rasa* . . . Genius is an intelligence capable of creating new things.'[26] *Pratibha* is imagination, insight, and seems to be spontaneously creative, playful, an overflow of the interaction between self-luminosity and self-awareness; it flows forth, aided by craft and learning. The Indian aesthetic theorists were 'philosophers who dealt with the philosophy of awareness and the philosophy of language,' but they seem to have not been very interested in biographies of literary effort and failure.[27] The only reference to the costs of poetic effort I've come across is from Rajashekara, who insists that 'When the poet after the intense activity of poetic composition wishes for relaxation, the inmates of his family and his followers should not speak without his desire.'[28] Which makes me believe that Rajashekhara and Avantisundari got a bit cranky by the end of the poetry-writing quarter of their day.

But the Indian phenomenology of literary pleasure perhaps provides a way to think about literary effort: making a narrative come to life within you requires that you bring alive your own *samskaras* and *vasanas*, make active all those latent impressions that lie submerged within the layers of your consciousness. This is why stories are not only constructed, but formed, found. They *emerge* through an alchemical process which requires significant concentration, *samadhi*. The writer experiences these stories as events happening within himself.

'The poet is, indeed, comparable to the spectator,' Abhinavagupta says. 'The origin of the *rasa* that emerges within the reader is the generalized consciousness of the poet . . . the *rasa* which lies within the poet.'[29] The implication here is that in the moment of creation, the poet must be both creator (the one who is producing or constructing the aestheticized object) and the audience (the subject that is experiencing the generalized consciousness thus produced). That is, you must simultaneously be in multiple cognitive modes: to produce any semblance of *rasa* you must remove your ego-self or I-self from the narrative that is forming within yourself, you must allow *sadharanikarana* or generalization to occur. And yet, the ego-self cannot be allowed to slip effortlessly into the continuous dream of the narrative, it must stay alert and conscious of the very language it is deploying to construct the story—the story, that living, moving thing which is a part of itself, is another aspect of the self. Experientially, this results in a hypersensitive self-awareness, the very opposite of flow; the writer's ego-self knows at every moment the abrading of generalization and the terror of its own ephemerality. It is a slow, continuous suicide, a 'civilized self-destruction.'

So the experience of the writer during *samadhi* is more akin to the mental state '(laboriously) milked by yogin' than it is to the effortlessly achieved *rasa* of the *sahrdaya*. The yogin know well these beautiful, bleak landscapes of our inner worlds. I once heard the scholar, Tantric practitioner and teacher Paul Muller-Ortega speak about the terrors the yogi faces on the path towards self-realization. Yogic practices didn't just bring bliss or pleasure, he said. The 'yogic ordeal' also made you feel that 'you are dying.' And this was true, Muller-Ortega said. 'You *are* dying.' That is, the ego-self that most of us believe to be our true self must die if the identification with the larger, undivided self is to occur. The yogi must confront the *mysterium tremendum* and pass through it. The path of the yogi is not for the faint-hearted.

The *sahrdaya*, on the other hand, is granted the spontaneous, temporary suspension of the ego-self through the encounter with art, while tasting—in a concentrated, wondrous manner—consciousness itself, the larger self of the world. The *Natyashastra* tells us that theatre was created by Brahma as a fifth Veda, available to people of all castes and conditions; art is thus a democratic meditation through which the ordinary person can taste bliss.

Is the writer then a kind of entry-level yogi, engaging in a daily practice that mingles asceticism, dangerous mental disciplines, multifarious cognitive states, suffering and joy? There have been many figurings of the artist in recent history: Romantic seeker-explorer, drunken hedonist, bohemian outcast, manic depressive, social reformer, truth teller, tortured confessor of secrets. Perhaps it would be apposite to set next to these a portrait offered by Madhuraja, Abhinavagupta's contemporary and student:

> [Abhinavagupta] sits in the middle of a garden of grapes, inside a pavilion made of crystal and filled with beautiful paintings. The room smells wonderful because of flower garlands, incense-sticks and (oil-) lamps . . . The room is constantly resounding with musical instruments, with songs and with dancing . . . Abhinavagupta is attended by all his numerous students, with Kṣemaraja at their head, who are writing down everything he says. To his side stand two women, partners in Tantric rites (dūtī), who hold in one hand a jug of wine, śivarasa, and a box full of betel rolls, and in the other hand a lotus and a citron. Abhinavagupta has his eyes trembling in ecstasy. In the middle of his forehead is a conspicuous tilaka made of ashes . . . His long hair is held by a garland of flowers. He has a long beard and golden (reddish-brown) skin; his neck is dark with shining yakṣaparīka powder . . . he sits in the Yogic position known as virāsana [the pose of the hero]. One hand is held on his knee holding a rosary with his fingers clearly making the sign (mudrā) that signifies his knowledge of the highest Siva. He plays on his resonating lute with the tips of his quivering fingers.[30]

In recent decades there has been something of an Abhinavagupta revival, an increasing interest—in India and elsewhere—in his work. This is due, in no small part, to a fascination with the person one glimpses in the texts—with the sheer range of knowledge, the confident voice, the subtlety of the mind; his contemporaries regarded him as 'Shiva incarnate,' and one feels the glamour across the centuries. As often happens with culture heroes, his life shades off into legend: around 1025 CE, he and 1200 followers are said to have entered a cave, singing a hymn Abhinavagupta wrote to Bhairava (the terrifying manifestation of Shiva); none of them were seen again. We have twenty-one of the books he wrote, and know of twenty-three other now-lost titles.[1] His grand masterwork, the *Tantraloka*, has been translated into Hindi and Italian, but still awaits an authoritative and complete translation into English. 'Abhinavagupta Studies' is a fast-expanding field because much remains to be done.

~

Efforts to restore Sanskrit to some semblance of its former glory are afoot. At the time of this writing, a non-profit group based in Bangalore, Samskrita Bharati, has begun the task of translating the *Amar Chitra Katha* comics into Sanskrit.[2] The organization's slogan is, 'Revive a language. Rejuvenate a culture. Revolutionize the world.'

Something of the same wide-ranging cultural aspiration

fuels some governmental attempts to bolster the teaching of Sanskrit. In 2010, the BJP-led Uttarakhand state government proclaimed two villages to be 'Sanskrit Villages,' which meant that funding was provided to teach all citizens—including Dalits—the language. Uttarakhand has 'a separate Sanskrit Education Department, 88 government-aided Sanskrit educational institutes, and 47 Sanskrit colleges giving "Shastri (BA)" and "Acharya (MA)" degrees.' But in one of the villages, 'people learnt to speak the language with much hope and now wait in vain for the gains that were to follow.'[3] The Congress government that followed dropped the project, so the villagers' ambitions of being appointed Sanskrit teachers for other villages remain frustrated.

The Special Centre for Sanskrit Studies at the Jawaharlal Nehru University in New Delhi has more explicit aims: Sanskrit computational linguistics, Sanskrit informatics, Sanskrit computing, Sanskrit language processing. There has also been an effort over the past two decades to reintroduce the Indian scholastic tradition into humanities departments, and students have responded with enthusiasm. Controversies have flared over some of the more clumsy attempts by academic nationalists to proclaim—by fiat—the continuing relevance and accuracy of 'Vedic astrological science' and similar subjects. Sanskrit departments are still Brahminical redoubts, within which Dalit students face active prejudice.

In 2004, the Department of Posts released a postage stamp honouring Panini, in the denomination of Rs 5.

~

After Abhinavagupta, *rasa-dhvani* theory became the predominant system of aesthetic analysis in the subcontinent, although it was by no means accepted universally. Many poets wrote poetry that displayed astonishing technical virtuosity rather than depths of *dhvani*; the great Anandavardhana himself, despite his stern pronouncements about 'picture poetry,' wrote a spectacular picture poem called the 'Devisataka' (The goddess's century) which when decoded syllabically according to the embedded instructions reveals an intricate, spoked wheel. He explains in the poem that the goddess appeared in a dream and not only told him to write the poem but also acted as his instructor.

Perhaps the goddess—who gives rise to fullness and void— understands that every form needs its opposite.

∼

The simple on–off operations of a computer's logic gates might mislead one into regarding that computer as a large and overly complicated abacus. But, as Ada Byron pointed out:

> The Analytical Engine, on the contrary, is not merely adapted for tabulating the results of one particular function and no other, but for developing and tabulating any function whatever. In fact the engine may be described as being the material expression of any indefinite function of any degree of generality and complexity[4]

In 1936, in his famous paper 'On Computable Numbers,' Alan Turing announced, 'It is possible to invent a single machine which can be used to compute any computable sequence,' and then showed how—at least in principle—to build such a machine. [5]

'Any indefinite function,' 'any computable sequence'—that simple word 'any' holds here a vastness perhaps equal to the universe, or your consciousness. Whether the universe is an *abhasa*—a simulation—or whether self-awareness can be produced by recursive algorithms are questions open to debate, but one thing is certain: the ability to materially express computable sequences and therefore move the world is unprecedented and extraordinary. 'Before ten years are over, the Devil's in it if I have not sucked out some of the life-blood from the mysteries of this universe, in a way that no purely mortal lips or brains could do,'[6] Ada Byron wrote to Charles Babbage, with an inkling of the uncanny powers they were beginning to glimpse. 'The Analytical Engine does not occupy common ground with mere "calculating machines,"' she wrote elsewhere.

> It holds a position wholly its own. . . . A new, a vast, and a powerful language is developed . . . in which to wield its truths so that these may become of more speedy and accurate practical application for the purposes of mankind than the means hitherto in our possession have rendered possible. Thus not only the mental and the material, but the theoretical and the practical in the mathematical world, are brought into more intimate and effective connexion with each other.[7]

This is why comparisons and analogies between programming and older disciplines can obtain only to a limited extent. When programmers say what they do is just like what writers do, or gardeners, or painters, the error is that they aren't claiming enough, the fault is that they are being too humble. To compare code to works of literature may point the programmer towards legibility and elegance, but it says nothing about the ability of code to materialize logic.

What programmers want to do in their investigations of the 'eloquence' of code, I think, is analogous to what Anandavardhana and Abhinavagupta tried to do with poetic language in the Sanskrit cosmopolis: to understand how the effects of a language can escape language itself. The Indian theorists were also dealing with a formal language tightly constrained by rules, a stable formal language that had been analysed only in stylistic terms, with catalogues of figures and reckonings of correctness. The *rasa-dhvani* theorists saw that this understanding of beauty was incomplete, and so they tried to formalize the processes of literary affect, to investigate how poetry moves across the borders of bodies and selves, and to understand how consciousness uses and is reconstructed by poetry, how poetry expands within the self and allows access to the unfathomably vast, to that which cannot be spoken.

Programmers also use formal languages, but programming is sui generis. It is unlike anything else. Programmers need to claim the extraordinary nature of what they do. Most discussions of the beauty of code I have encountered emphasize formal qualities of language—simplicity, elegance, structure, flexibility—what a riti- or style-inclined theorist might have described as the qualities of the code. But programs are not just algorithms as concepts or applied ideas; they are algorithms in motion. Code is uniquely kinetic. It acts and interacts with itself, with the world. In code, the mental and the material are one. Code moves. It changes the world.

Marcel Duchamp, who achieved chess-master rank at the royal game, observed in an interview:

> A game of chess is a visual and plastic thing, and if it isn't geometric in the static sense of the word, it is mechanical, since it moves; it's a drawing, it's a mechanical reality. The pieces aren't pretty in themselves, any more than is the form of the game, but what is pretty—if the word 'pretty' can be used—is the movement. Well, it is mechanical, the way, for example, a Calder is mechanical. In chess there are some extremely beautiful things in the domain of movement, but not in the visual domain. It's the imagining of the movement or of the gesture that makes the beauty, in this case. It's completely in one's gray matter.[8]

Code is also a mechanical reality, but it does not stay merely within one's grey matter. One does not have to merely imagine its movements and gestures. We already live in a world that abounds with computers, and we already filter experience through software—Facebook and Google offer us views of the world that we can manipulate, but which also, in turn, manipulate us. The embodied language of websites, apps, and networks writes itself into us. One of the pioneers of the newly minted field of Aesthetic Computing, Paul Fishwick, points out that digital watches and DVRs surface the abstract computer-science notion of 'finite state machines' in their menus—each time you press the 'mode' button you move from one state to another:

> The way in which our thinking is changing culturally surfaces deep abstract concepts in computing to us as we use these

devices: from number, to information structure, to process . . .
It is not just that the finite state machine is embedded within
the watch's silicon, but also that the human wearing the watch
becomes aware of this virtual machine's structure and its
components through the experience of using the watch. The
state machine *changes how the wearer thinks*, even though the wearer
is probably unaware of the formal mathematical notation
of a state machine. The watch's software internals become
embedded within our psychology and culture.[9]

So the locus of code's dance is not only logic gates or the
gleaming fields of random-access memory; code also moves
within the millions of humans who encounter its effects, not
just programmers. Code already shapes the world of the non-
programmers and embeds itself into their bodies, into their
experience of themselves, into lived sensation and therefore
the realm of experience and aesthetics. Soon, in the near future,
we will live *inside* an experience mediated by computers; all
those science-fiction fantasies of eyeglasses that can overlay
data over what you see, of new means of sensing the world
through android extensions of our bodies, all of these are already
possible, they already exist.

And this is not all. We will program ourselves and the world
we live in. Consider this: the four letters of the genetic alphabet
that makes up DNA—A (adenine), C (cytosine), G (guanine),
and T (thymine)—are really, quite literally, a programming
language. And this language can be represented in binary code,
which means that it can be manipulated on a computer. A recent
article in the *Atlantic* lays out the process and the possibilities:

The latest technology—known as synthetic biology, or 'synbio'—moves the work [of biotechnology] from the molecular to the digital. Genetic code is manipulated using the equivalent of a word processor. With the press of a button, code representing DNA can be cut and pasted, effortlessly imported from one species into another. It can be reused and repurposed. DNA bases can be swapped in and out with precision. And once the code looks right? Simply hit Send. A dozen different DNA print shops can now turn these bits into biology.[10]

The DNA print shop will send back several vials of 'frozen plasmid DNA,' which you will then inject into a host bacterial cell, causing this cell to 'boot up' using the DNA code you've created. The cell will metabolize, grow, and reproduce. Congratulations—you have just created a new form of life.

Synthetic biology is 'currently advancing at 5 times the speed of Moore's Law.'[11] The cost of synbio is falling exponentially, and the tools are already so easy to use that schoolchildren can wield them effectively. In 2012, the high-school division of the annual International Genetically Engineered Machine competition was won by a team of teenagers from Heidelberg.[12] Their winning entry was 'a new biological system in E. coli that reacts quantitatively to UV radiation.' Their planned application for their engineered E. coli is 'small tubes filled with bacterial suspension and integrated into trendy necklaces and bracelets.' That is, jewellery that changes colour in response to changing doses of ultraviolet radiation.[13]

The possibilities of programmed biology are awesome and terrifying: engineered T-cells that kill cancer but avoid the generalized depredations of chemotherapy; assassin viruses that leap harmlessly from person to person until they find their DNA-profiled target and cause a quick death; a terrorist cooking up a species-killing weapon in his garage. Bioluminescent trees that glow in the dark, providing lighting for city streets.[14] DNA hard drives—rewritable data-storage systems that can store information within cells.[15] Bioengineered plants that 'produce plastic exactly in a desired shape, from a drinking cup to a house.'[16]

And yes, engineered humans immune to disease, capable of recalling every fleeting experience like Funes the Memorious, no longer just *homo sapiens* but transformed by imported bits from other species. 'The interspecies barrier is falling as fast as the Berlin Wall did in 1989,' George M. Church writes in his book *Regenesis: How Synthetic Biology Will Reinvent Nature and Ourselves*.

> Not just occasional horizontal transfer but massive and intentional exchange—there is a global marketplace for genes. Not the isolating effect of islands or valleys resulting in genetic drift and xenophobia, but a growing addiction to foreign gene products, for example, humans 'mating' with wormwood for antimalarial drug precursor artemisinin, and with *Clostridium* for Botox.[17]

If you think that all this sounds comfortably science-fiction-like and distant, take a moment to consider how you might have reacted in 1985 if someone had told you that within your own lifetime, you would carry a Cray 2 supercomputer in your pocket, as would farmers in rural India. Synbio is here, and bio-hackers and programmers will change you and your environment much sooner than you think.

The effects of code will spill out from the compiler; its *vyanjana* or suggestiveness will echo through the world and the human body. Undoubtedly, artists will—and already do—arrange this suggestion to manifest *dhvani* and *rasa*. The question, really, is not whether code can be art; as Bhatta Nayaka—a tenth-century theorist—put it:

> Scripture is distinguished by its dependence on the primacy of the wording [that is, the Veda is more important for how it says than what it says, and it can therefore never be rephrased]. Historical narrative, for its part, is a matter of factual meaning [that is, what it says is more important than how it says it, and can be rephrased multiply]. When both these, wording and meaning, are subordinate, and the aesthetic process itself has primacy, we call it literature.[18]

If an artist can manipulate our attention to code so that 'the aesthetic process itself has primacy,' code becomes art. Recent filmic visualizations of cyberspace—William Gibson's 'mass consensual hallucination'—as networks of embodied logic gates and circuits begin to demonstrate how code can be manifested, how code can itself become the object of perception and therefore, perhaps, of savouring.

The more difficult and intricate problem, it seems to me, is understanding the self that will be paying attention to the embodied code. In the analyses of the classical Indian theorists, a model of the self is produced: this self is limited, bounded, local, but also diffused through the entire universe; it has boundaries, but those boundaries are porous, and can allow inflows from without; it has stability but is also capable of submergence and emergence; it dies but reappears; it forgets but has endless stores of latent memories; it is itself but has been everything else.

What is the nature of the self that codes and is coded itself, which resides in a biology transformed by code? How will it allow inflows across its borders? When will this self be limited, and how will it be diffused or expanded? What will be the distance this self adopts in relation to the objects of its cognition? When and how will its perceptions undergo *sadharanikarana* or generalization? Under what circumstances will it feel personally attached to emotions generated by external stimuli?

The Tantric systems promised profound transformations of outlook, and also *siddhis*, superpowers that allowed control over nature itself, over biology and physics: the ability to reduce one's body to the size of an atom, or to an infinitely large size; the ability to appear simultaneously in more than one place, or to move through space; the power to subjugate all. This was possible because reality itself was encoded in a primal, eternal language, in the alphabet of Sanskrit, in its *matrka*, the mothers of the universe. With Tantric mantras, strings of phonemes that emerged from the 'pre-cognitive, pre-linguistic, and pre-discursive layers' of the self, the practitioner could change himself and the world.[19]

In one of the Tantric visualizations used during meditation, the practitioner imagines himself sitting 'above the Lords of the world.' Then he, with the power of his mantra, burns his entire body, sees it 'blazing from the feet' upwards until nothing is left but a pile of ashes. He 'floods the ashes to the directions' with water that arises from his meditation. Having destroyed his gross body, his elemental image of himself, he now meditates upon 'the complete, solitary, pure body of the five true mantras, bursting with the energies of the mantras.' Now he enters this subtle mantra-body made of blazing phonemes, he becomes it. 'Then meditating on his own speech, which is the support of all the worlds, the complete word [the entire mantra] creates total satisfaction.'[20]

In the *Tantraloka*, Abhinavagupta writes:

> The more this uncreated overflowing reality is seen clearly, the more wonder unfolds. The various levels in which creative intuition is present follow from conventional language being immersed in what precedes it, and that in the primordial, transcendental phonemes. Those who repose in this creative intuition, overflowing with the primordial phonemes, become poetic and linguistic adepts. Resting in this consciousness-reality in its highest form, unlimited by conventional language, what would they not [be able to] know [and] what would they not [be able to] do?[21]

How do we imagine selves which can easily manipulate language to remake the world and themselves? How would they make art and experience it? Perhaps these are questions not for programmers but for novelists and poets, for thinkers who deal with 'the philosophy of awareness and the philosophy of language.' We await an Anandavardhana, an Abhinavagupta, for answers.

~

In March 1954, a few months before his tragic death, Alan

Turing sent four postcards to his friend, the logician Robin Gandy. Gandy kept only the last three of the series, which was labelled 'Messages from the Unseen World.' The second postcard contains the following lines in Turing's handwriting:

III. The Universe is the interior of the Light Cone of the Creation.

IV. Science is a Differential Equation. Religion is a Boundary Condition.

And on the third postcard, Turing writes:

V. Hyperboloids of wondrous Light
   Rolling for aye through Space and Time
   Harbour there Waves which somehow Might
   Play out God's holy pantomime.[22]

~

Red Earth and Pouring Rain was published in 1995. It feels now, of course, like it was written by somebody else, by another person with whom I am moderately familiar. When I try to recall its writing, what I remember is the heat haze of Houston afternoons; reading photocopied historical texts in a transit lounge at Dubai airport; moments of uncertainty and thirty-something unpublished-writer panic in Bombay when I ran into school friends who already had jobs, spouses, children, homes. I remember girlfriends, and loneliness, and the generosity of my teachers. And vividly, I remember computers, the machines I spent endless hours with, through which my characters came alive: the borrowed IBM PCjr I began writing the book on, with its abominable Chiclet keyboard and associated stack of WordStar floppies; my clone XT, the first computer I ever owned, bought with the entirety of a grant that was supposed to supplement my meagre TA stipend through a semester; 'Sikander,' the big beast of a 486 clone I indulged in once I was making money as a consultant and programmer.

Makers tend to fetishize tools that they use successfully, and computer geeks are no exception—hackers will tell you in exacting detail about the first computer they ever used, the first program they ever wrote. My writing life and my life with computers, in spite of their differences, seem mirrored, twinned. Both are explorations of process, of the unfolding of connections. Both reward curiosity, dogged patience. And perhaps it is just the double presence that I cherish, of art and logic, of deep historical roots and newness. All cognition is re-cognition, recognition; discovery and rediscovery are both nourishing. It has been pointed out to me that my fiction proliferates doubles, couplings, alter egos, layers within layers. Duchamp noticed that 'most artists only repeat themselves.'[23] If so, an obsession with contradiction, paradox, ambiguity, and mirroring has been my repetition, one that I'm happy with. Repetition need not only be a grim karmic necessity, or an endless rehearsal of trauma. In the practice of fiction, what is tasted—first and then again—is consciousness itself.

NOTES

Chapter 1: Hello, World!

1. Graham, 'Hackers and Painters.'
2. Ibid.
3. Ibid.
4. Lampson, 'Guest Editorial,' 195.
5. Ibid., 196.
6. Wright and Daintith, *A Dictionary of Computing*, 205.
7. Knuth, 'Literate Programming,' 99.
8. Ibid.
9. Mataes and Montford, 'A Box, Darkly,' 145.
10. Ibid., 194.
11. 'The IBM 650 Magnetic Drum Calculator'; Mataes and Montford, 'A Box, Darkly,' 194.
12. Oram and Wilson, *Beautiful Code*, loc. 482.
13. Ibid., loc. 473.
14. Mataes and Montford, 'A Box, Darkly,' 145.
15. Ceglowski, 'Dabblers and Blowhards.'
16. Graham, 'Design and Research.'
17. Graham, 'Hackers and Painters.'
18. Ceglowski, 'Dabblers and Blowhards.'
19. Ibid.

Chapter 2: Learning to Write

1. Simon, *Spies and Holy Wars*, 98.
2. Jcoll [pseud.], 'For Most of You, This Is Surely Child Play, but Holy Shit, This Must Be What It Feels Like to Do Heroin for the First Time.'

Chapter 3: The Language of Logic

1. Rob P., 'How Do Computers Work?'
2. Jong89 [pseud.], 'Razorlength—1036 Early Winter by Jong89.'
3. 'Computer Scientists Build Computer Using Swarms of Crabs.'

4. Petzold, *Code*, 101–02.
5. See Gleick, *The Information*, loc. 2056–69.
6. Rob P., 'How Do Computers Work?'
7. Ganssle, 'Microprocessors Change the World.'
8. Winegrad and Akera, 'A Short History of the Second American Revolution.'
9. Ganssle, 'Microprocessors Change the World.'

Chapter 4: Histories and Mythologies

1. Rosenberg, *Dreaming in Code*, 300–01.
2. Nather, 'The Story of Mel.'
3. Ibid.
4. Ibid.
5. Ibid.
6. Used with permission from Microsoft. Lippert, 'Cargo Cultists, Part Three: Is Mort a Cargo Cultist?'
7. Ibid.
8. Ibid.
9. Ibid.
10. Ibid.
11. Nather, 'The Story of Mel.'
12. Ibid.
13. Wozniak, 'And Then There Was Apple.'
14. Livingston, *Founders at Work*, 45.
15. Ibid., 49.
16. DFectuoso [pseud.], 'Solo Development—Are There Any Famous One-Man-Army Programmers?'
17. 'Programming the ENIAC.'
18. Ensmenger, *The Computer Boys Take Over*, 14–15.
19. Ibid., 37.
20. Ibid., 39.
21. Ibid., 74.
22. Ibid., 238.
23. Ibid., 16.
24. Ibid., 69.
25. Ibid., 79.
26. Ibid., 137.
27. Ibid., 144.

28. Ibid., 231.
29. Ibid., 168.
30. Ibid., 239–40.
31. Griffin, 'The Place of the Bengali in Politics,' 812.
32. Ibid., 813.
33. Barrett, 'Why We Don't Hire .NET Programmers.'
34. Ibid.
35. Ibid.
36. Solnit, 'Diary.'
37. Ibid.
38. See Lacy, 'And You Thought SF Cabs Were Bad? BART Strike Is Crippling Fledgling Mid-Market Tech Corridor.'
39. Silver, 'In Silicon Valley, Technology Talent Gap Threatens G.O.P. Campaigns.'
40. Barbrook and Cameron, 'The Californian Ideology,' 44.
41. Ibid., 55.
42. Matyszczyk, 'Woz: Microsoft Might Be More Creative Than Apple.'
43. Torvalds, 'Re: Stable Linux 2.6.25.10'; Leonard, 'Let My Software Go!'; Raymond, 'Microsoft Tries to Recruit Me.'
44. Bailey, 'Dear Open Source Project Leader: Quit Being a Jerk.'
45. Alec Scott, email to author, November 29, 2012.
46. Brockmeier, 'How Casual Sexism Put Sqoot in the Hotseat.'
47. Bassett, 'Aligning India in the Cold War Era,' 786.
48. Bassett, 'MIT-Trained Swadeshis,' 215.
49. Ibid., 213.
50. Ibid., 215.
51. Ibid., 225.
52. Ibid., 227.
53. Ibid.
54. Ibid., 229–30.
55. Bassett, 'Aligning India in the Cold War Era,' 783.
56. Ibid., 791.
57. 'Immigrant Entrepreneurship Has Stalled for the First Time in Decades, Kauffman Foundation Study Shows.'
58. Khan, '40% of Startups in Silicon Valley Are Headed by India-Based Entrepreneurs.'
59. Stahl, 'Imported from India.'
60. Sivakumar, Dude, Did I Steal Your Job?, 33.
61. Mukherji, 'Student Suicides Soar 26% in 5 Years, Education System Blamed.'

62. Spectre, 'Twilio's Definitive Brogramming Primer.'
63. MacMillan, 'The Rise of the "Brogrammer".'
64. Scott, 'Lessons from Canada's Silicon Valley Diaspora.'
65. World Economic Forum, *Global Gender Gap Report*.
66. 'We believe that currently in most IT companies (IBM India, Accenture India, Infosys, Wipro, TCS, HCL, Cognizant, iGate, etc.), the percentage of women is also 30% at the lower level . . .' Alok Aggarwal (co-founder and chairman, Evalueserve), email to author, December 8, 2012; 'Household Data Annual Averages: Employed Persons by Detailed Occupation, Sex, Race, and Hispanic or Latino Ethnicity.'
67. Varma, 'Exposure, Training, and Environment,' 205; DuBow, 'NCWIT Scorecard: A Report on the Status of Women in Information Technology.'
68. Varma, 'Computing Self-Efficacy among Women in India,' 257.
69. Varma, 'Exposure, Training, and Environment,' 213.
70. Ibid., 215.
71. Ibid., 217.
72. Ibid., 219.
73. Ibid.
74. Alok Aggarwal (co-founder and chairman, Evalueserve), email to author, December 8, 2012.
75. Alok Aggarwal (co-founder and chairman, Evalueserve), email to author, February 15, 2013.
76. Varma, 'Exposure, Training, and Environment,' 219.
77. Fine, *Delusions of Gender*, 94.
78. Ibid., 181–82.
79. Sivakumar, *Dude, Did I Steal Your Job?*, 34.
80. Ibid., 140–46.
81. Ibid., 144.
82. Ibid., 141.
83. Wadhwa, 'The Face of Success, Part I: How the Indians Conquered Silicon Valley.'
84. See, for instance: Raj, 'Indian Mafia'; Warner, 'The Indians of Silicon Valley.'
85. Lanier, 'The Suburb That Changed the World.'

Chapter 5: The Code of Beauty: Anandavardhana

1. Ramanujan, *The Interior Landscape*, 74.
2. Ibid., 115.

3. Harpham, 'Aesthetics and the Fundamentals of Modernity,' 124–25.
4. See Leeming, *The Oxford Companion to World Mythology*.
5. Kiparsky, 'Paninian Linguistics,' 1.
6. 'Astadhyayi has two distinct bodies of sutras—the 14 Maheswara or pratyahara sutras of Sanskrit varnas, sounds, that are the primary building blocks of the Sanskrit language, that are enumerated before the sutrapatha begins. The sutrapatha has, according to the now ascertained authentic text (ed. by Pt. Narayana Mishra and published by Chowkhamba Varanasi) has 3976 sutras. Sometimes the 14 pratyahara sutras are conjoined to make the total 3990.' Kapil Kapoor, email to author, September 9, 2013.
7. Kiparsky, 'Paninian Linguistics,' 5.
8. See Matthews, *The Concise Oxford Dictionary of Linguistics*, 284.
9. Kiparsky, 'Paninian Linguistics,' 6.
10. Ibid., 7.
11. Panini, *Ashtadhyayi*, 47.
12. Kapoor, *Text and Interpretation: The Indian Tradition*, 74.
13. Joshi, 'Background of the Aṣṭādhyāyī,' 2.
14. Ganeri and Miri, 'Sanskrit Philosophical Commentary,' 193.
15. See Manjali, 'The "Social" and the "Cognitive" in Language: A Reading of Saussure, and Beyond.'
16. Emeneau, 'Bloomfield and Pānini,' 759.
17. Ibid., 758–59.
18. Bloomfield, *Linguistic Aspects of Science*, 2.
19. Kiparsky, 'Paninian Linguistics.'
20. Kiparsky, 'On the Architecture of Pāṇini's Grammar.'
21. Emeneau, 'India and Linguistics,' 150.
22. Ingerman, 'Panini-Backus Form Suggested,' 37.
23. Kelly, 'What Was Sanskrit For? Metadiscursive Strategies in Ancient India,' 103–04.
24. Pollock, *The Language of the Gods in the World of Men*, 50.
25. Houben, 'Sociolinguistic Attitudes Reflected in the Work of Bhartṛhari and Some Later Grammarians,' 169.
26. Muller-Ortega, *The Triadic Heart of Śiva*, 133.
27. Pollock, *The Language of the Gods in the World of Men*, 53.
28. Ibid., 54.
29. Ibid., 55–56.
30. Briggs, 'Knowledge Representation in Sanskrit and Artificial Intelligence,' 34.
31. Ibid., 36.

32. Ibid., 35–36.
33. Ibid., 39.
34. See Bhate and Kak, 'Panini's Grammar and Computer Science'; Staal, 'Context-Sensitive Rules in Pāṇini'; Subbanna and Varakhedi, 'Computational Structure of the Aṣṭādhyāyī and Conflict Resolution Techniques'; Saxena, Parul Saxena, and Pandey, 'Panini's Grammar in Computer Science.'
35. See 'Similarities between Sanskrit and Programming Languages'; 'Why Sanskrit Is Best Language for Computer?'
36. Jha and Mammaṭācārya, The Kāvyaprakāsha of Mammaṭa, 148–49.
37. Ingalls Sr, Masson, and Patwardhan, The Dhvanyaloka of Anandavardhana with the Locana of Abhinavagupta, 131.
38. Ibid., 130.
39. Ibid., 122.
40. Ibid., 113.
41. Translated from Anandavardhana's Dhvanyaloka (1.4 b) by Luther Obrock.
42. Translated from Anandavardhana's Dhvanyaloka (1.4 c) by Luther Obrock.
43. Translated from Anandavardhana's Dhvanyaloka (2.27 a) by Luther Obrock.
44. Bharata Muni and Rangacharya, The Nāṭyaśāstra, 55.
45. Translated from Anandavardhana's Dhvanyaloka (2.22 b) by Luther Obrock.
46. Ingalls Sr, Masson, and Patwardhan, The Dhvanyaloka of Anandavardhana with the Locana of Abhinavagupta, 312.
47. Translated from Anandavardhana's Dhvanyaloka (2.1 a) by Luther Obrock.
48. Ingalls Sr, Masson, and Patwardhan, The Dhvanyaloka of Anandavardhana with the Locana of Abhinavagupta, 204.
49. Ibid., 206.
50. Ibid., 105.
51. Hogan, 'Towards a Cognitive Science of Poetics: Anandavardhana, Abhinavagupta, and the Theory of Literature,' 164.
52. Ingalls Sr, Masson, and Patwardhan, The Dhvanyaloka of Anandavardhana with the Locana of Abhinavagupta, 546.
53. Ibid., 679.
54. Ibid., 714–15.
55. Ibid., 636.
56. Ibid.
57. Ibid., 641–42.
58. O'Connor, Mystery and Manners, 96.

Chapter 6: The Beauty of Code

1. Matsumoto, 'Treating Code as an Essay,' 478.
2. Ibid., 481.
3. Ibid., 477.
4. Purushothaman and Perry, 'Toward Understanding the Rhetoric of Small Source Code Changes,' 513; McPherson, Proffitt, and Hale-Evans, 'Estimating the Total Development Cost of a Linux Distribution.'
5. Knuth, 'All Questions Answered,' 320.
6. Foote and Yoder, 'Big Ball of Mud,' 653.
7. Paltrow and Carr, 'How the Pentagon's Payroll Quagmire Traps America's Soldiers.'
8. Ensmenger, The Computer Boys Take Over, 227.
9. 'The International Obfuscated C Code Contest.'
10. Ibid.
11. Scheffer, 'Programming in Malbolge.'
12. Hayes, 'Computing Science: The Semicolon Wars,' 299.
13. Dijkstra, 'How Do We Tell Truths That Might Hurt?', 14.
14. 'How SQLite Is Tested.'
15. 'Most Widely Deployed SQL Database Engine.'
16. Savoia, 'Beautiful Tests,' loc. 3010.
17. Bloch, 'Extra, Extra—Read All About It: Nearly All Binary Searches and Mergesorts Are Broken.'
18. Grimes, 'In His Own Words.'
19. Yegge, 'Foreword,' XVII–XVIII.
20. 'Hype Cycle Research Methodology.'
21. 'GitFaq—Git SCM Wiki.'
22. Wolfcore [pseud.], comment on 'Git Is Simpler Than You Think.'
23. 'Whatever Happened to Programming?'
24. Campbell, 'Where Does One Go to Find the Current "Good" Books to Read? (Or Blogs?)'
25. Ensmenger, The Computer Boys Take Over, 88.
26. Kwak, 'The Importance of Excel.'
27. Ibid.
28. Ibid.; Schlesinger, 'JPMorgan Chase Earnings: "London Whale" Cost $5.8 Billion.'
29. Oliver, 'Why I Still Love CQRS (and Messaging and Event Sourcing).'
30. Ibid.

31. Zihotki, 'Raven & Event sourcing.'
32. Chakrabarti, 'Arguing from Synthesis to the Self: Utpaldeva and Abhinavagupta Respond to Buddhist No-Selfism,' 203.
33. Ibid., 209.
34. Ibid., 211.

Chapter 7: The Code of Beauty: Abhinavagupta

1. Gnoli and Abhinavagupta, *The Aesthetic Experience According to Abhinavagupta*, 55.
2. Ibid., 54–55.
3. Ibid., 64.
4. Ibid., 64–65.
5. Ibid., 66.
6. Ibid., 113.
7. Ibid., 61.
8. Ibid., 81.
9. Ibid., XXXVI.
10. Ibid., 117.
11. Ingalls Sr, Masson, and Patwardhan, *The Dhvanyaloka of Anandavardhana with the Locana of Abhinavagupta*, 118.
12. Gnoli and Abhinavagupta, *The Aesthetic Experience According to Abhinavagupta*, XXXVI.
13. Ibid., 48.
14. Pandit, 'Dhvani and the "Full World",' 143.
15. Ibid.
16. Ibid., 148.
17. Ingalls Sr, Masson, and Patwardhan, *The Dhvanyaloka of Anandavardhana with the Locana of Abhinavagupta*, 70.
18. Masson and Patwardhan, *Aesthetic Rapture*, 10.
19. Ingalls Sr, Masson, and Patwardhan, *The Dhvanyaloka of Anandavardhana with the Locana of Abhinavagupta*, 192.
20. Ibid., 43.
21. Gnoli and Abhinavagupta, *The Aesthetic Experience According to Abhinavagupta*, 106.
22. McCrea, *The Teleology of Poetics in Medieval Kashmir*, 395.
23. Ibid., 395–96.
24. Ibid., 216–17.
25. Ingalls Sr, Masson, and Patwardhan, *The Dhvanyaloka of Anandavardhana with*

the Locana of *Abhinavagupta*, 671.

26. Ibid., 680–81.
27. Ibid., 681–82.
28. Gnoli and Abhinavagupta, *The Aesthetic Experience According to Abhinavagupta*, 59.
29. Ibid., 102.
30. Ingalls Sr, Masson, and Patwardhan, *The Dhvanyaloka of Anandavardhana with the Locana of Abhinavagupta*, 226.
31. Ibid., 592.
32. Ibid., 71.
33. Ibid., 193.
34. Ibid., 500, 505.
35. Ibid., 503–04.
36. Translated from Anandavardhana's *Dhvanyaloka* (3.20 e) by Luther Obrock.
37. Douglas, *Thinking in Circles*, loc. 403.
38. Ibid., loc. 43.
39. Ibid., loc. 57.
40. Witzel, 'On the Origin of the Literary Device of the Frame Story in Old Indian Literature,' 411.
41. Shulman, 'The Buzz of God and the Click of Delight,' 56.
42. Ibid., 58.
43. See Kapoor, *Dimensions of Pāṇini Grammar: The Indian Grammatical System*, 193.
44. Ingalls Sr, Masson, and Patwardhan, *The Dhvanyaloka of Anandavardhana with the Locana of Abhinavagupta*, 437.

Chapter 8: Mythologies and Histories

1. Gupta, Hoens, and Goudriaan, *Hindu Tantrism*, 6.
2. White, 'Introduction: Tantra in Practice: Mapping a Tradition,' 7.
3. Urban, *The Power of Tantra*, loc. 322–25.
4. Ibid., loc. 1091.
5. Ibid., loc. 1274.
6. Ibid., loc. 182–85.
7. Wezler, 'Do You Speak Sanskrit? On a Class of Sanskrit Texts Composed in the Late Middle Ages,' 331.
8. Freely adapted from Feuerstein, *Tantra*, loc. 3682.
9. Urban, *The Power of Tantra*, 1219.
10. Davidson, *Indian Esoteric Buddhism*, 179.
11. See Sanderson, 'Śaivism and the Tantric Traditions.'

12. Pomeda, The Heart of Recognition: A Translation and Study of Kṣemarāja's Pratyabhijñāhṛdayam, 46.

13. Dehejia, The Advaita of Art, 129.

14. Ibid.

15. Ratié, 'Remarks on Compassion and Altruism in the Pratyabhijñā Philosophy,' 350.

16. Ibid.

17. Muller-Ortega, The Triadic Heart of Śiva, 61–62.

18. Ratié, 'Remarks on Compassion and Altruism in the Pratyabhijñā Philosophy,' 361–62.

19. Sanderson, 'Śaivism and the Tantric Traditions,' 696.

20. Ratié, 'Otherness in the Pratyabhijñā Philosophy,' 363–64.

21. Wallis, 'The Descent of Power: Possession, Mysticism, and Initiation in the Śaiva Theology of Abhinavagupta,' 253–54.

22. Urban, The Economics of Ecstasy, loc. 1008.

23. Translated from the Bhaver Gita with the help of Dilip Misra, Rakesh Mishra, and Monidipa Mondal.

24. Urban, The Economics of Ecstasy, loc. 1351.

25. Ibid., 863.

26. Ibid., 579.

27. Sanderson, 'Purity and Power among the Brahmans of Kashmir,' 193.

28. Tharu and Lalita, Women Writing in India, 68.

29. Parashar and Rājaśekhara, Kāvyamīmāṃsā of Rājaśekhara, 157.

30. Tharu and Lalita, Women Writing in India, xviii.

31. Ibid., xx.

32. Ibid., 6.

33. Ibid., 116.

34. Urban, The Power of Tantra, loc.254; Urban, The Economics of Ecstasy, loc.556.

35. Tharu and Lalita, Women Writing in India, 8.

36. Ibid., 2.

37. Ibid., 145

38. Ibid., 3.

39. Ibid.

40. Ibid., 5–6.

41. Ibid., 6.

42. Wujastyk, 'Indian Manuscripts,'1–2.

43. Ibid.

44. Dominik Wujastyk, email to author, December 19, 2012.

45. Wujastyk, 'Indian Manuscripts,' 2.

46. Dominik Wujastyk, email to author, December 13, 2012.
47. Wujastyk, 'Indian Manuscripts,' 3.
48. Copyright © 1998 by Andrew Schelling. Reprinted with the permission of City Lights Books. Schelling, *The Cane Groves of Narmada River*, 48.
49. Ibid., 149.
50. Ibid.
51. Rotter, 'Gender Relations, Foreign Relations: The United States and South Asia, 1947-1964,' 523.
52. Ibid., 527.
53. Conrad, *Heart of Darkness and Selections from the Congo Diary*, loc. 1881, 2028, 1886.
54. Ibid., loc. 1011, 1454.
55. Gleick, *The Information*, 418.
56. Ibid., 436.
57. Ibid., 217.

Chapter 9: The Language of Literature

1. Translated from Anandavardhana's *Dhvanyaloka* (3.41 a) by Luther Obrock.
2. Bronner and Shulman, '"A Cloud Turned Goose": Sanskrit in the Vernacular Millennium,' 28–29.
3. Pollock, 'The Death of Sanskrit,' 394.
4. Dalmia, 'Sanskrit Scholars and Pandits of the Old School,' 334.
5. See Srinivas, 'Amarabhāratī: Sanskrit and the Resurgence of Indian Civilization,' 41–42.
6. Kapoor and Ratnam, *Literary Theory: Indian Conceptual Framework*, 1.
7. Ramaswamy, 'Sanskrit for the Nation,' 334–35.
8. Ibid., 373.
9. Pollock, 'The Cosmopolitan Vernacular,' 29.
10. Merwin, *East Window: The Asian Translations*, 36.
11. Eliot, *The Sacred Wood and Major Early Essays*, 58.
12. Eliot, *After Strange Gods*, 43–44.
13. Sanderson, 'Śaivism and the Tantric Traditions,' 675.
14. Christiansen, 'Computers.'
15. Pipher, *Writing to Change the World*, 81.
16. Tedd, 'Hours of Hell and Anguish,' 95.
17. Ibid., 97.
18. West, *Conversations with William Styron*, 9.
19. Review, *The Paris Review Interviews, III*, 22.

20. Ingersoll and Ingersoll, *Conversations with Anthony Burgess*, 73.
21. Fisher, *The Writer's Quotebook*, 18.
22. Acocella, 'Blocked: Why Do Writers Stop Writing?', 129.
23. Leeds, *The Enduring Vision of Norman Mailer*, 132.
24. Cowley, *And I Worked at the Writer's Trade*, 191.
25. Tedd, 'Hours of Hell and Anguish,' 99.
26. Ingalls Sr, Masson, and Patwardhan, *The* Dhvanyaloka of *Anandavardhana* with the Locana of *Abhinavagupta*, 120.
27. Matilal, 'Vakroti and Dhvani: Controversies about the Theory of Poetry in the Indian Tradition,' 381.
28. Parashar and Rājaśekhara, *Kāvyamīmāṃsā of Rājaśekhara*, 149.
29. Gnoli and Abhinavagupta, *The Aesthetic Experience According to Abhinavagupta*, XLIX.
30. Muller-Ortega, *The Triadic Heart of Śiva*, 46.

Chapter 10: Application.Restart()

1. Muller-Ortega, 'Seal of Sambhu,' 574.
2. 'Fwd: Amar Chitra Katha Comics in Samskritam: Participate in Readership Survey—Google Groups.'
3. Singh, 'New Life, Old Death for Sanskrit in Uttarakhand.'
4. Toole, *Ada, the Enchantress of Numbers*, loc. 2867–870.
5. Turing, 'On Computable Numbers, with an Application to the Entscheidungsproblem (1936).'
6. Toole, *Ada, the Enchantress of Numbers*, loc. 2131–133.
7. Gleick, *The Information*, loc. 2048–052.
8. Cabanne, *Dialogues with Marcel Duchamp*, 18–19.
9. Fishwick, 'Aesthetic Computing.'
10. Hessel, Goodman, and Kotler, 'Hacking the President's DNA.'
11. Kotler, 'Synthetic Biology for Dummies, Investors or Both . . .'; Carlson, 'The Pace and Proliferation of Biological Technologies.'
12. 'iGEM 2012 HS Is Officially Over!'
13. 'Team: Heidelberg LSL.'
14. Swain, 'Glowing Trees Could Light Up City Streets,' 21.
15. Brown, 'Stanford Team Turns DNA into a Hard Drive.'
16. Church and Regis, *Regenesis*, 7.
17. Ibid., 248–49.
18. Pollock, 'What Was Bhaṭṭa Nāyaka Saying?,' 154.
19. Skora, 'The Pulsating Heart and Its Divine Sense Energies,' 445–46.

20. Flood, 'The Purification of the Body,' 518–19.
21. Skora, 'Abhinavagupta's Erotic Mysticism: The Reconciliation of Spirit and Flesh,' 76.
22. Reprinted with the permission of P.N. Furbank. 'Messages from the Unseen World,' The Turing Digital Archive, King's College, University of Cambridge.
23. Cabanne, *Dialogues with Marcel Duchamp*, 98.

Acocella, Joan. 'Blocked: Why Do Writers Stop Writing?' *New Yorker* 80, no. 16 (2004): 80–129.

Bailey, Derick. 'Dear Open Source Project Leader: Quit Being a Jerk.' LosTechies.com, December 14, 2012. http://lostechies.com/derickbailey/ 2012/12/14/dear-open-source-project-leader-quit-being-a-jerk/.

Barbrook, Richard, and Andy Cameron. 'The Californian Ideology.' *Science as Culture* 6, no. 1 (1996): 44–72.

Barrett, David. 'Why We Don't Hire .NET Programmers.' Expensify (blog), March 25, 2011. http://blog.expensify.com/2011/03/25/ceo-friday-why-we-dont-hire-net-programmers/.

Bassett, Ross. 'Aligning India in the Cold War Era: Indian Technical Elites, the Indian Institute of Technology at Kanpur, and Computing in India and the United States.' *Technology and Culture* 50, no. 4 (2009): 783–810.

———. 'MIT-Trained Swadeshis: MIT and Indian Nationalism, 1880–1947.' *Osiris* 24, no. 1 (2009): 212–30.

Bharata Muni, and Adya Rangacharya. *The Nāṭyaśāstra: English Translation with Critical Notes*. Rev. ed. New Delhi: Munshiram Manoharlal Publishers, 1996.

Bhate, Saroja, and Subhash Kak. 'Panini's Grammar and Computer Science.' *Annals of the Bhandarkar Oriental Research Institute* 72 (1993): 79–94.

Bloch, Joshua. 'Extra, Extra—Read All About It: Nearly All Binary Searches and Mergesorts Are Broken.' Google Research Blog, June 2, 2006. http:// googleresearch.blogspot.com/2006/06/extra-extra-read-all-about-it-nearly.html.

Bloomfield, Leonard. *Linguistic Aspects of Science*. In *International Encyclopedia of Unified Science* 1:4. Chicago: University of Chicago Press, 1939.

Briggs, Rick. 'Knowledge Representation in Sanskrit and Artificial Intelligence.' *AI Magazine* 6, no. 1 (1985): 32–39.

Brockmeier, Joe. 'How Casual Sexism Put Sqoot in the Hotseat.' ReadWrite (blog), March 20, 2012. http://readwrite.com/2012/ 03/20/ how-casual-sexism-put-sqoot-in.

Bronner, Yigal, and David Shulman. '"A Cloud Turned Goose": Sanskrit in the Vernacular Millennium.' *Indian Economic & Social History Review* 43, no. 1 (March 1, 2006): 1–30. doi:10.1177/001946460504300101.

Brown, Eryn. 'Stanford Team Turns DNA into a Hard Drive.' *Los Angeles Times*, May 26, 2012. http://articles.latimes.com/2012/may/26/science/la-sci-synthetic-biology-q-a-20120526.

Cabanne, Pierre. *Dialogues With Marcel Duchamp*. Reprint, Boston, MA: Da Capo Press, 1987.

Campbell, Michael. 'Where Does One Go to Find the Current "Good" Books to Read? (Or Blogs?)' Programmers.stackexchange.com, August 25, 2011. http://programmers.stackexchange.com/questions/103619/where-does-one-go-to-find-the-current-good-books-to-read-or-blogs.

Carlson, Ron. 'The Pace and Proliferation of Biological Technologies.' *Biosecurity and Bioterrorism: Biodefense Strategy, Practice, and Science* 1, no. 3 (2003): 203–14.

Ceglowski, Maciej. 'Dabblers and Blowhards.' Idle Words (blog), April 4, 2006. http://www.idlewords.com/2005/04/dabblers_and_blowhards.htm.

Chakrabarti, Arindam. 'Arguing from Synthesis to the Self: Utpaldeva and Abhinavagupta Respond to Buddhist No-Selfism.' In *Hindu and Buddhist Ideas in Dialogue: Self and No-Self*, edited by Irina Kuznetsova, Jonardon Ganeri, and Arindam Chakrabarti, 199–215. Surrey: Ashgate, 2012.

Christiansen, Tom. 'Computers.' Wikiquote.com. Accessed February 3, 2013. http://en.wikiquote.org/wiki/Computers.

Church, George M., and Ed Regis. *Regenesis: How Synthetic Biology Will Reinvent Nature and Ourselves*. New York: Basic Books, 2012.

'Computer Scientists Build Computer Using Swarms of Crabs.' The Physics arXiv Blog, April 12, 2012. http://www.technologyreview.com/view/427494/computer-scientists-build-computer-using-swarms-of-crabs/.

Conrad, Joseph. *Heart of Darkness and Selections from the Congo Diary (Modern Library Classics)*. Edited by Caryl Phillips. New York: Modern Library, 2000. Kindle edition.

Cowley, Malcolm. *And I Worked at the Writer's Trade: Chapters of Literary History, 1918-1978*. New York: Viking, 1978.

Dalmia, Vasudha. 'Sanskrit Scholars and Pandits of the Old School: The Benares Sanskrit College and the Constitution of Authority in the Late Nineteenth Century.' *Journal of Indian Philosophy* 24, no. 4 (1996): 321–37.

Davidson, Ronald M. *Indian Esoteric Buddhism: A Social History of the Tantric Movement*. New York: Columbia University Press, 2002.

Dehejia, Harsha V. *The Advaita of Art*. Delhi: Motilal Banarsidass Publishers, 1996.

DFectuoso [pseud.]. 'Solo Development—Are There Any Famous One-Man-Army Programmers?' Programmers.stackoverflow.com, February 9, 2009. http://programmers.stackexchange.com/questions/47197/are-there-any-famous-one-man-army-programmers.

Dijkstra, E.W. 'How Do We Tell Truths That Might Hurt?' *ACM SIGPLAN Notices* 17, no. 5 (1982): 13–15.

Douglas, Mary. *Thinking in Circles: An Essay on Ring Composition*. New Haven, CT: Yale University Press, 2007.

DuBow, W. 'NCWIT Scorecard: A Report on the Status of Women in Information Technology.' Boulder, CO: NCWIT, 2009.

Eliot, T.S. *After Strange Gods: A Primer of Modern Heresy*. London: Faber and Faber, 1934.

———. *The Sacred Wood and Major Early Essays*. Mineola, NY: Dover Publications, 1997.

Emeneau, Murray B. 'Bloomfield and Pāṇini.' *Language* 64, no. 4 (1988): 755–60.

———. 'India and Linguistics.' *Journal of the American Oriental Society* 75, no. 3 (1955): 145–53.

Ensmenger, Nathan L. *The Computer Boys Take Over: Computers, Programmers, and the Politics of Technical Expertise*. Cambridge, MA: The MIT Press, 2010.

Feuerstein, Georg. *Tantra: The Path of Ecstasy*. Boston: Shambhala, 1998. Distributed in the USA by Random House.

Fine, Cordelia. *Delusions of Gender: How Our Minds, Society, and Neurosexism Create Difference*. Reprint, New York: Norton, 2011.

Fisher, Jim, ed. *The Writer's Quotebook: 500 Authors on Creativity, Craft, and the Writing Life*. New Brunswick, NJ: Rutgers University Press, 2006.

Fishwick, Paul A. 'Aesthetic Computing.' In *The Encyclopedia of Human-Computer Interaction*, 2nd ed., edited by Mads Soegaard and Rikke Friis Dam. Aarhus, Denmark: The Interaction Design Foundation, 2013. http://www.interaction-design.org/encyclopedia/aesthetic_computing.html.

Flood, Gavin. 'The Purification of the Body.' In *Tantra in Practice*, edited by David Gordon White. Princeton: Princeton University Press, 2000.

Foote, B., and J. Yoder. 'Big Ball of Mud.' *Pattern Languages of Program Design* 4 (1997): 654–92.

'Fwd: Amar Chitra Katha Comics in Samskritam: Participate in Readership Survey—Google Groups.' Accessed August 21, 2013. https://groups.google.com/forum/#!topic/samskrita/iQRm52cp0Aw.

Ganeri, Jonardon, and M. Miri. 'Sanskrit Philosophical Commentary.' *Journal of the Indian Council of Philosophical Research* 25, no. 1 (2010): 186–207.

Ganssle, Jack. 'Microprocessors Change the World.' Embedded.com, November 30, 2011. http://www.embedded.com/electronics-blogs/break-points/4231029/Microprocessors-change-the-world.

'Git Is Simpler Than You Think.' Reddit.com, September 7, 2011. http://

www.reddit.com/r/programming/comments/k7qvj/git_is_simpler_
than_you_think/.

'GitFaq—Git SCM Wiki.' Git.wiki.kernel.org. Accessed February 3, 2013. https://
git.wiki.kernel.org/index.php/GitFaq#Why_the_.27git.27_name.3F.

Gleick, James. *The Information: A History, a Theory, a Flood.* New York: Vintage, 2011.

Gnoli, Raniero, and Abhinavagupta. *The Aesthetic Experience According to Abhinavagupta.*
Varanasi: Chowkhamba Sanskrit Series Office, 1968.

Graham, Paul. 'Design and Research.' January 2003. http://www.paulgraham.
com/desres.html.

———. 'Hackers and Painters.' May 2003. http://www.paulgraham.com/
hp.html.

Griffin, Lepel. 'The Place of the Bengali in Politics.' *The Fortnightly* 57 (1892):
811–19.

Grimes, Roger A. 'In His Own Words: Confessions of a Cyber Warrior.'
InfoWorld.com, July 9, 2013. http://www.infoworld.com/d/security/
in-his-own-words-confessions-of-cyber-warrior-222266.

Gupta, Sanjukta, Dirk Jan Hoens, and Teun Goudriaan. *Hindu Tantrism.* Vol. 2.
4. Leiden: Brill, 1979.

Harpham, Geoffrey Galt. 'Aesthetics and the Fundamentals of Modernity.' In
Aesthetics and Ideology, edited by George Levine, 124–53. New Brunswick,
NJ: Rutgers University Press, 1994.

Hayes, B. 'Computing Science: The Semicolon Wars.' *American Scientist* (2006):
299–303.

Hessel, A., M. Goodman, and S. Kotler. 'Hacking the President's DNA.' *Atlantic,*
November 2012. http://www.theatlantic.com/magazine/archive/
2012/11/hacking-the-presidents-dna/309147/?single_page=true.

Hodges, Andrew. *Alan Turing: The Enigma.* New York: Walker, 2000. Kindle edition.

Hogan, Patrick Colm. 'Towards a Cognitive Science of Poetics: Anandavardhana,
Abhinavagupta, and the Theory of Literature.' *College Literature* 23.1
(February 1996): 164–79.

Houben, Jan E.M. 'Sociolinguistic Attitudes Reflected in the Work of
Bhartṛhari and Some Later Grammarians.' In *Ideology and Status of Sanskrit:
Contributions to the History of the Sanskrit Language,* 157–93. Leiden: Brill, 1996.

'Household Data Annual Averages: Employed Persons by Detailed Occupation,
Sex, Race, and Hispanic or Latino Ethnicity.' Bureau of Labor Statistics,
United States Department of Labor, 2012. http://www.bls.gov/opub/
ee/2013/cps/annavg11_2012.pdf.

'How SQLite Is Tested.' Sqlite.org. Accessed February 3, 2013. http://www.
sqlite.org/testing.html.

'Hype Cycle Research Methodology.' Gartner.com. Accessed February 3, 2013. http://www.gartner.com/technology/research/methodologies/hype-cycle.jsp.

'iGEM 2012 HS Is Officially Over!' Igem.org. Accessed February 3, 2013. http://2012hs.igem.org/Main_Page.

'The IBM 650 Magnetic Drum Calculator.' Columbia University Computing History. Accessed August 27, 2013. http://www.columbia.edu/cu/computinghistory/650.html.

'Immigrant Entrepreneurship Has Stalled for the First Time in Decades, Kauffman Foundation Study Shows.' Kauffman.org, October 2, 2012. http://www.kauffman.org/newsroom/immigrant-entrepreneurship-has-stalled-for-the-first-time-in-decades-kauffman-foundation-study-shows.aspx.

Ingalls Sr, Daniel H.H., Jeffrey Moussaieff Masson, and M.V. Patwardhan, trans. The Dhvanyaloka of Anandavardhana with the Locana of Abhinavagupta. Cambridge, MA: Harvard University Press, 1990.

Ingerman, Peter Zilahy. 'Panini-Backus Form Suggested.' Commun. ACM 10, no. 3 (March 1967): 137–38, 48. doi:10.1145/363162.363165.

Ingersoll, Earl G., and Mary C. Ingersoll, eds. Conversations with Anthony Burgess. Jackson, MS: University Press of Mississippi, 2008.

Jcoll [pseud.]. 'For Most of You, This Is Surely Child Play, but Holy Shit, This Must Be What It Feels Like to Do Heroin for the First Time.' Reddit.com, July 20, 2011. http://www.reddit.com/r/programming/comments/iv4e0/for_most_of_you_this_is_surely_child_play_but.

Jha, Ganganatha, and Mammaṭācārya. The Kāvyaprakāsha of Mammaṭa. Varanasi: Bharatiya Vidya Prakashan, 1995.

Jong89 [pseud.]. 'Razorlength—1036 Early Winter by Jong89.' Dwarf Fortress Map Archive, 2009. http://mkv25.net/dfma/poi-22127-dwarvencomputer.

Joshi, S.D. 'Background of the Aṣṭādhyāyī.' In Sanskrit Computational Linguistics, 1–5. Springer, 2009. http://link.springer.com/chapter/10.1007/978-3-540-93885-9_1.

Kapoor, Kapil. Dimensions of Pāṇini Grammar: The Indian Grammatical System. New Delhi: D.K. Printworld, 2005.

———. Text and Interpretation: The Indian Tradition. New Delhi: D.K. Printworld, 2005.

Kapoor, Kapil and Nalini M. Ratnam. Literary Theory: Indian Conceptual Framework. New Delhi: Affiliated East-West Press, 1998.

Kelly, John D. 'What Was Sanskrit For? Metadiscursive Strategies in Ancient India.' In Ideology and Status of Sanskrit: Contributions to the History of the Sanskrit

Language, edited by Jan E.M. Houben, 87–107. Leiden: Brill, 1996.

Khan, Taslima. '40% of Startups in Silicon Valley Are Headed by India-Based Entrepreneurs.' *Business Today*, March 21, 2013. http://businesstoday.intoday. in/story/google-executive-chairman-eric-schmidt-on-india/1/193496.html.

Kiparsky, Paul. 'On the Architecture of Pāṇini's Grammar.' In *Sanskrit Computational Linguistics*, 33–94. Springer, 2009. http://link.springer.com/ chapter/10.1007/978-3-642-00155-0_2.

———. 'Paninian Linguistics.' *The Encyclopedia of Language and Linguistics* 6 (1995): 59–65.

Knuth, Donald E. 'All Questions Answered.' *Notices of the AMS* 49, no. 3 (2002): 318–24.

———. 'Literate Programming.' *The Computer Journal* 27, no. 2 (January 1, 1984): 97–111. doi:10.1093/comjnl/27.2.97.

Kotler, Steven. 'Synthetic Biology for Dummies, Investors or Both . . .' Forbes.com, November 8, 2012. http://www.forbes.com/sites/stevenkotler/ 2012/11/08/synthetic-biology-for-dummies-investors-or-both/.

Kwak, James. 'The Importance of Excel.' The Baseline Scenario (blog), February 9, 2013. http://baselinescenario.com/2013/02/09/the-importance- of-excel/#.

Lacy, Sarah. 'And You Thought SF Cabs Were Bad? BART Strike Is Crippling Fledgling Mid-market Tech Corridor.' PandoDaily (blog), July 2, 2013. http://pandodaily.com/2013/07/02/and-you-thought-sf-cabs-were- bad-bart-strike-is-crippling-fledgling-mid-market-tech-corridor/.

Lampson, Butler W. 'Guest Editorial.' *Software: Practice and Experience* 2, no. 3 (1972): 195–196.

Lanier, Jaron. 'The Suburb That Changed the World.' *New Statesman*, August 18, 2011. http://www.newstatesman.com/scitech/2011/08/silicon- valley-computer.

Leeds, Barry H. *The Enduring Vision of Norman Mailer*. Bainbridge, WA: Pleasure Boat Studio, 2002.

Leeming, David. *The Oxford Companion to World Mythology*. New York: Oxford University Press, 2005.

Leonard, Andrew. 'Let My Software Go!' Salon.com, March 30, 1998. http:// www.salon.com/1998/03/30/feature947788266/.

Lippert, Eric. 'Cargo Cultists, Part Three: Is Mort a Cargo Cultist?' Eric Lippert's Blog: Fabulous Adventures in Coding, March 2, 2004. http://blogs.msdn. com/b/ericlippert/archive/2004/03/02/cargo-cultists-part-three-is- mort-a-cargo-cultist.aspx.

Livingston, Jessica. *Founders at Work: Stories of Startups' Early Days*. Berkeley: Apress,

2008.

MacMillan, Douglas. 'The Rise of the "Brogrammer".' *Businessweek*, March 1, 2012. http://www.businessweek.com/articles/2012-03-01/the-rise-of-the-brogrammer.

Manjali, Franson. 'The "Social" and the "Cognitive" in Language: A Reading of Saussure, and Beyond.' Hal.archives-ouvertes.fr/, 2012. http://hal.archivesouvertes.fr/halshs-00724036/.

Masson, Jeffrey Moussaieff, and M.V. Patwardhan. *Aesthetic Rapture: The Rasādhyāya of the Nāṭyaśāstra.* Poona: Deccan College, Postgraduate and Research Institute, 1970.

Mataes, M., and N. Montfort. 'A Box, Darkly: Obfuscation, Weird Languages, and Code Aesthetics.' In *Proceedings of the 6th Digital Arts and Culture Conference, IT University of Copenhagen* (2005): 144–53.

Matilal, Bimal Krishna. 'Vakroti and Dhvani: Controversies about the Theory of Poetry in the Indian Tradition.' In *Abhinavagupta: Reconsiderations*, edited by Makarand Paranjape and Sunthar Visuvalingam, 372–81. New Delhi: Samvad, 2012.

Matsumoto, Yukihiro. 'Treating Code as an Essay.' In *Beautiful Code: Leading Programmers Explain How They Think*, edited by Andy Oram and Greg Wilson, loc. 13832–6127. Sebastopol, CA: O'Reilly Media, 2007. Kindle edition.

Matthews, Peter Hugoe. *The Concise Oxford Dictionary of Linguistics*. 2nd ed. Oxford: Oxford University Press, 2007.

Matyszczyk, Chris. 'Woz: Microsoft Might Be More Creative Than Apple.' Technically Incorrect—CNET News, November 15, 2012. http://news.cnet.com/8301-17852_3-57550839-71/woz-microsoft-might-be-more-creative-than-apple/.

McCrea, Lawrence J. *The Teleology of Poetics in Medieval Kashmir*. Cambridge, MA: Harvard University, Department of Sanskrit and Indian Studies, 2008.

McPherson, Amanda, Brian Proffitt, and Ron Hale-Evans. 'Estimating the Total Development Cost of a Linux Distribution.' Linuxfoundation.org, September 2008. http://www.linuxfoundation.org/sites/main/files/publications/estimatinglinux.html.

Merwin, William Stanley. *East Window: The Asian Translations*. Port Townsend: Copper Canyon Press, 1998.

'Most Widely Deployed SQL Database Engine.' Sqlite.org. Accessed February 3, 2013. http://www.sqlite.org/mostdeployed.html.

Mukherji, Anahita. 'Student Suicides Soar 26% in 5 Years, Education System Blamed.' *Times of India*, November 2, 2011. http://articles.timesofindia.

indiatimes.com/2011-11-02/india/30349474_1_student-suicides-education-system-higher-education.

Muller-Ortega, Paul Eduardo. 'Seal of Sambhu.' In *Tantra in Practice*, edited by David Gordon White. Princeton: Princeton University Press, 2000.

———. *The Triadic Heart of Śiva: Kaula Tantricism of Abhinavagupta in the Non-dual Shaivism of Kashmir*. New York: State University of New York Press, 1988.

Nather, Ed. 'The Story of Mel.' May 21, 1983. http://www.cs.utah.edu/%7Eelb/folklore/mel.html.

O'Connor, Flannery. *Mystery and Manners: Occasional Prose*. Edited by Sally Fitzgerald and Robert Fitzgerald. New York: Farrar, Straus and Giroux, 1970.

Oliver, Jonathan. 'Why I Still Love CQRS (and Messaging and Event Sourcing).' Jonathan Oliver (blog), May 9, 2011. http://blog.jonathanoliver.com/2011/05/why-i-still-love-cqrs-and-messaging-and-event-sourcing/.

Oram, Andy, and Greg Wilson, eds. *Beautiful Code: Leading Programmers Explain How They Think*. Sebastopol, CA: O'Reilly Media, 2007. Kindle edition.

Paltrow, Scot J., and Kelly Carr. 'How the Pentagon's Payroll Quagmire Traps America's Soldiers.' Reuters, July 9, 2013. http://www.reuters.com/article/2013/07/09/us-usa-pentagon-payerrors-special-report-idUSBRE96818I20130709.

Pandit, Lalita. 'Dhvani and the "Full Word": Suggestion and Signification from Abhinavagupta to Jacques Lacan.' *College Literature* 23, no. 1 (1996): 142–63.

Panini. *Ashtadhyayi*. Vedic Literature Collection. Fairfield, IA: Maharishi University of Management, n.d.

Parashar, Sadhana, and Rājaśekhara. *Kāvyamīmāṃsā of Rājaśekhara: Original Text in Sanskrit and Translation with Explanatory Notes*. New Delhi: D.K. Printworld, 2000.

The Paris Review. *The Paris Review Interviews, III*. New York: Picador, 2008.

Petzold, Charles. *Code: The Hidden Language of Computer Hardware and Software*. N.p.: Microsoft Press, 2009.

Pipher, Mary. *Writing to Change the World*. New York: Riverhead Trade, 2007.

Pollock, Sheldon. 'The Cosmopolitan Vernacular.' *The Journal of Asian Studies* 57, no. 1 (February 1998): 6–37. doi:10.2307/2659022.

———. 'The Death of Sanskrit.' *Comparative Studies in Society and History* 43, no. 2 (2001): 392–426.

———. *The Language of the Gods in the World of Men: Sanskrit, Culture, and Power in Premodern India*. Berkeley: University of California Press, 2006.

———. 'What Was Bhaṭṭa Nāyaka Saying? The Hermeneutical Transformation of Indian Aesthetics.' *Epic and Argument in Sanskrit Literary History*. New Delhi: Manohar, 2010.

Pomeda, Carlos Gómez. *The Heart of Recognition: A Translation and Study of Kṣemarāja's*

Pratyabhijñāhṛdayam. Berkeley: University of California, 2001.

'Programming the ENIAC.' *Columbia University Computing History: A Chronology of Computing at Columbia University.* Last updated April 2, 2012. http://www.columbia.edu/cu/computinghistory/index.html

Purushothaman, Ranjith, and Dewayne E. Perry. 'Toward Understanding the Rhetoric of Small Source Code Changes.' *IEEE Transactions on Software Engineering* 31, no. 6 (2005): 511–26.

Raj, Ritu. 'Indian Mafia.' Medium (blog), February 17, 2013. https://medium.com/behind-the-scene-silicon-valley/7051c3f5e37c.

Ramanujan, A.K., trans. *The Interior Landscape: Love Poems from a Classical Tamil Anthology.* New York: Oxford University Press, 1994.

Ramaswamy, Sumathi. 'Sanskrit for the Nation.' *Modern Asian Studies* 33, no. 2 (1999): 339–81.

Ratié, Isabelle. 'Otherness in the Pratyabhijñā Philosophy.' *Journal of Indian Philosophy* 35, no. 4 (September 2, 2007): 313–70. doi:10.1007/s10781-007-9017-5.

———. 'Remarks on Compassion and Altruism in the Pratyabhijñā Philosophy.' *Journal of Indian Philosophy* 37, no. 4 (February 14, 2009): 349–66. doi:10.1007/s10781-009-9066-z.

Raymond, Eric S. 'Microsoft Tries to Recruit Me.' Armed and Dangerous (blog), September 8, 2005. http://esr.ibiblio.org/?p=208.

Rob P. 'How Do Computers Work?' Programmers.stackoverflow.com, June 5, 2011. http://programmers.stackexchange.com/questions/81624/how-do-computers-work.

Rosenberg, Scott. *Dreaming in Code: Two Dozen Programmers, Three Years, 4,732 Bugs, and One Quest for Transcendent Software.* New York: Three Rivers Press, 2008.

Rotter, Andrew J. 'Gender Relations, Foreign Relations: The United States and South Asia, 1947-1964.' *The Journal of American History* 81, no. 2 (1994): 518–42.

Sanderson, Alexis. 'Purity and Power among the Brahmans of Kashmir.' *The Category of the Person: Anthropology, Philosophy, History* (1985): 190–216.

———. 'Śaivism and the Tantric Traditions.' *The World's Religions* (1988): 660–704.

Saxena, Vinay, Parul Saxena, and Kuldeep Pandey. 'Panini's Grammar in Computer Science.' *Recent Research in Science and Technology* 3, no. 7 (2011): 109–11.

Savoia, Alberto. 'Beautiful Tests.' In *Beautiful Code: Leading Programmers Explain How They Think*, edited by Andy Oram and Greg Wilson, loc. 2958–3491. Sebastopol, CA: O'Reilly Media, 2007. Kindle edition.

Scheffer, Lou. 'Programming in Malbolge.' Accessed June 11, 2013. http://www.lscheffer.com/malbolge.shtml.

Schelling, Andrew. *The Cane Groves of Narmada River: Erotic Poems from Old India.* San Francisco: City Lights Books, 1998.

Schlesinger, Jill. 'JPMorgan Chase Earnings: "London Whale" Cost $5.8 Billion.' CBS Money Watch, July 13, 2012. http://www.cbsnews.com/8301-505123_162-57471697/jpmorgan-chase-earnings-london-whale-cost-$5.8-billion/.

Scott, Alec. 'Lessons from Canada's Silicon Valley Diaspora.' *The Globe and Mail*, February 23, 2012. http://www.theglobeandmail.com/report-on-business/rob-magazine/lessons-from-canadas-silicon-valley-diaspora/article535544/?service=print.

Shulman, David. 'The Buzz of God and the Click of Delight.' In *Aesthetics in Performance: Formations of Symbolic Construction and Experience*, edited by Angela Hobart and Bruce Kapferer, 43–63. New York: Berghahn Books, 2005.

Silver, Nate. 'In Silicon Valley, Technology Talent Gap Threatens G.O.P. Campaigns.' *New York Times*, November 28, 2012.

'Similarities between Sanskrit and Programming Languages.' uttiSTha bhArata. Accessed August 16, 2013. http://uttishthabharata.wordpress.com/2011/05/30/sanskrit-programming/.

Simon, Reeva Spector. *Spies and Holy Wars: The Middle East in 20th-Century Crime Fiction.* Austin, TX: University of Texas Press, 2011.

Singh, Sanjay. 'New Life, Old Death for Sanskrit in Uttarakhand.' *Indian Express*, June 29, 2013. Mobile edition. http://m.indianexpress.com/news/new-life-old-death-for-sanskrit-in-uttarakhand/1126773/.

Sivakumar, N. *Dude, Did I Steal Your Job? Debugging Indian Computer Programmers.* Bridgewater: Divine Tree, 2004.

Skora, Kerry Martin. 'Abhinavagupta's Erotic Mysticism: The Reconciliation of Spirit and Flesh.' *International Journal of Hindu Studies* 11, no. 1 (2007): 63–88.

———. 'The Pulsating Heart and Its Divine Sense Energies: Body and Touch in Abhinavagupta's Trika Śaivism.' *Numen* 54, no. 4 (October 1, 2007): 420–58. doi:10.1163/156852707X244298.

Solnit, Rebecca. 'Diary.' *London Review of Books.* Accessed February 7, 2013. http://www.lrb.co.uk/v35/n16/rebecca-solnit/diary.

Spectre, Rob. 'Twilio's Definitive Brogramming Primer.' YouTube video, 14:34. Twilio Conference, uploaded September 22, 2011. http://www.youtube.com/watch?v=Qi_AAqi0RZM.

Srinivas, M.D. 'Amarabhāratī: Sanskrit and the Resurgence of Indian Civilization.' In *Indian Knowledge Systems*, vol. 1, 33–48. Shimla: Indian

Institute of Advanced Study, 2005.

Staal, J.F. 'Context-Sensitive Rules in Pāṇini.' *Foundations of Language* 1, no. 1 (1965): 63–72.

Stahl, Leslie. 'Imported from India.' 60 Minutes. CBS Video. June 22, 2003.

Subbanna, Sridhar, and Srinivasa Varakhedi. 'Computational Structure of the *Aṣṭādhyāyī* and Conflict Resolution Techniques.' In *Sanskrit Computational Linguistics*, 56–65. Springer, 2009.

Swain, F. 'Glowing Trees Could Light up City Streets.' *New Scientist* 208, no. 2788 (2010): 21.

Swan, Rachel. 'Outside the Gates: Unions Versus Big Tech.' *SF Weekly*, July 3, 2013. http://www.sfweekly.com/2013-07-03/news/apple-google-seiu-sis-manny-cardenas/full/.

'Team: Heidelberg LSL.' Igem.org. Accessed February 3, 2013. http://2012hs.igem.org/Team:Heidelberg_LSL.

Tedd, Eugene. 'Hours of Hell and Anguish.' *Prairie Schooner* (1955): 95–108.

Tharu, Susie, and K. Lalita, eds. *Women Writing in India: 600 B.C. to the Present*. New York: The Feminist Press at CUNY, 1993.

'The International Obfuscated C Code Contest.' Iocc.org. Accessed February 3, 2013. http://www.ioccc.org/.

Toole, Betty Alexandra. *Ada, the Enchantress of Numbers: Poetical Science*. Sausalito: Critical Connection, 2010. Kindle Edition.

Torvalds, Linus. 'Re: Stable Linux 2.6.25.10.' Gmane.org, July 15, 2008. http://article.gmane.org/gmane.linux.kernel/706950.

Turing, Alan. 'On Computable Numbers, with an Application to the Entscheidungsproblem (1936).' In *The Annotated Turing: A Guided Tour through Alan Turing's Historic Paper on Computability and the Turing Machine*, by Charles Petzold. Indianapolis: Wiley, 2008.

Urban, Hugh B. *The Economics of Ecstasy: Tantra, Secrecy, and Power in Colonial Bengal*. New York: Oxford University Press, 2001.

———. *The Power of Tantra: Religion, Sexuality and the Politics of South Asian Studies*. London: IB Tauris, 2009. Kindle edition.

Varma, Roli. 'Computing Self-Efficacy among Women in India.' *Journal of Women and Minorities in Science and Engineering* 16, no. 3 (2010): 257–74.

———. 'Exposure, Training, and Environment: Women's Participation in Computing Education in the United States and India.' *Journal of Women and Minorities in Science and Engineering* 15, no. 3 (2009): 205–22.

Wadhwa, Vivek. 'The Face of Success, Part I: How the Indians Conquered Silicon Valley.' Inc.com, January 13, 2012. http://www.inc.com/vivek-wadhwa/how-the-indians-succeeded-in-silicon-valley.html.

Wallis, Christopher. 'The Descent of Power: Possession, Mysticism, and Initiation in the Śaiva Theology of Abhinavagupta.' *Journal of Indian Philosophy* 36, no. 2 (2008): 247–95.

Warner, Melanie. 'The Indians of Silicon Valley.' Money.cnn.com, May 15, 2000. http://money.cnn.com/magazines/fortune/fortune_archive/2000/05/15/279748/.

West, James L. III, ed. *Conversations with William Styron.* Limited ed. Jackson: University Press of Mississippi, 1985.

Wezler, Albrecht. 'Do You Speak Sanskrit? On a Class of Sanskrit Texts Composed in the Late Middle Ages.' *Ideology and Status of Sanskrit: Contributions to the History of the Sanskrit Language,* edited by Jan E.M. Houben, 327–46. Leiden: Brill, 1996.

'Whatever Happened to Programming?' News.ycombinator.com, March 3, 2010. http://news.ycombinator.com/item?id=1165623.

White, David Gordon. 'Introduction: Tantra in Practice: Mapping a Tradition.' In *Tantra in Practice.* Princeton: Princeton University Press, 2000.

'Why Sanskrit Is Best Language for Computer?' Yahoo! Answers. Accessed August 16, 2013. http://in.answers.yahoo.com/question/index?qid=20061108053328AAzdnNE.

Winegrad, Dilys, and Atsushi Akera. 'A Short History of the Second American Revolution.' *University of Pennsylvania Almanac* 42, no. 18 (1996): 4–7.

Witzel, Michael. 'On the Origin of the Literary Device of the Frame Story in Old Indian Literature.' In *Hinduismus Und Buddhismus: Festschrift Für Ulrich Schneider,* edited by Harry Falk, 380–414. Freiburg: Hedwig Falk, 1987.

World Economic Forum. *Global Gender Gap Report.* October 23, 2012. http://www.weforum.org/issues/global-gender-gap.

Wozniak, Steve. 'And Then There Was Apple.' Apple II History. Accessed August 10, 2013. http://apple2history.org/museum/articles/ca8610/.

Wright, Edmund, and John Daintith. *A Dictionary of Computing.* Online. Oxford University Press, 2008. http://www.oxfordreference.com/10.1093/acref/9780199234004.001.0001/acref-9780199234004-e-2050.

Wujastyk, Dominik. 'Indian Manuscripts.' In *Manuscript Cultures: Mapping the Field,* edited by Jörg Quenzer and Jan-Ulrich Sobisch. Berlin: Walter De Gruyter Inc., 2013.

Yegge, Steve. Foreword to *The Joy of Clojure: Thinking the Clojure Way,* XVII–XVI. Stamford, CT: Manning Publications, 2011.

Zihotki. 'Raven & Event Sourcing.' Ayende@Rahien. Accessed August 17, 2013. http://ayende.com/blog/4530/raven-event-sourcing.

COPYRIGHT ACKNOWLEDGEMENTS

Grateful acknowledgement is made to the following for permission to reprint copyright material:

Prose

1. The Wiley Press for extracts from 'Guest Editorial' by Butler W. Lampson from *Software: Practice and Experience* 2, no. 3 (1972): 195–96.
2. Maciej Ceglowski for extracts from 'Dabblers and Blowhards' from Idle Words (blog), April 4, 2006. Text available at http://www.idlewords.com/2005/04/dabblers_and_blowhards.htm.
3. David Barrett for extracts from 'Why We Don't Hire .NET Programmers' from Expensify (blog), March 25, 2011. Text available at http://blog.expensify.com/2011/03/25/ceo-friday-why-we-dont-hire-net-programmers/.
4. Derick Bailey for extracts from 'Dear Open Source Project Leader: Quit Being a Jerk' from LosTechies.com December 14, 2012. Text available at http://lostechies.com/derickbailey/2012/12/14/dear-open-source-project-leader-quit-being-a-jerk/.
5. Vivek Wadhwa for extracts from 'The Face of Success, Part I: How the Indians Conquered Silicon Valley' from Inc.com, last updated on January 13, 2012. Text available at http://www.inc.com/vivek-wadhwa/how-the-indians-succeeded-in-silicon-valley.html.
6. Roli Varma for extracts from 'Exposure, Training, and Environment: Women's Participation in Computing Education in the United States and India' from the *Journal of Women and Minorities in Science and Engineering* 15, no. 3 (2009): 205–22.
7. James Kwak for extracts from 'The Importance of Excel' from The Baseline Scenario (blog), February 9, 2013. Text available at http://baselinescenario.com/2013/02/09/the-importance-of-excel/#.
8. Joshua Bloch for extracts from 'Extra, Extra—Read All About It: Nearly All Binary Searches and Mergesorts Are Broken' from Google Research

Blog, June 2, 2006. Text available at http://googleresearch.blogspot.com/2006/06/extra-extra-read-all-about-it-nearly.html.

9. P.N. Furbank, copyright © P.N. Furbank, for permission to reprint two postcards (page 229) written by Alan Turing to Robin Gandy, from the series 'Messages from the Unseen World,' The Turing Digital Archive, King's College, University of Cambridge. Postcards available at http://www.turingarchive.org/viewer/?id=154&title=14 and http://www.turingarchive.org/viewer/?id=154&title=16.

Poetry

1. Oxford University Press for 'What could my mother be to yours?' by Cempulappeyanirar, translated by A.K. Ramanujan in *The Interior Landscape: Love Poems from a Classical Tamil Anthology*, Oxford University Press, 1994.

2. Susie Tharu and K. Lalita for 'A woman well set free!' by Sumangalamata and 'If I ask her not to get too close' by Muddupalani, translated by Susie Tharu and K. Lalita in *Women Writing in India: Love Poems from a Classical Tamil Anthology*, The Feminist Press at CUNY, 1993.

3. City Lights Press, copyright © 1998 by Andrew Schelling, for 'Black swollen clouds' and 'To Her Daughter' by Vidya, and 'Nights of jasmine & thunder' by Shilabhattarika, translated by Andrew Schelling in *The Cane Groves of Narmada River: Erotic Poems from Old India*, City Lights Books, 1998.

4. The Wylie Agency for 'A poet should learn with his eyes' by Kshemendra, translated by William Stanley Merwin and Jeffery Moussaieff Masson in *East Window: The Asian Translations*, Copper Canyon Press, 1998.

5. Columbia University Press for 'I don't know mantra from tantra' from *Karpūramañjarī*, 1.22–23, translated by Ronald M. Davidson in *Indian Esoteric Buddhism: A Social History of the Tantric Movement*, Columbia University Press, 2002.

Figures

1. Martin Howard for figures 3.13, 3.14, 3.15, 3.16 and 3.17. Images (and videos) available at http://randomwraith.com/logic.html.

Martin Howard is a physicist from the UK with a keen interest in mechanical computing.

2. Alex Papadimoulis of TheDailyWTF.com for figure 6.1. Image available at http://img.thedailywtf.com/images/201101/DependencyGraph.png.

3. MIT Libraries for figure 4.3.